ıt

No Child Left Different

No Child Left Different

EDITED BY SHARNA OLFMAN

FOREWORD BY MEL LEVINE, M.D.

Childhood in America

PRAEGER

**Westport, Connecticut
London**

Library of Congress Cataloging-in-Publication Data

Olfman, Sharna
  No child left different / edited by Sharna Olfman; foreword by
  Mel Levine.
    p. cm.—(childhood in America)
  Includes bibliographical references and index.
  ISBN 0–275–98522–9 (alk. paper)
  1. Pediatric psychopharmacology. 2. Behavior disorders in children—United
States—Chemotherapy. 3. Child psychiatry—United States—Differential
therapeutics. 4. Medication abuse—United States. I. Title. II. Series
  [DNLM: 1. Child Psychology—United States. 2. Mental Disorders—drug
therapy—Child—United States. 3. Mental Disorders—psychology—child—
United States.   ws 105.5.s6 N739 2006]
RJ504.7.N6 2006
618.92'89—dc22   2005022471

British Library Cataloguing in Publication Data is available.

Library of Congress Catalog Card Number: 2005022471
ISBN: 0–275–98522–9

First published in 2006

Praeger Publishers, 88 Post Road West, Westport, CT 06881
. An imprint of Greenwood Publishing Group, Inc.
www.praeger.com

Printed in the United States of America

The paper used in this book complies with the
Permanent Paper Standard issued by the National
Information Standards Organization (Z39.48–1984).

10 9 8 7 6 5 4 3 2 1

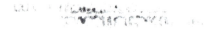

For my dear children Adam and Gavriela.

Contents

Acknowledgments

I wish to express my deep appreciation to each of the contributors to *No Child Left Different* for their excellent work on this volume and their tireless efforts to protect children's rights to grow up unfettered by cultural constraints and corporate predation. I felt particularly inspired by the research, writing, and advocacy of Laura Berk, Urie Bronfenbrenner, Raffi Cavoukian, David Healy, Mel Levine, and Meredith Small. Deborah Carvalko, senior acquisitions editor for Praeger Press, was—as always—a pleasure to work with. My parents Bess and Mitchell Olfman are a wellspring of generativity, and my dear children Adam and Gavriela inspire me always to make their world a better place. I give special thanks to my husband Daniel Burston, my constant companion in heart, soul, and mind.

Series Foreword

The rich diversity of cultures created by humankind is a testament to our ability to develop and adapt in diverse ways. But however varied different cultures may be, children are not endlessly malleable; they all share basic psychological and physical needs that must be met to ensure healthy development. The *Childhood in America* series examines the extent to which American culture meets children's irreducible needs. Without question, many children growing up in the United States lead privileged lives. They have been spared the ravages of war, poverty, malnourishment, sexism, and racism. However, despite our nation's resources, not all children share these privileges. Additionally, values that are central to American culture, such as self-reliance, individualism, privacy of family life, and consumerism, have created a climate in which parenting has become intolerably labor intensive, and children are being taxed beyond their capacity for healthy adaptation. Record levels of psychiatric disturbance, violence, poverty, apathy, and despair among our children speak to our current cultural crisis.

Although our elected officials profess their commitment to "family values," policies that support family life are woefully lacking, and inferior to those in other industrialized nations. American families are burdened by inadequate parental leave, a health care system that does not provide universal coverage for children, a minimum wage that is not a living wage, "welfare to work" policies that require parents to leave their children for long stretches of time, unregulated and inadequately subsidized daycare, an unregulated entertainment industry that exposes children to sex and violence, and a two-tiered public education system that delivers inferior education to poor children and frequently ignores individual differences in learning styles and profiles of intelligence. As a result, many families are taxed to the breaking point. In addition, our fascination with technological innovation is creating a family lifestyle that is dominated by screen rather than human interaction.

The *Childhood in America* series seeks out leading childhood experts from across the disciplines to promote dialogue, research, and understanding regarding how best to raise and educate psychologically healthy children, to ensure that they will acquire the wisdom, heart, and courage needed to make choices for the betterment of society.

Sharna Olfman

Foreword

BEGGING TO DIFFER...

Many years ago a child psychiatry resident named Vernon completed a month-long elective working in a behavioral pediatrics clinic that I ran at Children's Hospital in Boston. On the final day of his rotation, I took Vernon out to lunch and I asked him to identify the major difference between his pediatric and psychiatric clinic experiences. He surprised me when he responded without a moment's hesitation, "You call a lot more kids normal than we do."

Defining Normal

What's normal anyway? When should a pattern of behavioral or personality *variation* be construed as a form of *deviation*? When is it appropriate to interpret quirky or annoying behaviors, traits, or interests as clear indicators of psychopathology as opposed to the rough edges of childhood or of rugged individuality? How severe or recurrent must a child's troublesome or worrisome behaviors, or feelings—such as a bout of sadness—be before they are interpreted as evidence of a psychiatric disturbance that meets DSM-IV diagnostic criteria? How "bad" can a "bad boy" be and still be considered normal? When do we shrug our shoulders and say "boys will be boys," and when do we take him for a psychiatric evaluation? Aren't all kids entitled to an acceptable quota of such "badness"?

These are tough questions, and they are not new. But in an age in which diagnoses adhere tightly to developing children and the aggressive use of medication almost automatically follows suit, the distinctions between variation and deviation have more weighty consequences and far broader implications than ever before. *No Child Left Different* represents a timely and scholarly effort to articulate the complex psychological, philosophical, political, and economic factors that have blunted our capacity to distinguish between developmental or behavioral variation and psychiatric disturbance in childhood and adolescence, as well as our capacity to tolerate (let alone embrace) our children's differences.

Most mental health experts agree that the traditional medical model serves an important role in child psychiatry, pediatrics, and other disciplines involved in the diagnosis and treatment of *severe* conditions such as childhood schizophrenia, major depression, or extreme intellectual impairment. But today, most clinicians in the children's mental health field spend the bulk of their time caring for children who present with the so-called "high prevalence, low-severity" conditions, including problems with attention, learning difficulties, weak social skills, mood swings, or intermittent anxiety—and don't we all suffer from the latter? When clinicians assess children who exhibit these common symptoms, they must scale the controversial gradient that separates normal variation from actual pathology and run the very real risk of labeling too many kids as abnormal.

Disabling by Labeling

It is ironic that America, whose founding principles emphasize individual rights and freedoms, has developed a culture that demands homogeneity and uniformity in its children. In consequence, we are quick to interpret children's differences as mental illnesses, as opposed to unusual ways of being or divergent patterns of brain wiring, and we find diagnostic labels deeply comforting. When a child fails to fit an acceptable mold, he may only be tolerated after he is declared to be mentally ill, and given a label with its accompanying treatment regimen. Generally, the condition that he is assigned is accorded a concise taxonomic tag, one that is distilled even further to an abbreviation (e.g., "Aspy" for Asperger Syndrome or "ADHD" for Attention Deficit Hyperactivity Disorder). In fact, nowadays, parents are apt to state, "my son *is* ADHD" rather than my "son *has* ADHD," suggesting ever deeper penetration of the label into his identity!

Each of these popular childhood labels has its fan club—an ardent faction of loyal, sometimes fanatical, followers and a gaggle of closely affiliated dedicated scholars (generously subsidized and entertained by pharmaceutical companies). Together they saturate the media with articles and documentaries, fervently claiming that their diagnosis is much more common than we ever thought, and that it is being perilously underdiagnosed. In justifying this stance, they often broaden the "spectrum" of a condition, capturing milder and milder as well as younger and younger inheritors of their label. Publicity about the "hitherto unrecognized high prevalence of a condition" results in expanded funding for researchers and higher profits for drug makers.

The Diagnostic Risks of Labels

When a child elicits concerns about the way she acts or learns or interacts with others, a three-stage process is typically set in motion. First, an assumption is made—typically by her parents, family members, or teachers—that she is not normal. Second, there is a vigorous quest for a specific label for her "abnormality." Third, that diagnostic label is used to justify the use of a particular treatment—most often a psychoactive drug. Assigning psychiatric labels offers many hidden advantages:

- to doctors seeking a shelter from legal liability for their prescribing practices. They have a measure of protection if the psychiatric drug that they prescribe a child fits the standard for medical care of the given label (even if their assessment took place during a ten-minute office visit or the drug they prescribed was never clinically tested for use with children).
- to parents whose child's psychiatric label may be their only means of accessing special education services through their school district.
- to therapists struggling to pay the office rent!

Regrettably, these turnkey labels for "low-severity conditions" are often misleading and can engender serious consequences. Designating a child with a psychiatric label rests on the pessimistic assumption that she suffers from a mental illness (as opposed to simply being "different"). This implies that she has a chronic, "hard wired" condition and is destined to lead the life of an "abnormal" person. When one or more caregivers that a child loves and holds in high regard such as parents, teachers, or doctors label her as mentally ill, she will rarely disappoint their expectations, and over time the label may become a self-fulfilling prophecy.

Diagnostic labels are reductionistic. Complex, multifactorial problems get oversimplified into single words or abbreviations. Also, when a child is given a psychiatric label, it becomes easier to overlook or obscure his strengths and special endowments. This is particularly tragic because identifying, encouraging, and celebrating each child's unique potential is one of the most important missions for parents, and teachers.

Labels are generally based entirely upon outward symptoms that the child presents with. But many different pathways or mechanisms produce very similar symptoms. Physicians would mismanage countless patients if they assumed, for example, that everyone with swollen joints has the identical underlying illness. Similarly, a child may have trouble paying attention because he has weaknesses of receptive language, or memory, difficulty sequencing information, or because he processes incoming information slowly. Or he may tune out because he is anxious, or preoccupied, or he can't relate to the subject matter or to his teachers at school. In all of these instances, the outward signs might be identical: poor concentration, fidgetiness, and impulsivity. As a result, each of these diverse scenarios may result in the child being labeled as "ADHD" and being placed on stimulant medication rather than getting the kind of help he really needs.

Of course, some children may need and benefit from pharmacological treatments, but labeling results in far too many kids receiving drug therapy that is inappropriate. I prescribe medication for some of my patients, but I do so conservatively and only after a careful evaluation of a child's educational and parenting needs. By *describing* a child instead of labeling him, more often than not, medication can be put on the back burner. It is also the case that the more thoroughly you know a child the less prone you are to reach for the prescription pad; many other options present themselves.

Labeling negates the frequent finding that a weakness or problem at one age may evolve into an asset later in life. A highly distractible seven-year-old may emerge as an adult who is remarkably creative. A teenager with language gaps may acquire outstanding spatial and nonverbal thinking abilities largely because she can not rely on her verbal thinking. She could become a successful artist or fashion designer at age thirty. An eleven-year-old who is oppositional and perpetually determined to march to his own drummer may harbor the potential to become a world leader, but not if he becomes convinced that his ways of acting are all bad and that they comprise some kind of mental disease called mild "oppositional defiant disorder" (justifying the use of a drug to cure his insistent and persistent individuality and independence).

Labels, when invoked at the mild end of the spectrum run the risk of homogenizing our citizenry. We need to see value and beauty in a highly unique albeit quirky or eccentric child with odd-ball tastes or interests, a nonconformist who enjoys being by himself and is decidedly not a social butterfly. In a humane, tolerant, and pluralistic society, such a way of life ought to be a legitimate and laudable preference, rather than the occasion for the diagnosis of a psychiatric condition. Imbuing such a child with the label of Asperger Syndrome would be tragic, a very sad commentary on an increasingly conformist culture. Unfortunately, that is precisely what is taking place.

Avoiding the Medicalization of Differences

The extraordinary compilation of essays in this book points us in a new direction, one that informs and empowers us to observe and embrace children's individual differences and even seek to cultivate such diversity. As well, we can help kids get back on track when their differences cause them to go astray. All this can be accomplished without declaring them all to be mentally ill. Variation will always be harder to understand and manage than uniformity. But the long-term results are likely to have a significant payoff. We must acknowledge that to treat everyone the same is to treat them unequally. Differences call for different approaches.

In order for society to thrive and prosper, it must utilize the skills and talents of a seemingly endless cast of "kinds of minds"—people possessing a vast range of abilities, tastes, behavior patterns, and lifestyles. Their differences are essential in any productive culture. When we force conformity on our children, we risk losing the creativity and talents that we so urgently need in today's world. We must therefore embrace a philosophy of behavioral and cognitive pluralism. *No child should have to beg to differ.*

Mel Levine, M.D.

1

Introduction

Sharna Olfman

The number of American children being diagnosed with psychiatric illnesses has soared over the past decade and a half. The National Institute of Mental Health (NIMH) estimates that today, one in ten children and adolescents in the United States "suffers from mental illness severe enough to result in significant functional impairment."[1] During this same time period, psychotropic drugs have become the treatment of first choice rather than the treatment of last resort.[2] Recent years have witnessed a threefold increase in the use of psychotropic medication among patients under twenty years of age, and prescriptions for preschoolers have been skyrocketing.[3] Over 10 million children and adolescents are currently on antidepressants, and about 5 million children are taking stimulant medications such as Ritalin.[4]

In addition, "polypharmacy" has become a commonplace practice in child psychiatry. Recent studies indicate that 40 percent of children being treated with drugs for psychiatric conditions are taking two or more of them concurrently. Many of these drugs—such as atypical antipsychotics—have never been tested in clinical trials with children, *let alone in combination* with other potent drugs acting on the developing brain.[5] In a recent guest editorial for the *Journal of Child and Adolescent Psychopharmacology*, Julie Zito expressed the concern that "with these fancy combinations where there is *virtually no evidence base*, you should be exhibiting some clinical skepticism" (emphasis added).[6] But in the current climate, caveats such as these often go unheeded.

In light of these trends, the contributors to *No Child Left Different* investigated the following two questions:

- Why are so many children in the United States being diagnosed with psychiatric disturbances?
- Why have drugs become the treatment of first choice in their care?

To fully address these issues, it was necessary to piece together a number of complex and interrelated factors, including

- the role of the pharmaceutical and managed care industries in shaping how we regard and treat distressed and disturbed children;
- why the "medical model of mental illness" enjoys such a monopoly in the mental health field and whether it is serving us well;
- the meaning of mental health and mental illness;
- the nature of and conditions for optimal psychological development and whether we as a society are meeting these conditions; and
- how the interplay of genes and environment shapes brain development.

The story that unfolded has all of the drama and suspense of a first-rate detective novel. But it is not fiction. Rather, it is a very real account of the lives of millions of children who are suffering, and who in many cases are being given drugs that do not address the root cause of their suffering and that may even undermine their health and prospects for recovery. This inquiry went to the very heart of our understanding of what it means to be a child.

CHILDHOOD DEFINED

Over the past few years, I have had the pleasure of reading some of the classics of children's literature—spanning the nineteenth through the mid-twentieth centuries—with my own children. I have noticed that a common theme among these novels is that children *routinely* challenge their parents with impulsivity and a range of temperamental styles. Parents, in turn, understand that it is their role to guide their children toward maturity. With this guidance their children's wayward tendencies often evolve into their finest attributes in adulthood. Think of headstrong Jo of *Little Women*, whose fiery temper and blunt speech got her into endless scrapes; of Anne Shirley of *Anne of Green Gables*, whose rapturous highs and "depths of despair" evoked such wonder, mirth, and dismay among her friends and family; and of Fern from *Charlotte's Web*, who preferred the conversation of her beloved Charlotte and Wilbur— a spider and a pig, respectively—over the company of other children.

These novels express a timeless truth: children, by definition, are dependent and require consistent adult care in order to reach maturity. But this simple fact of childhood is becoming lost in the current discourse of "genetically determined chemical imbalances," which encourages us to see a "brain disorder" instead of a child struggling to find her way. In the following section, I present Anne (of Green Gables) as a "case study" to illustrate this point.

Anne: A Case Study

Anne's passionate and impulsive personality, vivid imagination, and exuberant connection to nature make her life and relationships rich with pathos and humor, albeit initially she is a trial to her adoptive mother, Marilla.[7] Nonetheless, Marilla understands intuitively that Anne—who in toddlerhood lost her mother —needs the guidance that has thus far been denied her. Marilla's brother Matthew, on the other hand, thinks that Anne is perfection personified, and from the start he is wholeheartedly devoted to her.

We might ask ourselves what role Anne's early deprivation played in the cultivation of her vivid fantasy life and her often overpowering emotions. But regardless of when these traits emerged and why, Marilla's reliable and firm guidance, Matthew's unwavering love, and the care and support of friends and neighbors—in a setting of pastoral beauty, in which Anne had freedom to roam—are precisely what Anne needed in order to mature into the caring, keenly intelligent, and accomplished young woman that she became.

Let us now imagine that Anne is growing up today, as opposed to the late nineteenth century. After reading the *Time* magazine cover story about the rising incidence of bipolar disorder in childhood and getting an earful from her neighbor, Rachel Lynde, about some "ADHD" children attending Avonlea School,[8] alarm bells go off for Marilla, who feels compelled to share Anne's "symptoms" with her family doctor. He in turn feels that a referral to a child psychiatrist is warranted. After interviewing Marilla and Anne, child psychiatrist Dr. Jones notes the following in her chart:

> Ten-year-old Anne Cuthbert is the only child of adoptive parents Marilla and Matthew Cuthbert. As a result I am unable to take a

family history for mood disorders. She presents with the following symptoms:

—Rapid cycling of manic and depressive episodes.

—Manic episodes are marked by expansive mood, pressured speech, racing thoughts, risky behavior, and psychotic features, including an unshakable and age-inappropriate belief in two imaginary friends.

—Depressive episodes are characterized by sleep and eating disturbances and suicidal ideas.

—Inattention: Anne is unable to follow through with household chores involving more than one or two simple instructions and has made careless errors that place her and others in harm's way.

—Impulsivity: In the course of the past year Anne has physically assaulted a classmate, verbally abused an elderly neighbor, inebriated a friend, dyed her hair green, and walked a ridge pole suffering a near fatal injury.

—Hyperactivity: Anne talks incessantly and is constantly active.

Given the frequency and intensity of these symptoms, Dr. Jones concludes that Anne meets the criteria for early-onset bipolar 1 disorder (BPD) with psychotic features and decides to follow the new treatment guidelines for children and adolescents published in the March 2005 edition of the *Journal of the American Academy of Child and Adolescent Psychiatry*.[9] Accordingly, Anne is prescribed both a mood stabilizer and an atypical antipsychotic for a minimum of one to two years after full remission of symptoms. Dr. Jones notes that Anne also meets the criteria for ADHD, which she knows to be commonly co-morbid with early-onset BPD. She decides to wait until Anne's bipolar features are under control before initiating a concurrent course of psychostimulants. Marilla and Matthew are referred to a psychoeducational counselor to learn more about the cause and course of Anne's illnesses as well as symptom management strategies. At their first session they learn that "BPD tends to be a chronic illness like diabetes or epilepsy."[10]

By fast-forwarding Anne to the present and recasting her as a psychiatric patient, we see how it is possible to isolate features of a child's emotional, behavioral, and inner life and to present them as a "symptom checklist." But in the process, Anne, the exuberant, sensitive, caring child, who generations of children and adults have loved, identified with, and emulated, is rendered invisible. Anne is transformed into a "brain disorder" that will require three concurrent psychiatric medications to cure. These drugs—the antipsychotic, in particular—will in all likelihood permanently alter Anne's brain, which is in a critical phase of rapid development. And so in this sense too, the Anne we know and love is lost to us.

Why might Anne's behavior be conceptualized so differently today than it would have been 125 years ago—or even 25 years ago? Why is she so much more likely to be the recipient of a medical diagnosis and multiple drug prescriptions? To answer these questions, we need to appreciate the extent to which the "medical model of mental illness" and the pharmaceutical industry currently influence the mental health field.

THE MEDICAL MODEL OF MENTAL ILLNESS

"Dr. Jones" diagnosed Anne in accordance with the medical model of mental illness, which asserts that psychological disturbance is symptomatic of an underlying medical illness. Adherents of the medical model widely assume that the cause of most mental illnesses is a heritable chemical imbalance or structural flaw in the brain. The *Diagnostic and Statistical Manual of Mental Disorders* (*DSM*) is a catalog of categories of psychological disturbances and diagnostic criteria in accordance with the medical model. Although other illuminating models of mental illness do exist and have been widely adopted in the past, health insurance and managed care companies in the United States today only recognize the diagnostic codes listed in the *DSM*, thus obligating *all* mental health professionals to speak the "language" of the medical model. For this and other reasons, the medical model exerts a powerful influence over how psychological disturbance is conceptualized and treated.

There *are*, of course, instances in which biology plays a role in the etiology of psychological disturbance and in which medication *can* be a valuable component of psychiatric treatment. But the medical model can only serve a useful function if it is applied more judiciously than it is at present. First, practitioners who use the medical model must acknowledge that genetically primed brain disorders are not the only valid biological explanations for psychological disturbance. For example, toxic exposure to pollutants such as lead, mercury, and pesticides is known to undermine brain development and has been linked to a variety of learning disabilities. Second, although the medical model defines mental *illness* through the presence of specific symptoms, it does not offer a description of mental *health*, through which a child's actual and potential strengths and abilities are taken into account. Third, the medical model does not acknowledge the remarkable extent to which the human brain develops in response to its social, emotional, and physical environs. Indeed, even our genes can be altered, activated, or inactivated by different environmental conditions.

In summary, the medical model of mental illness encourages us to conceptualize the mind as a machine whose software is a set of genes that we are learning to decode and recode and whose hardware can be corrected or enhanced pharmacologically. This emphasis on the heritability of mental illness echoes eugenic beliefs that have contributed to some of the most shameful episodes in human history more generally, and in the history of psychiatry in particular.[11] It excuses us from having to look critically at and take responsibility for the environments we create for our children. The medical model monopoly has also served as a catalyst for the unchecked proliferation of drug-based therapies and undue influence by the pharmaceutical industry.

PSYCHOTROPIC DRUGS AND THE PHARMACEUTICAL INDUSTRY

Three recent compelling books detail the role of the pharmaceutical industry in shaping prescription drug use: they are *The Truth about the Drug Companies* by former editor in chief of the *New England Journal of Medicine* Marcia Angell; *Let Them Eat Prozac* by former secretary of the British Association for Psychopharmacology David Healy; and *Mad in America* by Pulitzer Prize nominee Robert Whitaker. These meticulously documented accounts tell a remarkably consistent story of how pharmaceutical companies, whose sole mandate is profit—and certainly not patient care—exercise almost total control over the design, interpretation, and dissemination of research about the efficacy of the drugs they produce and sell.

Angell, Healy, and Whitaker describe a reliable formula, particularly in use since the early 1980s, for introducing new drugs into the marketplace. When a class of drugs becomes unprofitable after their patents expire, new drugs are developed to replace them. The fallibility and adverse side effects of the old drugs are then "revealed" to the public, and industry-funded research is conducted to "demonstrate" the remarkable efficacy and safety of the new drugs. A new market niche is then created for these drugs—either by promoting a different "diagnosis du jour" or by finding new populations for old diagnoses.

This may be business as usual in the corporate world, but it does not take much imagination to appreciate the magnitude of the potential danger posed for emotionally distraught children whose parents are looking to psychotropic drugs as a lifeline. Indeed, as Brody and Burke discuss in chapters 6 and 10 of this volume, it was recently made public that SSRI (selective serotonin reuptake inhibitor) antidepressants—which millions of children are using—are associated with a higher risk of suicide. As Healy points out, that this information was widely known by the drug companies manufacturing SSRIs but kept hidden from the public illustrates the grave risks of allowing drug companies to oversee their own research.

In *Let Them Eat Prozac* Healy recalls that

> it had become clear to me that the Prozac (SSRI antidepressant) drug group could trigger suicide and violence, and that companies producing these drugs knew of the problem.... The Prozac-and-suicide saga reveals a structural problem in the system that gives us drugs, biotechnology, and other health care products. And this structural problem, this fault line, is highly likely to produce a drug or health care disaster at least equivalent to that of thalidomide on the Richter scale of drug disasters. And very soon.[12]

Atypical Antipsychotics: The New SSRIs?

With the media frenzy surrounding SSRI antidepressants still fresh in our minds, it would be prudent to consider whether the atypical antipsychotics now being prescribed to children like Anne for bipolar disorder are poised to become the drug disaster that Healy predicts. In keeping with the "script" that Angell, Healy, and Whitaker describe in their respective books, the atypical antipsychotics came onto the market in the 1990s to replace an older class of antipsychotic drugs that had gone off patent and were no longer profitable. Soon thereafter, a well-orchestrated series of stories hit the media about the poor efficacy of the first generation of antipsychotic drugs, which were "exposed" as carrying a high risk of dangerous side effects (although this was in fact known for decades). The new atypical antipsychotics were widely touted in the media and medical journals alike as highly "precise" drugs for the treatment of schizophrenia and as having very few side effects.[13]

These claims were not actually borne out in the research, however. In fact, in the letter of approval to Janssen—the manufacturer of the atypical antipsychotic Risperdal—the FDA stated that "we would consider any advertisement or promotional labeling for Risperdal false, misleading, or lacking fair balance under 502 (a) and 502 (n) of the ACT if there is presentation of data that conveys the impression that risperidone [Risperdal is the trade name for risperidone] is superior to haloperidol or any other marketed antipsychotic drug product with regard to safety or effectiveness." Furthermore, once Risperdal came onto the market, researchers without ties to drug companies were free to test it, and study after study has raised serious concerns about its safety and efficacy. Studies from McMaster University in Canada, the NIMH, and the University of Pittsburgh demonstrated that even a low dose of risperidone could cause Parkinsonism, akathisia, and extrapyramidal symptoms. The prestigious medical journal *Lancet* wrote a scathing review of the research practices that Janssen's researchers had used to gain approval from the FDA and concluded that risperidone was a "marketing success, if nothing else."[14] But, lacking Janssen's PR budget, these findings were not aired in the media.

Similarly, even though Eli Lilly's atypical antipsychotic drug Zyprexa—the trade name for olanzapine—received FDA approval, in the drug trials that led up to FDA approval:

> ... [O]f the 2,500 patients who received olanzapine, twenty died, twelve killed themselves, and two of the remaining eight deaths, from "aspiration pneumonia," were seen by FDA reviewers as possibly causally related to olanzapine. Twenty-two percent of the olanzapine patients suffered a "serious" adverse event. Two-thirds of the olanzapine patients didn't successfully complete the trials. More than one-fourth of the patients complained that the drug made them sleepy. Weight gain was a frequent problem, and other problems documented included Parkinson's, akathisia, dystonia, hypotension, constipation, tachycardia, diabetic complications, seizures, increases in serum prolactin, liver abnormalities, and white blood cell disorders.[15]

A review of clinical trials involving more than 12,000 patients, which was published in the *British Medical Journal* in 2000, found "no clear evidence that atypical antipsychotics are more effective or better tolerated than conventional antiypsychotics."[16] Paul Leber, the former director of the FDA's Division of Neuropharmacological Drugs, concluded that "no one should be surprised if, upon marketing, events of all kinds and severity not previously identified are reported in association with olanzapine's use."[17]

Pediatric Bipolar Disorder: The New "Diagnosis du Jour"?

Both Risperdal and Zyprexa have been resounding financial successes. Zyprexa is in fact Eli Lilly's top-selling drug, even outselling Prozac. In 2004, atypical antipsychotics had sales of $8.8 billion dollars, "2.4 billion of which was paid for by state Medicaid funds."[18] Financial success of this magnitude cannot be sustained from the relatively small population of adult schizophrenics. So soon after the drugs were approved by the FDA, manufacturers of atypical antipsychotics expanded their markets by promoting their "off-label" use for a wide range of clinical disorders.[19] As a result, Risperdal and Zyprexa (as well as other atypical antipsychotics) are listed in the treatment guidelines for child and adolescent bipolar disorder as published in the March 2005 *Journal of the American Academy of Child and Adolescent Psychiatry*, despite the fact that atypical antipsychotics are known to have a multitude of adverse side effects in adult patients and have not been rigorously tested for safety or efficacy with children.[20]

Pediatric bipolar disorder—whose incidence in the United States has climbed significantly in recent years—was considered a rare disorder only a decade ago. Furthermore, as psychiatrist Jon McClellan points out, the diagnostic criteria for pediatric BPD are still under debate. First, the criteria currently in use are fundamentally different from those of adult BPD; second, the steep rise in the diagnosis of pediatric BPD is confined to the United States; and third, preliminary research does not indicate that children who are diagnosed with BPD become adults with classic adult BPD.[21] And so we are left to question what exactly we *are* diagnosing in a majority of cases.

In summary, we are now prescribing antipsychotic drugs—with well-established side effects, that were initially designed to treat schizophrenic adults—to children for an "illness" that is not even remotely well defined or understood. And to further complicate matters, the current guidelines for pediatric BPD recommend that children take atypical antipsychotics *in combination* with mood stabilizers. If the first combination of drugs does not eliminate their symptoms, the psychiatrist is directed to try another combination of drugs, and another, and so on through five different stages of drug combinations. *But nowhere in the treatment guidelines is the therapist encouraged to question the original diagnosis or the efficacy of the drugs themselves.*[22]

It is instructive that the treatment guidelines for early-onset BPD, which were published in the premier journal for American child and adolescent psychiatrists, were created at the request of the Child and Adolescent Bipolar Foundation (CABF), whose members served on the committee that developed them. CABF's website states that it receives *unrestricted educational grants from seven different pharmaceutical companies whose drugs are recommended in the guidelines*.[23] Also, the lead author of these guidelines, Robert Kowatch, has received research support and/or is on the advisory boards and speaker's bureaus of seven different pharmaceutical companies.[24] Thus we may surmise that pediatric BPD has become the "diagnosis du jour" that will keep atypical antipsychotic drug sales humming.

State Mental Hospitals, Clinics, and Prisons: A New Market Force

The new guidelines or algorithms for pediatric BPD are anticipated in the Texas Medication Algorithm Project (TMAP).[25] In the mid-1990s, around the time that the "atypicals" came on the market, the state of Texas issued medication guidelines for various psychiatric illnesses in which it mandated the use of the latest and most expensive drugs in public institutions such as state mental hospitals, prisons, and government-funded clinics.[26] More recently, Texas started to develop CMAP,[27] a children's algorithm project that has developed guidelines for drug treatments of ADHD and major depression. Nine other states including Pennsylvania have followed suit. In each case, drug companies have helped to fund the creation of the algorithms as well as subsequent education, training, and dissemination of information. President Bush's New Freedom Commission on Mental Health calls TMAP a "model program" and has initiated screening programs in the public school system for early detection of psychiatric disturbance in children.[28]

In 2001, Harvard-trained psychiatrist Stefan Kruszewski was asked to review psychiatric care in Pennsylvania's state-funded agencies. As journalist Rob Walters, who interviewed him, observed:

> Most shocking to him were the cases of children placed in state-funded residential treatment facilities, sometimes for years, and heavily drugged on the new antipsychotics and anticonvulsants.... "These kids were on multiple medications without the clinical diagnoses to support the medications," Kruszewski says. One drug, Neurontin, approved for controlling seizures, "was being massively

prescribed for anxiety, social phobia, PTSD, social anxiety, mood instability, sleep, oppositional defiant behavior, attention deficit disorder. Yet there's almost no evidence to support these uses in adults
and no evidence for kids whatsoever."[29]

CHILDHOOD LOST

When we compare the fortunes of American children with those
living in countries ravaged by poverty, war, disease, and famine, it
may seem self-indulgent to question whether American children
are getting what they need for optimal development when they
have so much—perhaps too much, in some respects. But this perspective fails to take two important facts into account. First, the
wealth of this nation is not equitably distributed, and the economic
gap between the "haves and the have nots" is growing apace. At
present, 16 percent of all children in the United States live in poverty, and this number rises to 34 percent for African American and
Hispanic children and 50 percent among children of single mothers.[30] Nine million children in the United States have no health
insurance.[31] The deepening disparities can also be seen in the two-
tiered system of public education that serves children in poor and
wealthy neighborhoods very differently and in the increasing violence and despair in inner-city neighborhoods.

Second, although the GDP (gross domestic product) is the standard measure that nations use to assess prosperity, it is actually a
poor instrument for revealing quality of life and mental health.
Once our essential needs for food and safety are met, mental health
is not well correlated with economic prosperity.[32]

As I have documented in *Childhood Lost*, children in the United
States at all income levels are being challenged by a variety of environmental assaults that undermine healthy physical and psychological development.[33] Many of these factors are so pervasive that
we no longer "see" or think about them. In the United States, children's mental health is being undermined by factors such as the
following:

- Weak or absent policies to support families. Parents' ability to provide
  consistent and loving care for their children is compromised by "welfare to work" policies that require mothers to return to forty-hour work
  weeks while failing to provide them with affordable, regulated, high-
  quality childcare, sufficient maternity leave, child sick leave, a living
  wage, and universal health care.

- A two-tiered public education system that delivers inferior education to poor children and frequently ignores individual differences in learning styles.
- An unregulated advertising industry that spends over $15 billion annually in direct marketing to children, shaping lifetime addictions to junk food, alcohol, and cigarettes and contributing to a childhood obesity epidemic that is poised to become the leading cause of death in the United States.
- Entertainment and gaming industries that have been given the mandate to police themselves. As a result, children can play video games that invite the "player" to murder, rape, and engage in acts of hatred toward minority groups.
- Easy access to pornography sites in which women are portrayed as objects of sexual pleasure for men.
- Hours of screen viewing each day, which usurps time for conversation, outdoor play, and reading.
- The disappearance of direct contact with nature.
- Weak environmental protection policies that have allowed tens of thousands of toxic pollutants to erode our air, soil, and water and undermine endocrinological and brain development.

PATHOLOGY OF NORMALCY

Industrialized nations in Europe, Scandinavia, and Asia have created national policies to address many of the issues I have just cited. The United States stands virtually alone among wealthy nations in its failure to create national policies that ensure the health, safety, and integrity of families and children.

Our cultural emphasis on individual rights and freedoms has encouraged us to conceptualize the domains of childcare, health, education, and work as private matters that should not be overseen by government. As a result, it has become the norm for mothers to return to work immediately after the birth of a new child, to juggle multiple low-wage jobs, and to pay exorbitant fees for substandard daycare, while their children play on lawns dripping with toxic pesticides and eat food brimming with growth hormones, artificial preservatives, and coloring. Yet these factors, which derail healthy development, are primary contributors to the rise in psychiatric disturbance among children that we are witnessing today.

Long ago, psychoanalyst Erich Fromm coined the term *pathology of normalcy* to describe widely shared attitudes of a given culture that are nonetheless antithetical to psychological well-being.[34]

Rampant individualism that is not constrained by the humane consideration of our collective responsibilities to children, families, and communities could aptly be described as a pathology of normalcy.

Indeed, the widely held conviction that millions of American children suffer from brain disorders that can be fixed with psychotropic drugs could also be an expression of the pathology of normalcy. Our misguided faith in the quick pharmacological fix might explain why one in five teens now abuses prescription drugs and why it is becoming increasingly common among children—particularly those at elite schools—to buy or borrow prescription stimulants from their classmates to help them perform well on exams.[35] Perhaps the crowning irony is that several researchers have found a link between pediatric prescriptions for stimulants and antidepressants (which are much more prevalent in the United States) and the rise in diagnoses for early-onset bipolar disorder (which is exclusive to the United States). It appears that in some cases, the drugs themselves are deregulating children's emotions in ways that make them *more* likely to be labeled with bipolar disorder—and being placed on yet *more* drugs.[36]

In the chapters that follow, rich with case examples, we take an in-depth look at the conditions that have led to our increasing intolerance of differences and psychiatric overmedication of children and then propose humane ways to heal our distressed children. In section 1, "Environments Matter," we consider how emotional, social, cultural, and physical environments influence psychological and brain development—thus challenging the notion that most psychological disturbance in childhood is of genetic origin. In the next section, "Medical Remodel," we examine the strengths and limitations of the medical model of mental illness as applied to children's psychiatric disturbances and offer correctives to this model. In the final section, "Pathologies of Normalcy," we examine the impact of current trends in American culture on children who have been diagnosed with ADHD, depression, anxiety, and eating disorders and consider sane approaches to treatment with and without medication.

Part I

Environments Matter

2

The Building Blocks of Children's Mental Health

Care and Community

Sharna Olfman

Urie Bronfenbrenner, one of the leading scholars in developmental psychology, found it sobering to discover that, after fifty years of work in the field, he was able to distill the necessary conditions for healthy child development down to two facts. In order to become fully intact human beings, he concluded, children need "the enduring, irrational involvement of one or more adults.... In short, *somebody has to be crazy about that kid.*" And caregivers, in turn, "need public policies and practices that provide opportunity, status, resources, encouragement, stability, example, and above all *time* for parenthood."[1]

To word it even more simply, children need unconditional love and consistent care from their families, and families in turn need a "village" to support their efforts. These two principles not only capture the essence of Bronfenbrenner's prolific research but also that of a number of towering figures in child psychology, including Diana Baumrind, John Bowlby, Erik Erikson, and Stanley Greenspan. They also echo the "child-honoring" philosophy of children's singer and advocate Raffi. In recent years, with the advent of brain-imaging techniques, researcher Allan Schore and his colleagues have documented that reliable, loving care during infancy and early childhood has a profound impact on the development of regions of the brain that are critical for regulating emotions and coping with stress. And the ability to regulate feelings and manage stress are the hallmarks of mental health.[2]

In this chapter, I describe the kind of care and community support that all children need and some of the adverse consequences for children's mental health when these needs are not met, as is increasingly the case in the United States. In so doing, I contest the prevailing belief that psychological disturbances in childhood are predominantly the result of genetically primed brain disorders. When brain disorders are in fact implicated, research suggests that neglect or trauma in early childhood is more likely the causal factor. Therefore, this alternative perspective emphasizes the role of families, communities, and the governments that serve them, in fostering children's mental health.

Talk of giving children "unconditional love" sounds clichéd unless we clarify what this means within the context of parents' daily routines of feeding and carrying infants, coping with tantrums and toilet training, and juggling domestic and work schedules. It is also necessary to explicate the kind of support that parents need in order to be fully present both emotionally and physically for their children.

A few generations ago, new parents expected to learn these precepts from their own parents, and through hands-on experience from helping care for younger siblings and cousins in stable family and community networks. But in recent decades, technological innovation and globalization have engendered radical changes in our lifestyles—often within a single generation—and as a result, the lessons to be learned from our parents and grandparents may seem obsolete. In addition, changes in the workplace require many adults to relocate frequently, separating young parents from their families of origin. And so new parents must often sort out the challenges and complexities of parenthood for themselves.

A PORTRAIT OF CARE

Time and again over the past half century, a veritable army of researchers has demonstrated that a relationship with at least one loving, responsive, and dependable caregiver is essential for a child's present and future psychological well-being. The quality of this relationship extends well beyond the mere provision of food and shelter; it impacts intellectual, social, emotional, and brain development as well as the development of language and personality. This caregiver–infant relationship is called "attachment."[3] It is not essential that the caregiver in the attachment relationship be the biological mother. Any adult—who, in Bronfenbrenner's inimitable

words, is "crazy about that kid"—can serve as an attachment figure, and in fact it is better for the child to have more than one caregiver to rely on.

As psychologist Robert Karen explains in *Becoming Attached*:

> The concept of "attachment," born in British psychoanalysis some
> forty years ago and nurtured to near maturity in the developmental
> psychology departments of American universities ... encompasses
> both the quality and strength of the parent–child bond, the ways in
> which it forms and develops, how it can be damaged and repaired,
> and the long-term impact of separations, losses, wounds, and de-
> privations. Beyond that, *it is a theory of love and its central place in
> human life.*[4]

Attachment: An Anthropological Perspective

Beyond the immediate pleasure that tender loving care might
give an infant or young child, why does its presence or absence have
profound psychological consequences that reverberate throughout
our lives? In *Childhood Lost*, anthropologist Meredith Small helps us
to understand why the attachment between parent and child is of
such central importance. Small explains that

> Humans, like all primates, are designed to be involved with the
> upbringing of their offspring for many years, but as we will see,
> particular evolutionary pressures have rendered the human
> caregiver–child relationship especially intense and long-lasting.
> About four million years ago ... when early humans stood up and
> started to walk on two legs, that type of locomotion required an in-
> crease in the gluteus maximus and minimus muscles which in turn
> pushed for a short and broad bony pelvic shape. As a result, the pel-
> vic opening, or birth canal, also changed; the opening became essen-
> tial ovoid instead of round with the sacrum tilted inward forming a
> bowl. This change in pelvic architecture was not a problem at first
> because our earliest ancestors still had small brains—comparable in
> size to the brains of modern chimpanzees—and infants could easily
> navigate the birth canal. The real crisis came about 1.5 million years
> ago when there was intense pressure for brain growth in the human
> lineage and suddenly babies had much bigger heads relative to the
> size of the pelvic opening.
>
> At this point, evolution had to make a compromise because there is
> only so far you can push the width of the pelvis to accommodate
> infant head size; if the human pelvis were any wider, women would
> not be able to walk. Instead, Natural Selection opted for another

route; human infants are born too soon—neurologically unfinished compared to other primates. As a result they are physically and emotionally very dependent. But this level of dependence could not have appeared if there hadn't been some corresponding evolutionary shift in parental behavior that facilitated the capacity to respond to infant needs. And so, there must have been a "co-evolution" of dependent infants and responding adults for human infants to have survived. *A human newborn, therefore, is designed by evolution to be "entwined" with an adult of its species.* In other words, human infants have evolved to be "attached" both emotionally and physically to their caregivers and when that attachment is denied, the infant is at risk.[5]

Small also reminds us that for 95 percent of human history, we were all hunter-gatherers. And it was in this physical and social milieu that our species evolved. And so, studying the few extant hunter-gatherer and horticultural groups reveals the rich diversity of beliefs, values, and lifestyles that is typical of our species. But despite these variations, a common pattern emerges: in the preindustrial milieu, infants are in almost constant skin contact with their caregivers, who respond immediately to their needs and never leave them to cry. This style of infant care is not just a "third world phenomenon" born of poverty or lack of resources but is also standard practice in technologically advanced countries such as Japan. In fact, even today it is typical of infant care in the vast majority of human societies. *And this style of care is precisely what a half century of "attachment" research tells us that infants need for optimal psychological and neurological development.*

The Premature Push for Independence

It is striking that the United States—where so much attachment research is conducted—is one of the few countries in which parents do not routinely care for their infants in these physically responsive ways that are optimal for psychological and neurological development. Why is this so? As Small suggests:

The primary goal of Western—that is North American and European parents, but especially American—parents is independence and self-reliance for children. This push for independence is most striking in infancy when babies are expected to sleep alone and are fed on a schedule. Western parents also expect infants to "self comfort" when they cry so many parents delay responses to crying or do not respond at all but believe in a policy of letting the infant "cry it out."

This caretaking style results in many hours during which infants are not held and are not part of a social group. Western babies are held 50% less than in all other cultures, spend 60% of day time alone, and the West is the only culture in which babies are expected to sleep alone.[6]

Paradoxically, infants who are in constant physical contact with their caregivers and never left to cry—as opposed to infants who are "trained" to be independent by being left alone to "cry it out" several hours a day—are much more likely to become confident, independent children. This is not too difficult to understand when we place ourselves in comparable circumstances. Imagine that you are alone in your bedroom. You have fallen and broken your ankle, or perhaps you have awakened with a high fever, or from a terrifying dream. Your spouse is in the next room. You call out in anguish, and he pops his head in, smiles benevolently, and suggests that you settle down and go to sleep. You cry out to him repeatedly, but he does not return. The familiar sounds of the household—conversation, music, laughter—surround you, but you are alone, too incapacitated to move, and unable to effectively communicate how desperately ill or frightened or sad you feel. Eventually you fall silent because your efforts to reach out to your loved one are fruitless. Over the coming weeks you are routinely ignored by your spouse. But you are a competent adult with many personal and interpersonal resources. If your relationship with your husband does not improve, you are free to leave and seek out a more gratifying one.

An infant, on the other hand, does not have these competencies or freedoms. She is utterly dependent on her caregivers. When left for hours to cry herself to sleep, day after day, week after week, she will eventually stop crying and become "well behaved." But inwardly she may be paralyzed with fear, seething with anger, or overwhelmed with sadness. And in the process, she is acquiring an overarching orientation of mistrust—of herself, of others, of her world. While learning to self-comfort and not to cry, the infant is learning other important lessons as well: that her needs and feelings are insignificant, that she can't rely on others to help her when she is in pain, that how she feels is not particularly informative, and that how she communicates is not particularly effective. By contrast, the infant who is in continual contact with her caregivers, who take her seriously and respond quickly to her needs as they arise, builds up an image of herself as competent, of her family as loving, and of her world as safe. And it is this infant who will acquire the confidence with which to exercise true independence.

The Dance of Attachment

Given how vital attachment is to the infant's survival, it should not come as a surprise that human infants are born with a number of characteristics and instinctive behaviors that help to "woo" the parent into a loving relationship. Research has shown that infants' physical characteristics—their round faces and eyes, soft skin, their gentle grasp, the way they mold their bodies when held, their radiant smiles, coos, and babbles—are deeply appealing to adults. In addition, from birth infants are attracted to the smell of their mother's breast milk, the sound of her voice, the rhythm of her heart beat, the touch of her skin.[7] Daniel Stern's analysis of videos of infants and mothers revealed that quite unconsciously they engage in a synchronous dance as first one and then the other gaze, touch, and communicate with each other verbally and nonverbally.[8] Infants are so attuned to and dependent on this dance of attachment that they become distressed when a beloved caregiver does not return their smile. Touch is a key element in the attachment relationship. Research has shown that when premature infants are held and stroked each day, they show more rapid neural and physical development than those who receive standard hospital care.[9]

Born Too Soon

Because babies are "born too soon"—neurologically unfinished—during the first several months of life, human infants are not yet capable of regulating their bodies. Therefore, the attachment or entwined relationship is one of physiological and not just emotional dependency. Sleep expert James McKenna has demonstrated that when nursing mothers and their infants sleep beside one another, their heart rates, brain waves, breathing patterns, and sleep cycles become synchronized.[10]

Breast-feeding also helps to regulate and augment their physiological processes. Over and above the nourishing proteins, minerals, vitamins, fats, and sugars, breast milk also supplies antibodies to assist the infant's immature immune system, growth factors that help in tissue development and maturation, and a variety of hormones, neuropeptides, and natural opioids that subtly shape brain development and behavior. The breast has been described as the "external counterpart of the placenta, picking up where [it] left off the task of ushering the infant toward physical and neurological completion."[11]

Learning to Feel

The attachment relationship helps infants to modulate, interpret, and communicate emotions. Sue Gerhardt describes this process in *Why Love Matters: How Affection Shapes a Baby's Brain*:

> To become fully human, the baby's basic responses need to be elaborated and developed into more specific and complex feelings. With parental guidance, the basic state of "feeling bad" can get differentiated into a range of feelings like irritation, disappointment, anger, annoyance and hurt. Again, the baby or toddler can't make these distinctions without help from those in the know. The parent must also help the baby to become aware of his own feelings and this is done by holding up a virtual mirror to the baby, talking in baby talk and emphasizing and exaggerating words and gestures so that the baby can realize that this is not mum or dad just expressing themselves, this is them "showing" me my feelings. It is a kind of "psychofeedback" which provides the introduction to a human culture in which we can interpret both our own and others' feelings and thoughts. Parents bring the baby into this more sophisticated emotional world by identifying feelings and labeling them clearly. Usually this teaching happens quite unselfconsciously.[12]

Brain Development

In recent years, with the help of brain-imaging technologies, Allan Schore and his colleagues at the UCLA School of Medicine have documented that brain development in the first few years of life is dependent on the social and sensory stimulation that is part and parcel of the attachment relationship.[13] Despite a growth industry in flash cards, videos, toys, and software that boasts it can turn your baby into the next Einstein, it is human rather than electronic stimulation that grows a baby's brain. The human touch, voice, gaze, and smile trigger a complex cascade of neurochemicals that catalyze growth in regions of the brain that play a critical role in our ability to empathize, control our impulses, and develop a sense of self. One of the most vital brain regions to develop as an outgrowth of attachment relationships is the orbitofrontal cortex.

The orbitofrontal cortex plays a key role in emotional life. It enables us to empathize with others and to control our emotional responses. Although social emotions such as the pain of separation from a loved one and shame originate in the amygdala and hypothalamus, the orbitofrontal cortex serves to control our impulses and express ourselves in socially appropriate and reflective ways. It is very significant that the prefrontal cortex in general, and the orbitofrontal cortex in particular, has a growth spurt when the child is between six and twelve months of age, corresponding exactly with the period when the attachment bond is being consolidated. There is a second growth spurt in early toddlerhood, around the time the child begins to walk—which is also a period of intense pleasure between parent and child.[14]

In a study conducted with Romanian orphans who had had no opportunity to form attachments with caregivers during infancy and early childhood, brain imaging revealed a black hole where the orbitofrontal cortex should be. People who sustain damage to the orbitofrontal cortex become insensitive to social and emotional cues. They may also be prone to dissociation or even to sociopathy.[15]

After the orbitofrontal cortex has matured, other areas of the social-emotional brain begin to mature, including the anterior cingulate, which helps us to tune into our feelings. Soon thereafter the dorsolateral prefrontal cortex—the primary site of working memory—begins to develop. Together the anterior cingulate and dorsolateral cortex facilitate verbal and nonverbal communication of feelings. During a child's third year of life, the hippocampus, which plays a key role in long-term memory, begins to mature and becomes strongly linked to the anterior cingulate and the dorsolateral prefrontal cortex. The hippocampus enables the child to create a personal narrative with a past and a future, and so for the first time she has an enduring sense of self and no longer lives just in the moment. *This sequence of postnatal brain development is largely dependent on the sensory, intellectual, and emotional stimulation that is integral to the attachment relationship.*[16]

Beyond Attachment

The style of parenting that fosters attachment is ideal during infancy and early toddlerhood. But what then? Although space constraints prevent me from exploring their work at length, Diana Baumrind's parenting research and Erik Erikson's psychosocial theory of development provide excellent guidelines beyond the intense early months of "attachment" parenting.

Authoritative Parenting

In the 1970s, Diana Baumrind conducted research to discern what style of parenting is optimal for psychological development. She discovered that an approach to parenting that she named "authoritative" has the best long-term outcomes for children. In the decades that have ensued, her research has been replicated and elaborated, and there is now wide consensus among parenting experts that this approach fosters healthy development.[17]

Authoritative parents are warm, attentive, and sensitive to their child's needs. At the same time, they consistently assert age-appropriate expectations and responsibilities. So, for example, their young children know that they are not to eat cookies before dinner and that they must do their homework, complete household tasks, and treat others with respect. When making their expectations known, these parents provide their children with a cogent rationale. As a result, over time the children internalize their parents' underlying motives and values so that they don't remain dependent on authority figures to "do the right thing." As children get older, authoritative parents grant their children increasing autonomy over decisions that affect them, thereby gently ushering them along their journey toward adulthood.

Authoritative parenting has been linked to a variety of positive outcomes. During the preschool years, children of authoritative parents are happier, they have better impulse control, they persevere at challenging tasks, and they are more cooperative at school. Older children have higher self-esteem, are more socially and morally mature, and perform better at school.[18]

Psychosocial Stages

Psychoanalyst Erik Erikson's theory of psychosocial development describes the central psychological challenges that confront all human beings at different stages of the life cycle.[19] The central psychological challenge of infancy is the acquisition of *trust*. Securely attached infants whose caregivers consistently respond to their needs in a loving and timely fashion come to approach life with optimism. Children who are imbued with trust find it easier to acquire *autonomy* in toddlerhood. Toddlers have a burgeoning sense of self that is ushered in by an explosion of new intellectual, linguistic, and motor skills. Suddenly they are walking, talking, climbing, and exploring. Parents who allow their toddlers to "do for themselves"—whether it be climbing the stairs, putting on their own shirt, or feeding themselves—without providing absolute freedom on the one hand (which would be unsafe) or too little freedom on the other hand (which conveys a message of incompetence) provide optimal support during their bid for autonomy. During the preschool years, children need time for unstructured imaginative play in natural settings in order to develop *initiative*. Psychologically healthy school-age children feel a natural desire to develop the capacity for *industry*. When children find their passion, whether it be tennis, literature, or woodwork, they will work with great diligence toward mastery when parents and teachers facilitate their efforts as mentors and guides.

The predominant psychological challenge of adolescence is to acquire a coherent and meaningful sense of *identity*. Adolescents who begin their search for identity with a healthy sense of trust, autonomy, initiative, and industry are greatly advantaged. And when they enter adulthood knowing who they are, what they believe in and value, and where they are going in life, they are more capable of achieving the central tasks of adulthood: the capacity for enduring *intimacy* and *generativity*. Generativity refers to our desire to nurture the next generation. While parents and "helping professionals" such as teachers and therapists may nurture children in direct ways, everyone, whether they be artists, managers, environmentalists, or politicians, can make "generative" choices that inspire or secure the safety and prospects of the next generation.

And now we come full circle. Adults who were securely attached infants with authoritative parents who helped them to successfully negotiate the central psychological challenges of childhood will acquire a healthy sense of identity, which is a precursor for intimacy and generativity. The capacity to sustain intimacy and act generatively is in turn necessary to successfully parent one's own children. In other words, adults who lack trust, autonomy, initiative, industry, and a strong sense of identity will be greatly compromised in their ability to offer intimate and altruistic care to their children.

PORTRAIT OF COMMUNITY

As anthropologist Meredith Small reminds us, there is an evolutionary push toward an "entwined" or "attachment" relationship with our children that is as old as our primate history. But our potential for intimacy and generativity will not be actualized unless we ourselves have been the recipients of responsive and responsible care from our own parents. Harlow's research with monkeys revealed that infant monkeys who were separated from their mothers at birth were incapable of nurturing their own offspring.[20] But even when we were well parented ourselves, our natural desire to parent must be augmented by direct experience with childcare as well as a healthy dose of intelligence and energy. And still these circumstances do not suffice. In Bronfenbrenner's evocative words: "The heart of our social system is the family. If we are to maintain the health of our society, we must discover the best means of nurturing that heart."[21] In other words, parents must be supported in myriad ways by their communities and the wider culture.

What Parents Need

If adults are to have the time, resources, and the physical and emotional health necessary to parent their children, they need

- family, friends, and neighbors who can provide practical and emotional support;
- health care for themselves and their children that is affordable, comprehensive, and not contingent on the whims of an employer;
- affordable housing in safe neighborhoods with amenities that support family life, such as parks, community centers, libraries, and grocery stores;
- paid parental and child sick leave that is generous enough to enable parents to form secure attachments with their children and that never obligates them to choose between nursing a sick child or paying the rent;
- daycare that is affordable and of the highest quality;
- a living wage so that their "second shift" can be at home with their children;
- flexible work arrangements—ones that allow them to complete work at home or share a position—without forsaking essential benefits such as health care or permanently compromising opportunities for career advancement;
- public schools that are safe, with small teacher–child ratios, and that utilize developmentally sensitive approaches to education;
- media regulation so that their children are no longer relentlessly exposed to violence, pornography, sexism, racism, and commercials for products that undermine their health; and
- clean air, soil, and water.

American parents who read this wish list may dismiss it as utopian, and yet it describes the status quo in many industrialized nations. In fact these conditions should be regarded as fundamental human rights because they are the preconditions for fostering attachments and authoritative parenting, which in turn are essential for healthy psychological and neurological development.

When Care and Community Break Down

How can a mother who must return to work only days after giving birth—while placing her newborn in substandard care—establish a secure attachment with her infant? If a single mother must work two or three low-wage jobs to make ends meet while her children return to an empty home, how can she scaffold their arduous journey toward adulthood? And how can she protect them from the tidal wave of violence, hatred, racism, sexism, and pornography that pervade the media? And if this mother is the second or third generation to have raised children under these compromised circumstances, how will she herself have acquired the psychological maturity and wisdom to relate lovingly and responsibly toward her children? But these are precisely the conditions under which millions of American parents are obligated to raise their children. As Bronfenbrenner has lamented, "the comparative lack of family support systems in the United States is so extreme as to make it unique among modern nations."[22]

Sadly, it appears that support for families in the United States continues to deteriorate in lockstep with the rise in psychiatric disturbances. Psychologist Laura Berk described this downward spiral in *Childhood Lost*:

> American children and adolescents of all walks of life are experiencing more stress than their counterparts of the previous generation. An examination of hundreds of studies of nine- to seventeen-year-olds carried out between the 1950s and the 1990s revealed a steady, large increase in anxiety over this period. A combination of reduced social connectedness and increased environmental dangers (crime, violent media, fear of war, etc.) appeared responsible.... Interestingly, whereas societal indicators of diminished social connectedness ... showed strong associations with children's rising anxiety, economic conditions such as poverty and unemployment had comparatively little influence. *A child's well-being, it appears, is less responsive to whether the family has enough money than to whether it promotes close, supportive bonds with others.* Other changes in the American

family also point to a withering of social connectedness. For example, Americans are less likely to visit friends, join community organizations, and volunteer in their communities than they once were....[P]arents and children converse and share leisure time less often than they did in the past.

Simultaneously, young people's sense of trust in others has weakened. In 1992 only 18.3 percent of high school seniors agreed that one can usually trust people, compared with 34.5 percent in 1975. Young people's increased anxiety is a natural response to lower quality relationships. *As social connectedness in the United States declined, youth suicide rates rose.* Between the 1950s and 1970s, they rose by 300 percent for fifteen- to twenty-five-year-olds; and between 1980 and 1997, by 109 percent for ten- to fourteen-year-olds.[23]

CONCLUSION

The current and ongoing breakdown in caregiving and community support is largely responsible for the epidemic of psychiatric disturbances that we are now witnessing among children in the United States. That view is not very popular, however, because policy-based efforts to heal communities, empower parents, and regulate industry do not generate profits for the pharmaceutical or genetic technology industries. And stellar careers in research are not built on promoting practices that many of our grandmothers and great grandmothers knew intuitively to be true. In contrast, the claim is so widespread that mental health or illness is encoded in our genes that social psychologist Carol Travis apparently had no qualms about including the following statement as part of a list of false assumptions that have been "resoundingly disproved by research": "The way that parents treat a child in the first five years (three years) (one year) (five minutes) of life is crucial to the child's later intellectual and emotional success."[24] And this statement was published in the *Chronicle of Higher Education*, one of the most widely read and respected newspapers in academic circles.

As a result of our skewed emphasis on the heritability of mental illness, public funds are being used to develop screening programs in schools to detect early signs of mental illness in children and to create "medical algorithms" that mandate drug therapies. Meanwhile, and in spite of all the bipartisan talk about "family values," we are not providing even the most rudimentary support to our families, which is what we *must* do if we are to address the root cause of children's psychological disturbances. I close with a quote from Bronfenbrenner:

> One telling criterion of the worth of a society—a criterion that stands the test of history—is the concern of one generation for the next. As we enter our third century, we Americans, compared to other industrialized societies, appear to be abandoning that criterion. . . . It would appear that the process of making human beings human is breaking down in American society. To make it work again, we must reweave the unraveling social fabric and revitalize the human bonds essential to sustaining the well-being and development of both present and future generations.[25]

3

The Dance of Nature and Nurture

How Environment Impacts Brain Development and Genetic Expression

Jane M. Healy

Deep in the cavern of the infant's breast, the father's nature lurks and lives.

Horace, 15 B.C.

Men are like plants; the goodness and flavour of the fruit proceeds from the peculiar soil and exposition in which they grow.

Michael Guillaume Jean de Creve-Coeur, 1782

One of the oldest conundrums of the human condition concerns whether we are shaped more by our genes or by our environments. Opinions about the so-called nature–nurture debate have, over the centuries, shaped philosophies, confounded psychologists, and intrigued parents and teachers. The question, for example, of what percentage of one's intelligence derives from genetic endowment and what percentage from parenting, schooling, and other external influences (is it 40–60 percent? 60–40? 50–50?) has been endlessly studied, debated, and used as a rationale for everything from progressive education to eugenics. Studies of identical and fraternal twins, long the most common research tool in this field, have been cited to support both sides of the argument. While often useful in parsing out complex developmental issues, they have nonetheless failed to settle the question. Why, for example, if schizophrenia is known to be "inherited," is it only from 30 to 65 percent concordant for identical twins?[1] In other words, if you are a twin with an inherited gene pattern identical to that of your brother and your brother is diagnosed with schizophrenia, you have no more than about a 50 percent statistical likelihood of getting schizophrenia yourself.

Times are rapidly changing since the decoding of the human genome opened entirely new avenues of investigation. Behavioral genetics, the study of how genes and environment interact to make us who we are, has shown that an intricate dance between nature and nurture begins even before birth and very possibly even before conception. Throughout a lifetime, these two forces twine and intertwine, until it becomes virtually impossible to unravel them. Are genes or environment more important? The short answer is yes.

For the purposes of this book, the most important implication of this new information is to render absurd the following sorts of beliefs:

> If it's in the genes, there's nothing we can do about it—except give him drugs.
>
> It's hopeless; she must have inherited my gene for math phobia.
>
> Why should we bother with behavioral therapy or changing our lifestyle—it's in his genes!
>
> There's no point struggling to teach this kid—look at her parents!

As silly as they sound, I often hear these themes in one form or another not only from parents but also from professionals who should know better. With the exception of a handful of single-gene disorders (e.g., Huntington's, Tay-Sachs), most scientists now agree that each aspect of human behavior results from many genes interacting with each other and with multiple influences from the environment. In fact, what we mean by the word *environment* itself is so complex that the term *environmental variables* is a better way of describing the situation. These days the disagreement between nativists, who focus on inborn traits, and empiricists, who believe the environment is mainly responsible, is much more quantitative than qualitative.

INDIVIDUALS MOLD ENVIRONMENTS; ENVIRONMENTS MOLD INDIVIDUALS

No one denies that genetic endowment can predispose someone to certain types of temperament and behavior, which in turn act on the variables in the individual's environment. A child born with a "difficult" temperament may elicit different types of responses from parents and caregivers than one perceived as "easy"—which in turn may either exacerbate or ameliorate the behavioral problems. Nonetheless, new research described later in this chapter indicates that a seemingly innate "difficult" personality style can be considerably modified by early competent and nurturing caregivers.

As children mature, they tend to select friends who share similar likes and dislikes, which in turn reinforces native propensities. They also tend to be drawn to certain types of activities, or even of activity level. The power of innate qualities shows up not only in families with long pedigrees of accomplishment in certain fields (think Bach or Barrymore), but also with so-called resilient children who emerge relatively unscathed from unspeakably bad environments. In looking at such cases, however, we inevitably find powerful contributing environmental variables: musically and creatively enriched family environments in which certain types of achievement are valued, in the case of the Bachs or Barrymores, and invariably one influential individual (relative, teacher, older child) who believed in and encouraged those "resilient" ones.

Can a superstimulating environment make a Bach or a Barrymore out of any of our children? Probably not, unless some degree of innate potential exists. As Jerome Kagan suggests, "it may be helpful to think of some genetic factors as constraining certain outcomes rather than determining a particular trait."[2] For example, height is one of the most genetically influenced of all human traits, yet the influence of environment is evidenced by the fact that people on average are getting taller with each generation. Parents determined to engineer the development of a prodigy, a scholarship-level athlete, or a seven-footer might be better advised to provide a wide variety of stimulating activities, while observing and guiding the child's own nature and talents. Likewise, it is sensible to accept the fact that although a jumpy, disorganized infant may not become the calmest kid on the block, and a fearful, withdrawn one may never be a raging extrovert, supportive nurturance can enable each to succeed happily within the parameters of his or her own temperament.

Environmental influences and experience—which include, of course, teaching, learning, and practice—remain a significant force throughout our lifetimes, with the power to alter even the adult brain, as can be seen in stroke patients, who with effort develop new brain circuitry for some sorts of activities. Brain scans reveal that adult experts, such as musicians or chess players, differ from nonexperts; they have developed so-called expert circuits that enable their superior level of performance. In the case of musicians, the networks are more robust in those who took up their instrument before adolescence when the brain was still more "plastic,"[3] but new connections are possible even in those who start playing as adults.

In the past we have seen what damage crude determinism, either genetic or environmental, can do. Genetic determinists have claimed (and some still suggest)[4] that intelligence and academic ability are so strongly inherited that not much can be done about it—an argument that could be used to justify educational inequality, at the very least. On the opposite end of the pole, pure environmentalists once blamed "refrigerator mothers," whom they judged to be emotionally cold and distant, for their children's autism. We know now, of course, that although early and intensive treatment can mitigate the course of autism, it is a genetically influenced brain disorder and certainly not a reason to lay blame on an already distraught mother.

The bottom line: neither biology nor environment is necessarily destiny. For our purposes here, this realization sets the stage for understanding why genes do not always act deterministically and why biological solutions are not necessarily the only—or even the best—ones when a child has problems. In this chapter we explore how genes work and interact and look at the traits that are most powerfully genetically influenced. We then turn to an examination of the developing brain and how it can be significantly changed as genes interact with the child's experiences.

Genes: Mechanisms, Not Causes

A few basics of behavioral genetics can help us understand why the question "nature *or* nurture?" is outdated. The notion of "nature *via* nurture" captures much better the dynamic, self-organizing dance of human development and why the variables in each child's environment are so instrumental in determining how—or even whether—his or her genes express themselves.[5]

Probing the Genome
The human genome is comprised of some 33,000–50,000 genes, at least half of which may be expressed in the brain. Two species

(e.g., apes and men) can have almost identical genes, but if they are arranged in a different order, we see quite a different outcome. Genes do their work through the activity of proteins, the letter sequences for which are contained in their DNA. In the human genome, even a minute change in one gene's DNA code (e.g., a one-letter difference in a string of over a thousand letters) may have measurable results.[6]

Genes set the basic parameters within which each of us develops both as a member of the human race and as an individual. For example, all humans come programmed to acquire a language, but the quality of exposure and one's national/local environment— always interacting with individual genetic patterns—determine which language sounds, what vocabulary, what grammatical rules, and what level of language competence (reflected, of course, in reading, writing, and social conversation) become embedded in the brain. Human infants and even some primates are born with a basic number sense (are five objects greater than two?), but whether or not one learns to write numerals, which numerals one learns, and whether multiplication or calculus is mastered depends on culture, experience, and teaching.

Susceptibility or "risk" genes can increase the likelihood that an individual will develop certain problems, but most complex human traits are *polygenic*—that is, they are influenced by many genes which can combine in multiple variations. Just as the term *cake* may imply countless different mixtures of similar ingredients, the term *dyslexia* may signify multiple variations of certain genetic elements, which are then stirred up by each individual's particular environment. Perhaps this fact explains why similar combinations of genes may result in quite different behavioral (phenotypic) expressions in different individuals.

Even in the case of "risk" genes, environment may still play a role. For example, infants born with PKU, a single-gene disorder that prevents them from properly digesting protein foods, will suffer brain damage and retardation from toxins produced if they ingest protein. Obviously, however, if the child's diet is managed correctly—which is now possible—the problematic DNA will remain inactivated and little or no damage will be done.[7] "The example of PKU serves as an antidote to the mistaken notion that genetics implies therapeutic nihilism, even for a single-gene disorder," states Robert Plomin, a prominent researcher in the field of behavioral genetics.[8]

Each gene can be set to either on or off, yielding about 10 billion possibilities for individual variation.[9] Either environmental factors or other genes can pull this switch; genes thus become both the cause and the consequence of our actions.

Genes and the Environment

There are several reasons why genetic expression is so responsive to the environment. First, it is a long-term process, with new genes being activated even into adulthood. Such adult-onset diseases as Alzheimer's or Parkinson's are obvious examples of this point, but many other genetically influenced traits are similarly involved—and amenable, to a greater or lesser degree, to environmental influence.

Second, DNA, which encodes all our genetic information, is itself malleable to environmental variables.[10] "The truth of the matter," states one noted neuroscientist, "is that DNA is both inherited and environmentally responsive."[11] Such modification occurs through the action of gene promoters and transcription factors, with the intermediary of messenger RNA (mRNA). RNA is a genetic material that helps determine how cells of the body (including the brain, of course) function. It can have powerful effects on genes; RNA interference can "paralyze" a gene or act to up-regulate or down-regulate genetic activity.[12] Experimental rats exposed to mentally and physically stimulating environments show changes in mRNA, which then "turns on" DNA activity and increases cellular protein expression and development in certain areas of the brain's cortex. An interesting example of such effects in humans involves the effects of stress. Stressed-out medical students before and during exams experience hormonal changes, which in turn reduce mRNA activity in the immune response system, thus lowering the subjects' resistance to infection.[13]

"Inherited Characteristics"

Any parent realizes that children are not simply "blank slates" but that they come with distinct personalities, quirks, and talents—even if they have the same parents and similar genetic makeup. Of course, no two children—not even identical twins—have identical environments, since family and other dynamics inevitably differ among children. *Heritability* studies, however, which examine the fraction of the variance of a trait that is the result of genetic inheritance, have found several personality variables that seem to be most clearly influenced by genes. Let us look at two of the areas that have been most intensely studied to discover how genetic endowment lays down basic templates of our selves.

Personality and Temperament

In study after study, personality traits come up as some of our most "heritable" characteristics. The three most salient examples of strongly heritable dimensions of personality are labeled *novelty seeking* (risk taking, extraversion), *harm avoidance* (fearfulness, neuroticism), and *reward dependence* (persistence, attachment to others, sentimentality, warmth).[14] The underlying biology of these traits appears to depend on systems of brain chemicals called catecholamines (e.g., dopamine, serotonin). Novelty seeking (as in impulsivity) and harm avoidance (such as fearfulness, withdrawal) are under particularly close scrutiny because they are associated with problems such as attention-deficit/hyperactivity disorder, depression, and antisocial personality disorders, for which medications are often prescribed. As we shall see, however, environmental factors may mitigate or even reverse negative outcomes.

Cross-cultural studies have suggested that these characteristics are universal human traits. A study in China found heritability in similar aspects of temperament: activity level, approach/avoidance behavior, intensity of reaction, mood, and responsiveness threshold.[15] Yet once again, no one has suggested that "heritability" of such complex traits implies that a trait can't be modified—or even radically changed. In short, no matter what your genetic inclinations, life experiences will account for a significant amount of the outcome. Even in the womb, a pregnant mother's level of stress may "set" the infant's chemical balance and responsiveness,[16] and as we shall see when we examine brain functioning, experiences throughout life continue to have powerful effects.

Intelligence

Psychologists still argue about definitions of intelligence, and scientists have searched fruitlessly for a gene that controls it. After thousands of studies and unlimited quantities of speculation and opinion, what we call intelligence (usually as tested by some IQ measure) comes out as even more responsive to the environment than personality. Aspects of intelligence, such as reaction time and some aspects of language processing, as well as the amount of gray matter in the brain appear to be at least partially inherited,[17] but so many different factors comprise our "smarts" that they are hard to pin down. In addition, recent studies show the dramatic potential of environmental interventions to change not only tested mental ability but also lifetime outcomes.

It is beyond the intention of this chapter to detail the enormous literature, which includes studies of at-risk children adopted into enriched surroundings, comparisons of identical twins adopted into different socioeconomic groups, and intensive preschool enrichment programs for at-risk children and families. In each instance, appropriate early stimulation raises IQ scores and school readiness. Although these numerical gains tend to fall off somewhat with age, they are not lost. Even more impressive are the data on long-term life outcomes now available for participants in such early enrichment programs as Head Start, the Perry Preschool Project, and the Abecedarian Project. When these individuals are compared with those in a control group who did not receive the enrichment, we find repeatedly that such interventions engender lasting gains in life skills, school completion, social adjustment, and self-esteem, as well as financial and personal success.[18]

To understand more fully how such influences operate, we turn to an examination of the growing brain and the phenomenon of neural plasticity throughout the lifetime.

THE ENVIRONMENTALLY RESPONSIVE BRAIN

It's a fortunate person whose brain

Is trained early, again and again,

And who continues to use it

To be sure not to lose it

So the brain, in old age, may not wane.[19]

Albert Galaburda, neurobiologist

One of the most provocative scientific findings in recent decades has been that of neuroplasticity—the fact that the brain is significantly changed, throughout the lifetime, by interaction with the environment. Although plasticity is at its height in early years, examples abound of how adult mental activity retains power to effect positive change.

Two types of genes set the parameters of brain development within which these changes occur: *structural genes*, which build the brain and control the arrangement of its cells (neurons and glial cells), and *functional genes*, which keep it working.[20] The brain's functions are powered mainly through chemical and hormonal substances (neuromodulators, neurohormones, neurotransmitters) that convey messages over vast relay systems of synapses between neuronal networks.

Neuroplasticity: Powerful Implications

Both structure and function of the brain are "plastic" in the sense that they develop depending on input and use. At birth, the brain is *structurally* overendowed with immature neurons and synaptic potential; during the years of childhood and adolescence, some synapses are strengthened and others lost as it is gradually pruned into a strong and efficient operating system. As neural maps develop, relationships are built between their circuits, and these are reinforced by environmental experience. Recent studies portray this process as one in which synapses actually compete to grow; those successful in making connections survive, whereas others do not—a real "use it or lose it" situation. The originator of this idea, Nobel laureate Gerald Edelman, is careful to emphasize that all brain development takes place within a dynamic, developing human organism. The plastic brain is exquisitely responsive to environmental variables as the individual interacts, thinks, feels, and builds up a custom-tailored network of brain connections for his unique environmental demands. Edelman pointedly eschews "reductionism" that looks only at biological causes for human behavior: "To reduce a theory of an individual's behavior to a theory of molecular interactions is simply silly, a point made clear when one considers how many different levels of physical, biological, and social interactions must be put into place before higher order consciousness emerges."[21]

Functionally, the brain's plasticity results from the malleability of chemical transmission patterns in its circuits. Although a person inherits certain genetic predispositions for neurochemical activity and balance in the brain, this balance is continually shifting, both affecting and affected by internal variables (e.g., mood, thoughts) and external ones (e.g., vigorous exercise, dietary substances, drugs, amount of sleep). As with the neurons and their physical connections, repeated use of certain patterns of chemical transmission (e.g., high levels of stress) may eventually become habituated in the brain. Much more research is needed before we can parse the neurochemical effects of certain types of events in children's lives, but there is no doubt that often-repeated mental and emotional responses leave enduring marks. Animal experiments cited in a later section are only the beginning of our new understanding. Eventually we may be able to answer questions such as the following: How does early and repeated exposure to television and computer screens affect young children's neurotransmitter functions, and could exposure contribute to attention problems? What effect does scary or exciting/addictive content (e.g., video games) have on dopamine or serotonin levels in developing brains—and what are the behavioral consequences? Does inappropriate academic pressure, particularly in early grades, set the brain up for later imbalances? What are the exact effects of vigorous exercise—or the life of a couch potato—on the functionality of the brain? What environmental factors—physical, emotional, or cognitive—contribute to the current "epidemic" of childhood disabilities and disorders? These would seem to be pressing questions, but they have scarcely been addressed. Is it because the "quick fix" of a psychoactive drug (which often turns out to be neither "quick" nor a "fix") enables us to blame something inside the child rather than objectively examining—and maybe even doing something about—the factors in our culture that may be contributing to the problem?

How the Brain—and Psychoactive Drugs—Work

The various brain chemicals that make the system work are pumped into the synapses, or tiny gaps between cells, where they then transmit the electrical impulses carrying messages to receptors in other cells on the other side of the gap. Genetic differences play a role in setting up this process; some individuals appear to have systems that either enhance the presence of certain neurotransmitters in the synapse or suck them up too quickly. Here is where psychoactive drugs do their work; by altering the function of either the pumps or the "reuptake inhibitors" that suck up the substance, it is possible to manipulate the neurochemical balance in the synapse. For example, drugs used to control children's attentional behavior have thus far focused on increasing the presence of the neurotransmitters dopamine and/or norepinephrine in the synapse.

Because there are billions of synapses in the brain, and numerous families and types of chemicals, this entire system is both incredibly complex and a long way from being totally understood. What will be the long-term neurochemical effects of pharmaceutically manipulating the neurotransmitter levels in a developing brain? Thus far we have entirely too little research to answer this question with confidence, although we may be quite sure that these exogenous (external) agents will not all be benign. We do know that artificial neurochemistry, however efficient it may seem, does not in and of itself effect any permanent changes in behavior. Without some accompanying form of treatment directed at helping the individual and those around him manage his symptoms, the gains are commonly lost when the drugs are discontinued.

Another important question concerns whether chemical intervention is the best way to achieve the desired outcome. In adults, selective serotonin reuptake inhibitors (SSRIs) such as Prozac have been used to alleviate severe depression. Newer research demonstrates, however, that cognitive behavioral therapy, which teaches the individual to positively change and manage thoughts and behavior, may achieve an equal improvement in symptoms in some forms of depression and is a valuable adjunct even if it is necessary to use drugs.[22] Whereas drug effects are short term, behavioral change may offer long-term improvement.

It is impossible to separate the brain's structure from its function, as changes in structure will obviously cause it to work differently, whereas changes in function create structural change by strengthening and enlarging certain sorts of connections. I have written elsewhere of how lifestyle changes and today's fast-paced technological world may be quite literally altering children's brains in attention and language areas.[23] Those concerned about the current "epidemic" of psychoactive drugs being administered to children are well advised to remember that "habits of mind" eventually become structures of brain. Surely, it should be our first priority to help children develop adaptive connections in the first place rather than attempting to patch them up with drugs that might have been unnecessary in an environment better suited to the child's individual needs.

When assessing any child for problems, therefore, it is critical to take into account the entire scope of influences that may be affecting the efficiency of brain functioning. In only one example, lack of sleep—which appears to be increasingly chronic for kids in our "stressed-out" culture—may mimic the symptoms of attention deficit disorder.

STAGES OF DEVELOPMENT

Prenatal Gene–Environment Interaction

Structurally, genes set general parameters for the architecture of brain cells (cytoarchitecture) and its stages of development. From at least the moment of conception, however, the environment starts to exert its influence. Even prenatally, the diet, drug use, or general physical condition of the parents may impact the egg or sperm.

The fetal brain develops from a neural tube, from which cells are generated, proliferate, and migrate to form the brain's structure. Nature dictates a clear plan for this development, with genes directing the manner in which cells develop and place themselves throughout the brain. Yet even in the fetus' first weeks, the brain is vulnerable to external forces. The well-publicized finding that a folic acid deficiency in the mother's diet may result in birth defects related to malformation of the neural tube, such as spinal bifida or cleft palate, is only one example. Lead or other heavy metal exposure at any point in the process is a well-recognized factor in causing learning and/or attention disorders. Toxic chemicals, infectious agents, and even the mother's stress level continue to exert effects throughout pregnancy, and nature and nurture become increasingly difficult to sort out as this complex dance progresses. The newborn infant is an extraordinary bundle of genetic complexity, but from the time of birth on, the gene–environment equation becomes increasingly rebalanced toward environmental influences.

Postnatal Environments: Nurture, Genes, and the Brain

A provocative line of research from animal studies has recently demonstrated how early environments can either switch on or suppress genetic tendencies. Certain genes have been identified for the constellations of personality factors (temperament) mentioned earlier: tendencies toward depression or fearfulness on the one hand, and impulsivity, aggression, social problems, and risk taking on the other. These characteristics, which become evident even in very young infants, appear to be mediated by inherited differences in genes that regulate concentrations of the neurotransmitters serotonin and dopamine. Studies of rhesus monkeys, who genetically are very close to humans, have identified certain individuals with a genetic susceptibility to disregulation of these agents; the affected monkeys are more likely to show what researchers term "high reactivity," that is, stress and anxiety or impulsivity and social difficulties. The crucial finding, however, is that *the troublesome genes become activated only if the infant receives inadequate or inconsistent early nurturing*.

In one study, newborn monkeys with a genetic marker for high reactivity and serotonin disregulation were cross-fostered (i.e., reared from birth) with either low-reactivity or high-reactivity mothers. Those raised by the low-reactivity foster mothers, who were themselves calm and expert at soothing and nurturing the babies, showed a surprising outcome. Rather than developing the difficulties—behavioral and neurochemical—that they would have experienced otherwise, the expertly nurtured youngsters developed low-reactivity characteristics and went on to take leadership positions in their group. Notably, their serotonin brain chemistry was normalized. On the other hand, those reared by highly reactive mothers, who tended to be jumpy or fearful, showed the troublesome characteristics—as well as the serotonin imbalances—that usually accompany this genetic profile.[24]

Commenting on this study and other similar ones, developmental psychologist Richard Lerner says that "the recent findings that specific polymorphisms in the serotonin transporter gene are associated with different behavioral and biological outcomes for rhesus monkeys as a function of their early social rearing histories suggest that more complex gene–environment interactions actually are responsible for the phenomenon. It is hard to imagine that the situation would be any less complex for humans."[25] Indeed, studies looking at comparable genes that affect neurotransmitters in the human brain found that the genes have significant effects on depression and antisocial behavior—but only in persons exposed to particular life stressors.[26]

Continuing work with rhesus monkeys has also emphasized the lasting neurochemical effects of forming a positive emotional bond with an adult caregiver. In another series of studies, infants were either raised by adult monkeys or isolated, placed in a nursery, and allowed to play with three or four peers. All infants in the peer-reared group developed lower brain concentrations of serotonin; those who were also genetically susceptible had the least of all and were most likely to develop social problems, aggression, depression, and impulsivity.[27] This line of research also supports the idea that early rearing environments can alter the genome in positive or negative ways.

A recent study of variations in maternal behavior in rats came up with similar findings. Some rats, seemingly, are better at mothering newborns than others; they tend to groom and nurse more effectively, which appears to lower the rat infant's level of stress and produce offspring that retain their calm temperament throughout life. Did these "mellow" young rats simply inherit their mother's neurochemistry or is there something about the very early nurturing that has its own effects? To answer this question, researchers cross-fostered the infants. Those born to stressed-out mother rats were placed with calm dams; as adults, these babies resembled the normal offspring of nonstressed mothers. The authors conclude that the state of a gene can be established through "behavioral programming" that has "tissue-specific effects on gene expression."[28] These effects often become cross-generational, because poorly nurtured animals are subsequently likely to themselves be poor at mothering.[29]

Clinical and anecdotal evidence suggests that similar effects may be found in susceptible human infants in severely emotionally deprived circumstances, such as abusive or neglectful orphanages. Even children in so-called enriched environments may have their biological potential "dampened" by caregivers who fail to respond *contingently*—that is, at the child's level and as a direct response to the child's need or interest.[30] On the other hand, researchers are now demonstrating how human brain function—and later achievement—can be enhanced by appropriate early stimulation. In only one example, Dennis Molfese has shown how a newborn infant's brainwave measurements (event-related potentials, or ERPs) in certain language areas can predict that child's reading and language abilities at age eight. Molfese is careful to point out that the influence of these biological—and certainly genetic—factors can be modified by environmental interventions. In a series of studies, he has demonstrated how even brief periods of language stimulation can speed up and refine the brain's language-processing responses.[31]

One of the major issues in the lives of children today is the sometimes constant presence of electronic media, beginning at birth or even before. "Screen time" and electronic toys and gadgets not only detract from the development of interactive human language and social skills, but they are also noncontingent. There is no way in which such mechanisms can give each child a personal, emotionally, and cognitively custom-tailored response that is directed specifically at his or her level of ability and need. *Yet it is clear that both animal and human brains have critical developmental periods—some very early in life—in which they need this sort of contingent, face-to-face adult responsiveness.*

Later Stages of Brain Development: The Interaction Intensifies

Throughout childhood, adolescence, and even early adulthood, the brain develops through a series of stages that correspond with

the acquisition of more advanced learning abilities. Myriad environmental variables continue to intertwine with each child's
genetic program. One useful way of sorting out this complex
interaction contrasts "experience-expectant" versus "experience-
dependent" development.[32] Experience-expectant neural networks
are those responsive to stimuli that might ordinarily be found in a
human environment, such as features of the visual field or some
sort of language. These are thought to be robust across different
cultures. Experience-dependent connections, on the other hand, are
formed by each individual's idiosyncratic environment interacting
with the basic, genetically directed structures—a child's particular
language, accent, degree of sensitivity to certain types of visual
stimuli, and so forth.

In the very early years, as experience-expectant stages assert
themselves, this type of connectivity is active and rapid. Stages, or
waves, of rapid developmental change continue as the brain opens
new windows for certain types of thinking and learning even into
early adulthood; at the same time, brain development is increasingly influenced by culturally specific experiences.

For example, normally developing infants and toddlers pass
through a relatively predictable series of physical advances—hand
and eye movements, crawling, walking, hopping, and so forth—but
whether a teen becomes a soccer player depends, first, on the game's
existence and popularity in his particular culture and, second, on
the individual's degree of training and practice. Likewise, infants
throughout the world babble in a "universal language," but by six
months of age, the infant's brain is already sorting out the sounds of
the prevailing dialect, meanwhile strengthening neural connections
for those sounds and weakening or even eliminating those not present in the environment (such as *l* and *r* for Japanese speakers).[33]

During the young teen years, waves of maturation in the executive centers (prefrontal cortex) and other areas of the brain, as well as
hormonal upheavals, create both confusion and a profusion of new
abilities. Clearly, cultural influences during the teen years play a significant role in determining into which of many potential directions
this developing adult—and the synapses in her brain—may go.

TEACHING TO CHANGE THE BRAIN

Recent research confirms that brain processing can be changed
by various types of input and teaching. In another series of evoked
potential studies, changes in brain waves in children between the

ages of three and eight, as shown in electrophysiological recordings of those waves, depended on the amount and quality of language stimulation in the child's home environment. Children in enriched language environments appeared to learn to use their brains more efficiently and effectively in a listening task.[34]

Dyslexia has been known for some time to be strongly genetically influenced, with a special brain "signature" that shows up when the brain is scanned during reading tasks. Nonetheless, some notable recent studies have shown that different teaching methods in the primary grades can significantly alter the way dyslexic children's brains work—and the skill that they show—when they perform reading tasks.[35] At the beginning of the studies, scans revealed that the dyslexic students were using their brains in a maladaptive way—evoking the same pattern as that identified in adult dyslexics. In overly simple terms, the students were trying to read with the "wrong" parts of their brains. After a targeted educational intervention, not only had the students' reading improved, but *their brain function had shifted to a normal pattern, which seems to have become permanent.* Perhaps these children were lucky that no drug has thus far emerged as an "easy fix" for the problem of dyslexia, as it seems they are now greatly improved while still drug free. It simply took some additional effort on the part of everyone—especially the adults—involved.

The take-home message from current research is clear: the brain is continually changed by environmental variables, and targeted interventions *at a behavioral level* may have dramatic effects. One such effort was described by Michael Posner at the 2003 annual convention of the American Psychological Association. Posner believes it is possible to teach children to use their brains more effectively in paying attention. "The fact that we can now trace the development of neural networks in the human brain that are at the very heart of the educational experience means that we can try to change them for the better," he stated.[36] Using scalp electrical recordings to measure brain wave changes, he has looked at results from children after they participated in a program of concentration-enhancing computer simulation exercises. Although this research is in its infancy, Posner has noted improvement both in some aspects of attention and in the children's efficient use of relevant brain systems. Just because genes are involved in setting differences in attentional efficiency, he says, doesn't mean that people are sentenced to a fixed level of attentional disorder. Because the brain is so plastic in both structure and function, networks for positive behavior change may be developed by both specialized and everyday experiences.

The Glue of Experience

"People don't come pre-assembled but are glued together by life," quips Joseph LeDoux in his book *Synaptic Self*.[37] This situation is especially true of the developing brain. New genomic research reveals the awesome power of nurture to reach into the DNA itself, knitting together each individual self. As adults guiding this process, we surely have a responsibility to scaffold the process with wisdom, nurturance, and appropriate stimulation—themselves glued together by a deep respect for the fundamental nature and unique pattern of every child.

4

Toxic World, Troubled Minds

Varda Burstyn and David Fenton

Port Huron, Michigan, sits just across the Blue Water Bridge from Sarnia, Ontario. The St. Clair River flows between them, carrying the waters of the Great Lakes of Michigan, Superior, and Huron south. From Sarnia and Port Huron past the recreational shores of Lake St. Clair to the industrialized southern reaches of Detroit, the St. Clair water system picks up the wastes of one of the most highly industrialized regions of the world. Eventually it discharges these into Lake Erie just north of Toledo, Ohio. One of the largest installations of petrochemical plants on the continent, Sarnia hosts, among many others, Suncor Energy, Imperial Oil (Exxon), Shell, DuPont, and Dow Chemical. Twenty of its plants produce daily emissions that are large enough that they must be reported to Environment Canada's national registry of pollution releases. In the 1980s the so-called Sarnia Blob of toxic chemicals was discovered in the St. Clair River, and the river is one of the sites where federal scientists have found wildlife with blurred sexual characteristics. Just as Illinois, Indiana, and Ohio send their toxic airborne fuel emissions north and east to cover a territory that ranges from Windsor to Quebec City, sometimes for weeks at a time, gagging Toronto, Ottawa, and Montreal as well, so Sarnia sends its harsh, concentrated pollution south, down the river to the United States. Pollution doesn't recognize borders.

On the Aamjiwnaang First Nations Reserve just south of Sarnia, literally in the midst of those petrochemical installations, children play on lawns and suburban streets. Yet less than one hundred yards away at the plants, the workers have dressed for some years in biohazard suits. And in recent years the community has begun to figure out why: the births of girls outnumber the births of boys two to one, and the ratio continues to worsen; women have been reporting multiple miscarriages; and many children are having problems with normal sexual development. As in other jurisdictions, these frightening problems have gone hand in hand with an equally frightening phenomenon: a striking rise in the number of children with problems of neurological development and mental health. Large numbers of children at the local elementary school have below-average intelligence, developmental delays, learning deficits, and behavioral problems.[1]

Living in the shadow of a toxic industry may be a worst-case situation, but it would be a mistake to believe that anyone not surrounded by chemical plants or directly living in their plumes is out of harm's way. Scientific investigations have repeatedly shown us that, through many forms of dispersal, the persistent organic pollutants (POPs) these plants produce have been carried to the remotest places on earth and that we all carry them in our bloodstreams. Science has also demonstrated that extremely low levels of these toxicants can cause significant, lifelong damage to children's sexual, neurological, and immunological development; the damage is especially problematic when they affect fetuses, infants, and toddlers.

Many scholars and commentators have been pointing out for years that growing numbers of American children are failing to thrive. In the wealthiest country on earth, we are witnessing yearly increases in youth violence, emotional volatility, depression and even suicide, substance abuse, and plummeting educational achievement.[2] Along with "emotional" problems—volatility, anxiety, panic, depression, suicide—we're witnessing an epidemic of neurodevelopmental disorders. These include learning disabilities, dyslexia, mental retardation, attention deficit disorders, and autism, and they now affect 5–15 percent of the 4 million babies born in the United States each year. Without question many sociocultural factors are contributing to this troubling state of affairs. This article sheds additional light on the role of environmental toxins and, in the briefest of terms, points toward some solutions.

Over 85,000 synthetic chemical compounds are now registered for commercial use in the Environmental Protection Agency's Toxic Substances Control Act (TSCA) inventory, and 2,800 high-production-volume (HPV) chemicals are currently produced in quantities of 1 million pounds or more per year. Arguably, not one has ever been properly tested for its toxicity—because none has undergone transgenerational studies on humans. But even at a less demanding level, hundreds have not been tested for potential toxicity to humans, and most—80 percent—have not been tested for toxicity to children.[3] This failure to test for safety in children is crucial, because in utero and early life exposures to lead, mercury, polychlorinated biphenyls (PCBs), certain pesticides, and other environmental neurotoxicants are known by many epidemiologists and toxicologists to contribute to the causation of very serious conditions. A report from the U.S. National Research Council concluded that 3 percent of developmental disabilities are the direct consequence of neurotoxic environmental exposures and that another 25 percent arise out of the interplay of environmental factors and individual genetic susceptibility.[4] (Note that without the "environmental factors," the genetic susceptibility would not be triggered—so finally this too is reducible to pollution, not genetics.) The NRC, like virtually every institution and researcher in the field, notes that the poor are particularly at risk.

This chapter focuses on three environmental toxins that are widely known to compromise children's neurological development and mental health: lead, mercury, and a class of toxins known as persistent organic pollutants (POPs). But first we explore how children come into contact with environmental toxins and why they are so much more vulnerable to their effects than are adults.

One caveat is crucial at the outset, however. Set aside are the huge health implications for children of the sex-hormone-disrupting effects of POPs—the chemicals so often seen in connection with neurological harm. Also left aside are the industrial uses of synthetic hormones and antibiotics in agriculture and environmental problems such as global warming, extreme weather, water shortages, and other various and pressing environmental challenges. Nevertheless, it is important to understand that all serious environmental health impacts have a bearing on mental functioning and emotional health—and may indeed lead to the inappropriate psychotropic drugging of children. For example, children whose homes and schools are contaminated with toxic mold as a result of damage from severe weather, such as ice storms or hurricanes, are at risk for poor academic performance and depression due to the effect of mold on the immune and nervous systems. Children who are the victims of precocious puberty (girls) or retarded sexual development (boys), problems to which POPs contribute, are at great risk for emotional problems.[5] By the same token, petroleum-based artificial food additives and dyes now ubiquitous in processed foods have been shown repeatedly to provoke extreme reactions in a great many children, ranging from inability to sit still or to write, to storms of temper and other forms of distressed and distressing behavior. Large numbers of such children have been drugged and therapized repeatedly and without success. But where a parent or physician, or indeed a school principal or school board, thought to eliminate the additives from the food, recovery for many children has been very significant, sometimes complete.[6]

TOXIC WORLD, BODY BURDEN

How do our children come into contact with chemical environmental hazards? First, let's note that such hazards are virtually everywhere. It is not possible to catalog the whole picture, but we can use a study of Colorado's water, reported in January 2005, to get an idea. In that state, scientists working for the U.S. Geological Survey reported that by-products of everyday activities such as antibacterial hand soap or bug spray are winding up in streams and groundwater that reach from the Denver area to remote spots in the Colorado mountains. Bill Battaglin, a coauthor of the study, said scientists expected to find chemicals associated with detergents, disinfectants, and pesticides in urban waterways but were surprised to find some of them in more remote areas. Fire retardants, caffeine, steroids, prescription drugs, and a host of insecticides and pesticides were all found in the waterways. Some of the compounds were found in rural water wells, although in fewer numbers and lower concentrations than in urban areas. Possible sources, the study suggested, include feed lots, industrial sites, wastewater treatment plants, septic systems, and water runoff.

Some of the chemicals documented in the U.S. Geological Survey, according to the scientists, are suspected of disrupting fish reproduction and of increasing resistance to antibiotics. The compounds that are regulated were within limits deemed safe, but—and here is the crucial problem—no standards exist for most of the sixty-two chemicals. In a similar study done of Minnesota waters, seventy-eight chemicals were found, and many of these too were associated with disruptions to the physical and sexual health of wildlife. The Colorado Department of Public Health and Environment responded that it was closely tracking the findings. "The ubiquitous nature of the chemicals was a bit surprising, but I guess nobody's looked that closely before," the director of Colorado's water quality division told Associated Press reporter Judith Kohler. Determining the potential long-term effects of the chemicals and their sources, and figuring out how to reduce them, perhaps through more advanced wastewater treatment, likely would take several years and several million dollars, he added.[7]

The Colorado and Minnesota studies are all too typical. Indeed, the Environmental Protection Agency (EPA) has issued advisories for mercury, dioxins, PCBs, and other persistent organic pollutants for more than one-third of U.S. lakes and nearly one-quarter of its rivers. In 2004 EPA officials said people should severely limit consumption of fish caught recreationally. Many studies over the last fifteen years have shown very high levels of multiple persistent chemical and agricultural contaminants in vast tracts of waterways, and in much soil and air besides. These chemicals have been found nearly everywhere studies have been done on North American air, soil, and water. In January 2005, the *Toronto Globe and Mail* released the results of a specially commissioned study on PBDEs (flame retardants), which found them not only in soil and water but also in food, household carpets, and dust bunnies under beds.[8]

Since these chemicals are found in the water, air, and soil, it should not surprise us that a high "body burden" of toxicants has been found inside us too. In November 2004, the European Public Health Alliance (EPHA) reported on a major study that found a "toxic cocktail" in human *blood*. This "cocktail" was flowing in the veins of every one of the 155 volunteers from different parts of the United Kingdom who participated in a scientific study. The subjects were tested, and showed positive, for a host of sex-disrupting PCBs, flame retardants, and organophosphates (pesticides)—the same chemicals that show up in American waterways. The study focused on seventy-seven chemicals known to be "very persistent" in the environment and to accumulate in people's bodies. It was among the most comprehensive of studies done to date. Just how persistent these chemicals are—and this is among the very greatest concerns for children and future generations—was demonstrated by the fact that 99 percent of the people tested had breakdown products of the pesticide DDT in their blood, even though this pesticide was banned more than thirty years ago in the United Kingdom and Europe. Worse, the blood levels of most of the chemicals were comparable to those found in people exposed to chemicals through their work. And finally, women were found to have lower levels of certain PCBs than men. These *levels were lowest in women who had carried and breastfed more children*, prompting the researchers to speculate in support of a thesis advanced more than ten years ago by U.S. scientists, Theo Colborn among them (*Our Stolen Future*), that this might demonstrate the "off-loading" of chemicals in the women's bodies to their offspring.[9]

Last fall, similar results were obtained from testing the blood of the environment ministers from thirteen European Union countries—Britain, Cyprus, the Czech Republic, Denmark, Estonia, Finland, France, Hungary, Italy, Lithuania, Slovakia, Spain, and Sweden. Their blood was contaminated with a mix of the usual suspects. All the ministers bore traces of twenty-two PCBs, toxic chemicals banned in Europe during the 1970s and among the "dirty dozen" being phased out internationally. The WWF (formerly known as the World Wildlife Fund), which sponsored the test, said that we do not have enough public safety information about 86 percent of the 2,500 industrial chemicals most commonly used, even though research has linked many of them to cancers, allergies, reproductive problems, and neurological and growth defects. A total of fifty-five different chemicals was found in the ministers' blood. The most highly concentrated chemicals found across the sample were the phthalate additive (used to soften plastics, including babies' toys and pacifiers, and known as one of the pseudo-estrogen chemicals) and the DDT toxin.[10]

John Spengler at Harvard's School of Public Health is one of those in the United States working in the new field of body burden, the emerging science of chemicals that accumulate in the human body. His work and that of other Harvard colleagues show results similar to the studies done by the Europeans.[11] For if the chemicals are in the water, the air, the food, and the furniture, if their spread knows no countries or borders, it is unavoidable that they'll be in the blood and tissues of North Americans too.

It should come as no surprise, then, that groups such as Boston Physicians for Social Responsibility want to alert the public to the dangers and the damage of environmental toxicants to children. Their report, *In Harm's Way*, presents a number of key findings:

- An epidemic of developmental, learning, and behavioral disabilities has become evident among children.
- Animal and human studies demonstrate that many chemicals commonly encountered in industry and the home are developmental neurotoxicants that can contribute to developmental, learning, and behavioral disabilities.
- Recent research has produced a glut of information not readily understood by nonspecialists.

- Genetic factors are important, but particular vulnerability to toxic chemicals may be the result of a single gene or multiple-interacting genes.
- Neurotoxicants are *not merely a potential threat* to children.
- Vast quantities of neurotoxic chemicals are released into the environment each year.
- As scientific knowledge advances, the "safe thresholds" for known neurotoxicants have continuously been revised down.
- Protecting our children requires a precautionary policy that can only occur with basic changes in the regulatory process.[12]

WHY CHILDREN ARE UNIQUELY VULNERABLE

Until recently, regulatory agencies set acceptable tolerances for the safety of industrial chemicals based on their apparent effects on adults—usually males—and with a focus on whether or not the chemicals were carcinogenic. Now we know that men and women have different tolerances for different kinds of chemicals; we know that the effects of toxins may not show up for decades or until the next generation; and we know that there are many other diseases besides cancer that are caused by environmental poisons. But most compellingly, we now know fetuses, infants, and children *do not respond to environmental hazards as though they were small adults*. In fact, they are much more vulnerable than adults in ways that are qualitatively different and have consequences for their whole lives. In the words of the Children's Environmental Health Network (CEHN), "the elegance and delicacy of the development of a human being from conception through adolescence affords particular windows of vulnerability to environmental hazards. Exposure at those moments of vulnerability can lead to permanent and irreversible damage."[13]

The implications of this fact are simple: *when we pollute our environment, we place the greatest burden on our children*—a finding now well documented.[14] The following factors, a list drawn from several authoritative sources, explain why children are so vulnerable:[15]

- Fetuses in the womb are physically unable to process or defend against serious toxicants because their nervous, respiratory, reproductive, and immune systems are far from fully developed, and they are in the process of dynamic change.
- Fetuses may be grievously, even irreversibly, harmed by toxins arriving via the placenta. Toxins most known to cause harm to the nervous system are lead, PCBs, mercury, ethanol, PBDEs, and nicotine from tobacco smoke in the environment.

- In their first year, babies spend hours close to the ground, where they may be exposed to toxicants in dust, soil, and carpets as well as to pesticide vapors in low-lying layers of air on lawns and porches. For the first few years of children's lives, even after they learn to walk, stature and play patterns keep them much closer to the ground—where toxicants are concentrated.
- These chemicals mimic the body's hormones and have been shown to disrupt reproductive and hormone systems in wildlife, including thyroid hormones crucial to neurological development, and are implicated in similar disruptions during human fetal and early childhood development.
- Children have higher metabolic rates and a higher proportionate intake of food and liquid than do adults. Their cells are multiplying and their organ systems are developing at a very rapid rate.
- Children absorb nutrients and toxicants from the gut at different rates. Children need more calcium than adults, for example. But when lead is present, they will absorb it in preference to calcium. So adults will absorb an average of 10 percent of ingested lead, but a toddler will absorb closer to 50 percent.
- Developing metabolic systems in children are much less capable of detoxifying and excreting toxins than are those of adults—hence buildup is greater, and greater per unit of body weight.
- A lot of hand-to-mouth exposure is a normal part of childhood and provides another route for exposure to such toxicants as lead in paint dust and pesticide residues. Recently, mercury has been found in soil as well as water.
- Children breathe more rapidly and respire more air per unit of body weight than do adults, and they often spend more time outdoors. Their developing respiratory systems and greater exposure mean they are at risk for even greater adverse effects—such as childhood asthma, for example—due to air particulates, ozone, and other outdoor pollutants. Recent research has also shown that tiny particulates of air pollution penetrate the blood/brain barrier (also weaker in children) and affect the brain as well as the lungs and the circulatory system.
- Children eat more fruits and vegetables and drink more liquids in proportion to their body weight than do adults. Consequently, their potential exposure to ingested toxicants such as lead, pesticides, and nitrates is greater. Consider that the average infant's daily consumption of six ounces of formula or breast milk per kilogram of body weight is equivalent to an adult male drinking fifty eight-ounce glasses of milk a day. The average one-year-old eats two to seven times more grapes, bananas, pears, carrots, and broccoli proportionally than does an adult.
- Exposure to toxicants at an earlier age means children have more time to develop environmentally triggered diseases with long latency periods, such as cancer and possibly Parkinson's disease, but also allergies,

autoimmune disorders, and chemical sensitivities, and, of course, mental and emotional disorders.

These factors set the backdrop for the particularly devastating effects of a host of chemicals and heavy metals on fetuses and children. In the sections that follow we focus on lead, mercury, and a number of POPs, leaving aside, due to space limitations, a large number of other chemicals now doing harm to children. Perhaps this brief catalog can inspire readers to find out more about these other problems too.

THE DAMAGE OF HEAVY METALS: LEAD AND MERCURY

It's now well established that exposure to a variety of heavy metals can cause serious problems in fetuses and children. Still, many people, even specialists in health and education, believe that such problems are small in scale or confined to very limited populations. This misapprehension hinders any attempt to tackle the tremendously damaging effects of these substances.

Lead

Howard Hu of Harvard University has written a great deal about heavy metals, including lead, in recent years. In 2002, he had this to say about lead:

> The general body of literature on lead toxicity indicates that, depending on the dose, lead exposure in children and adults can cause a wide spectrum of health problems, ranging from convulsions, coma, renal failure, and death at the high end to subtle effects on metabolism and intelligence at the low end of exposures. Children (and developing fetuses) appear to be particularly vulnerable to the neurotoxic effects of lead. A plethora of well-designed prospective epidemiologic studies has convincingly demonstrated that low-level lead exposure in children less than five years of age (with blood lead levels in the 5–25 µg/dL range) results in deficits in intellectual development as manifested by lost intelligence quotient points. As a result, in the U.S., the Centers for Disease Control (CDC) lowered the allowable amount of lead in a child's blood from 25 to 10 µg/dL and recommended universal blood lead screening of all children between the ages of six months and five years. Recent research has clearly demonstrated that maternal bone lead stores are mobilized at an

accelerated rate during pregnancy and lactation and are associated with decrements in birth weight, growth rate, and mental development. Since bone lead stores persist for decades, it is possible that lead can remain a threat to fetal health many years after environmental exposure had actually been curtailed.[16]

Herbert L. Needleman, of the University of Pittsburgh's School of Medicine, was responsible for much of the influential research that led the U.S. government to ban lead in fuel in 1979. He was among the early researchers who established that children with elevated lead levels had lower IQs, poor reading skills, and problems paying attention. His work was important because it showed that problems traditionally defined as genetic or psychogenic could also be the results of simple, if grievously harmful, toxicants.

As well as deficits in intelligence and learning capacities, lead has been linked to disruptive classroom behavior, failure to graduate high school, violent tendencies, addictive predispositions, and other behavioral and emotional problems resulting in self-destructive and criminal behaviors.[17] Studies covering hundreds of communities have shown that those with larger percentages of children with high levels of lead in their blood are significantly more likely to have higher rates of violent crime and higher rates of educational failure. Needleman, a pioneer of such studies, began looking at the possible connections between lead and crime in the 1980s. He studied a sample of 300 seven-year-old boys in primary school, measuring the concentration of lead in their bones; he then looked at these findings against reports of antisocial behavior from the students' teachers, parents, and the children themselves. He retested two years later, and then again when the subjects were eleven years old. A report on his findings notes the following:

> At age 7, parents reported no significant problems associated with lead, but teachers, by contrast, were beginning to spot social problems and delinquent and aggressive behavior. By 11, both parents and teachers of high-lead children were reporting significantly more social problems, delinquent and aggressive behavior, acting out, anxiety and/or depression, and attention problems. High-lead students also reported more delinquent behavior themselves. These behavior problems "went up in direct relation to the lead levels in the bone," Needleman said in an interview. He also found much higher lead rates in a group of juvenile delinquents than in a control group. He used 416 youths—216 delinquents and 200 in a control group. Adjusting for such factors as race, parental education, occupation,

family size, and crime rate in the neighborhood the youths came from, he found those with high lead levels were twice as likely to be delinquent than those with low levels.[18]

Needleman estimates that 11–38 percent of the nation's delinquency is attributable to high lead exposure, a finding he presented at a recent pediatric meeting in Boston. Needleman explains that lead creates biochemical changes that result in lower IQ, an inability to sit still, and problems with language and reading.

Roger D. Masters, a Nelson A. Rockefeller, professor emeritus of government at Dartmouth College and president of the Foundation for Neuroscience and Society, who has studied heavy metals such as lead, manganese, and cadmium, has found that heavy metals affect the neurotransmitters. Manganese, for example, has the opposite effect of Prozac. It reduces serotonin. Studies of young delinquents and long-term prison inmates present a biochemical picture that shows how nutritional status, particularly with respect to minerals, differs, and how enzyme deficiencies, possibly genetically determined, predispose some people to accumulate heavy metals.[19]

Although lead is gone from gasoline in developed countries (although not worldwide) and progress is being made toward ridding houses and institutions of old lead-based paint, a new mechanism for lead exposure has arisen. Masters has found a disturbing correlation between high lead rates and the use of silicofluoride to fluoridate water systems in given communities. Among most of the states in which he has measured high lead levels, he has found the levels to be much higher when silicofluoride is in the water. "If you look at violent crime," he has said, "you find the same kind of thing. A kind of doubling of the crime rates where silicofluoride is used. It seems to have the effect of breaking down barriers between the blood and the gut. It appears that silicofluoride increases the amount of toxins that get into the blood." Masters looked at towns in Massachusetts that had had more than ten toxic spills over a two-year period. If silicofluoride was not in the water, fewer than 1 percent of children had high lead levels. If silicofluoride was in the water, five times as many children had high lead levels."[20]

Nutritional status is very important in cases of lead exposure. Lead and calcium bind to the same place. A child low in calcium will pick up a lot more lead than one with adequate levels. So here, too, poverty, which affects nutritional status, becomes a risk factor for lead poisoning.

Mercury

"From a global perspective," writes Howard Hu, "mercury has been increasing in importance as a widespread contaminant. About half of the National Priority List toxic waste sites in the U.S. contain mercury. Mercury dispersion through atmospheric deposition has increased markedly through waste incineration; ironically, the medical industry is one of the largest contributors to mercury pollution in this fashion.... Fish, particularly tuna, king mackerel, and swordfish, can concentrate methyl mercury at high levels." Although mercury toxicity at any age is a health risk, "of greatest concern on a global scale," writes Hu,

> is the sensitivity of the fetal and infant nervous system to low-level mercury toxicity. The 1955 disaster in Minamata Bay, Japan, first alerted researchers to the dangers that mercury can pose to neurological development in the fetus. Women who were victims of this disaster gave birth to infants with mental retardation, retention of primitive reflexes, cerebellar symptoms, and other abnormalities. Recent research in the Faroe Islands has demonstrated that, even at much lower levels, mercury exposure to pregnant women through dietary intake of fish and whale meat, an important regional food staple, is associated with decrements in motor function, language, memory, and neural transmission in their offspring. Organic mercury, the form of mercury bioconcentrated in fish and whale meat, readily crosses the placenta and appears in breast milk.[21]

A nationwide survey by the U.S. Centers for Disease Control (CDC) found that one in twelve women of childbearing age already have unsafe blood levels of mercury and that as many as 600,000 babies in the United States could be at risk. This number is staggering. Researchers at the Mount Sinai Center for Children's Health and the Environment released a study in March (in the journal *Environmental Health Perspectives*) in which they combined a number of previous studies to determine that hundreds of thousands of babies are born every year with lower IQs associated with mercury exposure. Using work examining the effects of lead exposure on IQ, researchers determined that even a 1.6 point drop in IQ could cost a person $31,800 in lifetime earnings because of missed educational opportunities or jobs. From there, the researchers calculated that mercury damage in the womb probably costs the United States $8.7 billion a year in lost earnings potential. The research found the IQ losses linked to mercury range from one-fifth of an IQ point to as much as twenty-four points.[22]

For some time, some researchers have feared that thimerosal, a mercury derivative used as a preservative in vaccines, was causing autism in children. Other researchers claimed that this was simply not possible. But only a month ago from this writing, a study released by scientists at the University of Texas Health Science Center in San Antonio and to be published in an upcoming edition of the peer-reviewed journal *Health and Place* looked at 254 counties and 1,200 school districts in Texas, comparing 2001 mercury emission levels with rates of autism and special education services.[23] It reported a strong correlation between higher mercury release levels from coal-burning plants and the developmental disorder marked by communication and social interaction problems. Once thought to occur in 1 of every 10,000 children, autism today is estimated to afflict 1 in 250!

Because mercury is a neurotoxin that affects the brain, spinal cord, kidneys, and liver, it is thought by many to play a part in the etiology of autism. Coal-burning power plants are the largest source of mercury in the United States today—producing forty-eight tons of the poison annually. Texas plants release more than those in any other state. The researchers found a 17 percent increase in the autism rate for every 1,000 pounds of mercury released into the environment.

It was long thought that methylmercury—the toxic form—was found primarily in water, where bacteria broke it down from plain mercury. But within the last twelve months a veritable flood of information on mercury studies has revealed that toxic mercury is concentrated on land as well, and often in "mercury hot spots"; that it's found in the blood of non-fish-eating birds; and that we do not understand how widespread and bio-available it really is—except that things are considerably worse than previously suspected. A scientist with the Mercury Connections study, which found mercury poisoning in small birds on a Vermont mountaintop, remarked that "this is a wake-up call for us as a species to reflect on how much mercury we are putting in the atmosphere. There's mercury all over the place. The thrush may be a canary in the coal mine."[24]

The amount of progress that has been made in cleaning up this toxicant is a matter of considerable controversy. Certain measures in reducing medical waste incineration have brought about some reductions, but the potential for more coal-burning plants with inadequate pollution controls is a bleak one. A Harvard study estimated the potential public health benefits from cutting mercury pollution from coal-burning power plants in half fifteen years from now at $5 billion a year. The EPA has estimated that these benefits could be as high as $50 million a year. It's a thought-provoking discrepancy.[25]

PERSISTENT ORGANIC POLLUTANTS AS NEUROLOGICAL DISRUPTORS

Solvents

In October 2004, a new study, done at the MotherRisk program of the internationally renowned Hospital for Sick Children in Toronto, showed that children born to mothers exposed to solvents in the workplace had significant developmental delays as a result.[26] (Solvents are chemicals used by hair stylists, medical technologists, scientists, and others.) These children exhibited lower IQs and poorer language skills, and were inattentive and hyperactive. Despite the use of protective equipment such as masks and gloves to minimize their exposure to the chemicals, the mothers were obviously not sufficiently protected from the seventy-eight chemicals involved. Concerns about fetal exposure to workplace toxins have been expressed for decades by pioneers in the environmental field such as Theo Colborn and Doris Rapp. [27] But for a long time these scientists were voices in the wilderness. The MotherRisk research is now part of a growing body of evidence, in animals and in humans, that demonstrates the neurological, mental, and emotional health risks of exposure to such solvents.

Pesticides

In June 2004, Pesticide Action Network North America (PANNA), based in Washington, DC, released its report, *Chemical Trespass: Pesticides in Our Bodies and Corporate Accountability*. For the first time PANNA made public an analysis of pesticide-related data collected by the U.S. Centers for Disease Control and Prevention (CDC) that measured levels of chemicals in 9,282 people nationwide. The PANNA research demonstrated that the body burden of toxic pesticides that U.S. residents carry is far above government-assessed "acceptable" levels. PANNA noted that many of the pesticides found in the test subjects have been linked to serious short- and long-term health effects, including infertility, birth defects, and childhood and adult cancers.

The analysis found that children first, followed by women and Mexican Americans, shoulder the heaviest "pesticide body burden." Of particular concern were the findings that children have been exposed to the highest levels of nerve-damaging organophosphates. The PANNA analysis of the CDC data revealed that six- to eleven-year-olds in the subject pool had been exposed to the organophosphate pesticide chlorpyrifos (commonly known by the product name Dursban) at four times the level the EPA considers "acceptable" for long-term exposure.

Similar results were reported by the Ontario College of Family Physicians, which published a comprehensive study in 2004 on the chronic effects of pesticide exposure in the home, the garden, and at work. The study found links between common household pesticides and fetal defects, neurological damage, and the most deadly cancers. The college instructed its members to urge citizens to avoid pesticide exposure in any form. The study also found consistent links between parents' exposure to certain agricultural pesticides at their jobs and increasing fetal damage or death. The risks, they concluded, can come even from residue on food, ant spray, and the flea collar on the family pet. Their findings were supported by the Canadian Cancer Society, the Learning Disabilities Association of Canada, the Registered Nurses Association of Canada, and the Ontario Public Health Association, all of whom have called for the bans as well.[28]

There is compelling evidence, based on animal studies, that organophosphates, carbamates, and organochlorine pesticides cause neurobehavioral damage, but to date there is a paucity of research on children. As reported by Charles W. Schmidt in *Environmental Health Perspectives*, Elizabeth Guillette, an anthropologist and adjunct professor in the Bureau of Applied Research in Anthropology at the University of Arizona in Tucson, has gathered evidence as part of a battery of developmental end points in a study of indigenous children living in the Yaqui Valley of northwestern Mexico. "The results of a simple test show[ed] that young children exposed to pesticides were practically unable to draw a simple picture of a person.... The random undifferentiated lines drawn by exposed children averaged only 1.6 body parts per figure, whereas nonexposed children produced reasonably lifelike figures averaging 4.4 body parts each." For Schmidt, these results "provided one of the most compelling illustrations to date of a possible neurodevelopmental effect of pesticides in children."[29] This research replicates the findings of Doris Rapp, who in *Is This Your Child?* has published drawings made by children she tested. Also, according to her research, children exposed to the pesticides showed a decrease in stamina and thirty-minute memory, and a loss of gross and fine eye-hand coordination.[30]

The greatest challenge at present is that virtually all the toxic chemicals classed as persistent organic pollutants were passed into manufacture without the kind of testing we now know is needed to determine their real effects, particularly on fetuses and young children. At the same time, the length and the demanding protocols of scientific research mean that retrospective investigations are very slow and not adequate to the task at hand—that of identifying safe levels of exposure to any given chemical.

CONCLUSION

Problems with the neurological development of children that have been identified so far as related to toxicants can be grouped as follows: lowered concentration and information processing power; reduction in the ability to handle stress, hence an increase in frustration, volatility, and failure; an increase in depression, hence a greater predisposition to violence, addiction, and criminal behavior; and finally, a deleterious effect on the development of intelligence per se. A five-point drop in mean population IQ is estimated to reduce by half the number of gifted children (IQ over 120) and increase by half the number with borderline IQ (below 80).[31] Talk about the "dumbing down" of society!

On an individual basis, a child who is unable to concentrate, to read, or to process complex ideas because of pesticide exposures or heavy metal poisoning will often be diagnosed with attention and learning deficits. In the search for the cause of her problems, the parents may be unfairly targeted as neglectful, or the child may well be given psychotropic medication, often exacerbating the problem or creating new neurological and metabolic challenges. Rather than drugs or psychotherapy, children such as these need detoxification treatment and nutritional remediation.

At the community and societal levels, children who have lowered IQs, learning deficits, or volatile behavior as a result of toxic chemical exposure represent an unconscionable squandering of our social capital and a tragic testament to our cavalier disregard for the well-being of our young. Poor children are most at risk for multiple hazardous environmental exposures as well as for multiple sociocultural risk factors. Their plight testifies to our society's willingness to make poor children pay in the most devastating terms for our affluence.

Finally, what is happening to all the children who are poisoned by our way of life, across class, ethnic, race, and gender lines, threatens the future intelligence (and fertility) of our larger society and represents a major crisis not only in our notions of equality and justice but in our very viability.

If we are to make meaningful headway in addressing these pressing issues, it is essential that researchers and professionals in the fields of environmental epidemiology, biostatistics, occupational health, toxicology, medicine, education, and mental health pool their research and clinical practices to ensure accurate diagnosis and effective treatment of children with mental and emotional disorders. And in order to make the necessary advances in understanding, treating, and preventing the harms this essay has described, we need to act on three broad levels. Before discussing these, however, a word about the political and economic contexts in which we must act.

Environmental Madness

The problems this chapter chronicles have been in the making for a long time. Some of their origins were laid down during the industrial revolution, but they really began to take root after the explosion of petrochemical use in the 1950s. Like a wave that starts slowly and then more and more rapidly gains momentum and height as it reaches the shore, these problems have been swelling and accelerating so that we are now facing a veritable tsunami of dangers whose impact on individuals and society is extremely destructive. We have created more than 100,000 chemicals for which neither our biosphere nor our bodies were designed. We have altered our environment so that our water, air, and soil send back the poisons we've dispersed into them; we've flooded the capacity of the earth's natural systems and our own to handle all these pollutants. To turn things around, we must make significant changes, and rapidly. These changes range from shifting our production technologies from toxic to green, to supporting families and communities as they struggle to deal with the results of the fallout of our old technologies close to home.

It is to the credit of countless individuals, organizations, communities, industries, and governments that many positive actions have been taken. Many new technologies have been developed, and many programs have been launched to address the challenges. Still, despite improvements made by committed and caring people everywhere, overall environmental quality continues to decline. A study released last December, for example, based on Canadian government statistics, showed *that air and water pollution have increased by 50 percent over the last seven years*, a finding that shocked and surprised many because of big business' claims that it was on the pollution case. These findings would be equally relevant to the northern United States.[32]

Unlike many countries, especially in the less developed world, the United States has the wealth, the technology, and the expertise in abundance to address the problems this chapter has described. But while many states and municipalities are taking positive initiatives on a number of fronts, at the federal level this is not happening. In fact, we seem to have an environmentally challenged administration in place today. Between the midterm elections of 2002 and December of 2004, the Bush administration took more than 101 rollback initiatives that sought to de-fang or to gut the environmental regulations that were the product of thirty years of legislation. Taking the sum of these initiatives, the League of Conservation Voters cited President Bush and his allies for "consistently siding with corporate interests over the interests of American citizens in a clean and healthy environment."[33]

In April 2005 the Millennium Ecosystem Assessment, the first-ever global inventory of natural resources, was published. The report cost $24 million and took more than 1,300 scientists in ninety-five countries four years to complete. It is backed by the UN, the World Bank, and the World Resources Institute. The assessment reached the overwhelming conclusion that we are living way beyond our environmental means. Approximately 60 percent of the planet's natural products and processes that support life, such as water purification, are being degraded or used unsustainably.[34] Yet the current U.S. administration has resisted placing new limits on pollutants and industrial toxins and has rolled back many existing limits. Even when some limits are put in place, as in the EPA's recent mercury reduction order, the recommendations of industry are followed rather than those of public health professionals, environmentalists, or state governments.[35] And of course because pollution knows no borders, what is generated in the United States is shared—first with North American neighbors and ultimately with the whole world.

It is not possible to believe in an infinitely malleable environment and still put credibility in the environmental reports and alarms raised by scientists in every field, in and out of government, in the United States and globally. And so, as many people have observed with great disquiet, the Bush presidency has simply chosen to ignore science. In February 2004, the Union of Concerned Scientists published a report about the record of the Bush administration with respect to the treatment of scientists, scientific method, and evidence, which rang alarm bells throughout the country and around the world. They found that "there is a well-established pattern of suppression and distortion of scientific findings by high-ranking Bush administration political appointees across numerous federal agencies."[36] And they noted that there is "significant evidence that the scope and scale of the manipulation, suppression, and misrepresentation of science by the Bush administration is unprecedented."

This administration's agenda presents a special challenge to Americans who care about children. But even in Washington, DC, not all is lost; so much is possible at state, municipal, and local levels that there is abundant hope.

What We Need to Do

If we are to protect children's minds and bodies from toxic pollutants, action is needed by families, communities, and government.

Parents

Books such as Herbert Needleman and Philip Landrigan's *Raising Children Toxic Free: How To Keep Your Child Free from Lead, Asbestos, Pesticides and Other Environmental Hazards*[37] and Doris Rapp's *Our Toxic World* provide parents with a wealth of information to help them help their children. It suggests alternatives to toxic household products, provides help in recognizing the signs and symptoms of environmental illnesses, and details resources in the medical community to assist sick children. But children who are suffering from toxic exposure to environmental pollutants generally require medical interventions that are not part of standard health insurance plans, and this can be costly and daunting. In addition, children who have a high body burden of environmental toxicants often need to eat organic food and to live and go to school in environments in which nontoxic cleaning and construction products are used. These choices are beyond the scope of many families because of financial or time constraints. Clearly then, it is essential that other members of the community, and governments, partner with and support parents' efforts. As well, it must be said that no parent can fully protect a child from ubiquitous toxins that are invisible and inescapable. Hence, individual efforts, while important, simply aren't enough to address these health issues.

Community Efforts

Educators have the potential to play a pivotal role in helping to protect children from environmental toxins. Teachers spend several hours a day with their students and have access to parents, on the one hand, and local public authorities and policymakers, on the other. School administrators and school boards, in addition to teachers, are in a unique position to disseminate information about environmental hazards and to represent the interests and needs of children.[38] Schools should become community resource centers on environmental issues. Already there are many positive examples of this kind. For example, in 2005, California celebrated six years of "safe schools"[39]—a policy fought for by parents, children's activists, and enlightened educators. California's schools have banned the use of toxic pesticides, and many other school boards in different parts of the country have followed their example.

If, in the same spirit, schools were to decide to purchase only organic foods for their cafeterias (further extending the protection from pesticides to their children) and to use only nontoxic cleaning and construction materials, they would create a huge market for these benign goods. Such a positive economic incentive would quickly provoke a production response, even from corporations that now make harmful products, as companies would seek to profit from this substantial "green" market.

Health practitioners also see children and parents routinely and have a vital role to play in protecting children from environmental pollutants. It is critical that training programs for health professionals begin to integrate information about environmental harms into their curricula and that continuing education programs be made available to professionals already in practice. Health professionals can and should play a much expanded role in helping to identify and treat environmental illnesses as well as to encourage the creation of policies aimed at prevention. It is essential that health professionals pool research and resources with epidemiologists, occupational health experts, and toxicologists.

Public health officials must be part of community efforts. By any other epidemiological standards, the health-related environmental problems of today's children, and the damage being done to their mental and emotional health, constitute a public health crisis in the present and developing into the future. Further, individual parents and teachers are not in a position to effectively advocate alone for environmental cleanups in the community, nor to support all the families and children who have been negatively affected by environmental poisons. As a result we need to revive and expand our public health system as a matter of urgent public and economic policy. We need to do so for many health reasons, including the potential spread of infectious diseases, old (e.g., tuberculosis) and new (e.g., SARS). But environmental health—causes and solutions—must be included in the active mandates of these bodies, and public health bodies must be expanded to include experts in this field. For ultimately only these bodies can play the kind of leadership and coordinating roles we need as a society to practically identify and address the environmental assaults on children.

Government: Local, State, and National

For all three community groups, as well as for parents, new roles, or even the adequate fulfillment of old ones, are not possible without awareness, education, and resources. Environmental problems were not created by individuals. Rather they were caused by a particular industrial mode of production that involved toxic products and technologies that placed profit over all other considerations. Logically, such problems cannot be solved by individual action. It takes the whole of society to protect the biosphere for future generations. To ask families, professionals, and individual communities to take responsibility for protecting children from pollutants, without giving them the resources and the power to do so, is like asking chickens to guard their henhouse against an army of foxes. It won't work. We must also accomplish a multitude of tasks on the big political board as well as at the family and community levels.

The American people need government to act as guardian of the environment and children's health. Given what appears to be a vacuum of environmental leadership in Washington, DC, at present, one call to action everyone could unite behind is for each state government to create an official interdepartmental body with adequate funds, personnel, and power capable of animating citizens and community groups as well as its own departments and agencies into a system that makes the term *guardian* real in practice as well as in rhetoric. Such a system should be supported by municipal and county governments and, when the nation's capital regains its environmental senses, by generous federal support.

To address children's unique vulnerability to the adverse effects of environmental toxins, we must institute policies and initiatives based on the Precautionary Principle at all levels of government. This principle, which has already been adopted in many national and international forums dealing with health and the environment, amounts to a commonsense approach that uses a standard of reasonable doubt as the basis for policy, rather than waiting for irrefutable scientific proof (which can take years, even decades to achieve, long after irreparable damage has been done).

To effect the broad range of efforts and changes involved in societal environmental protection of children, we need the following:

- Public agencies with resources and clout, and free of personnel with conflicts of interest, to determine with more accuracy and honesty what harms are being done by what substances, processes, and technologies (for starters, bring back the Office of Technology Assessment and improve and expand it) and what alternative technologies exist or need to be devised to replace the harmful ones. This requires big budgets.
- Serious prioritizing inside the justice system. We need new norms that do not permit the endless postponement of trials in which toxic emissions are in question. Clearly, sending CEOs of polluting companies to jail for a long time or setting fines that break the profitability of a company's business (instead of fines that are virtual licenses to pollute) are ways to make this strategy meaningful in the short term. These are the big sticks, and we'll need them for a while.
- Economic carrots that are even bigger than sticks are, in the medium and long terms, the only really effective means of bringing about massive change. At the *economic* level, government's role should first and foremost be to devise a series of programs and incentives (rebates, tax reductions, subsidies, and more) to favor green technologies and disincentives (manufacturer-take-back laws, extra taxes, ending subsidies, and so forth) to discourage dirty ones. Using the purchasing power of all publicly funded institutions to create the basis for organic agriculture and nontoxic products can make an extraordinary difference. Either the existing corporate players will respond to these incentives or other organizations of people will—because given the right incentives, people interested in making green products will have the wherewithal to move ahead. Crucially, such public policies would provide a much-needed foundation for economic renewal on the basis of a living wage and productive work. Hence we should all support a national and worldwide campaign for a "Green Deal" to address the crisis, just as the New Deal addressed the crisis of the Great Depression. A campaign

for a Green Deal can link efforts with campaigns for children's, family, and worker's rights, providing crucial economic support to employers and employees alike while shifting us to sustainable ways of living and production.

The good news—the great news—is that new clean technologies exist: from wind turbines and solar panels, to plant-based plastics, to nontoxic pesticides and scientifically enhanced methods of organic farming, to filtration systems that use plants to produce pure drinking water without depositing one ounce of sewage in our waterways, to methods of manufacturing that take no resources from the biosphere and even give some back; from government regulations that make manufacturers reduce packaging to a biodegradable fraction of what it was, to programs that conserve energy and reduce mercury emissions to zero, to programs that help us feed our kids healthy food at school. We *can* help our biosphere to survive and protect our children and their children after them—*if* we can prioritize health and control the deployment of technology and the major actors that drive it.

If we are to succeed in turning the tide, we must stop separating environmental issues from economic or health issues in the belief that somehow we'll be able to deal with those later. The costs of degrading human health and the environment must be borne by the industries that do the degrading and not treated as "externalities"—for it is citizens who end up paying for them. True "life-cycle costs"—from cradle to grave—must be integrated into all products. Not to do so is a form of subsidy to business, which cannot continue if we are to preserve our children's health. It is time to put environmental issues front and center in all fields and to start to live our lives, as communities and nations as well as individuals, with the knowledge that we are natural beings, dependent on a natural environment, and committed to becoming its guardians—and in the process we will become better guardians for our own children and all future generations.

5

Media Violence
The Drug of Choice for Young Males

JOHN P. MURRAY

It is not unusual to describe media violence as a drug. Parents who have watched their young children sit mesmerized in front of the television screen, viewing fast-action and fast-paced programming, often comment on the zombie-like or drugged expression on the children's faces. Yet we know that the drug reference is merely a metaphor—or do we? Our recent research mapping children's brain activation patterns while they watch violent video clips suggests that there may be a basis for thinking about the addictive quality of media violence.

Of course, concern about media violence is not a new issue. Early in the twentieth century, parents, teachers, and legislators raised concerns about violence in comic books, the "penny dreadful" illustrated material, as well as radio and movies. In the middle of the twentieth century, television arrived on the scene and quickly became a focus of concern. And, of course, the recent explosion of video game violence adds to the list of growing concerns in the twenty-first century.

All of these concerns are real and important. The culture of childhood, particularly in the United States, is rife with violence in entertainment—portrayed as socially acceptable and even "fun" in the latest breed of video games. The largest body of research on media violence is research on televised violence. More recent research efforts have addressed video game violence, but this is merely an extension of the extensive research on TV violence. We can benefit from the fifty years of research on television[1] to begin to understand the "drugging" effects of all media violence. In reviewing the research of the past fifty years, we have cataloged almost 2,000 studies (1,945 to be precise) conducted on various aspects of television's impact, with about 600 studies related directly to the issue of violence.

The violent face of television has been presented to audiences from the first broadcasts of this medium. Television broadcasting in the United States began in the early 1940s, with full development of the medium following the Second World War. Although extensive broadcast schedules did not begin until the late 1940s, and violence was not as graphic as it would become in later years, the first public concerns about violence were evident in the 1950s. The early congressional hearings set the stage for similar expressions of public concern that have continued through the twentieth and into the twenty-first century.[2] What have we learned from all of this research and discussion on the "violent face of television" and what can be done to mitigate the harmful influences?

EARLY RESEARCH AND SOCIAL CONCERNS

The early studies of television's influence began almost simultaneously in England, the United States, and Canada in the mid-1950s. In England, a group of researchers at the London School of Economics and Political Science, under the direction of Hilde Himmelweit, a reader in social psychology, began the first study of children's television-viewing patterns while TV was still relatively new (only 3 million TV sets were installed in the 15 million households in England). This study was proposed by the Audience Research Department of the British Broadcasting Corporation (BBC) but was conducted by independent researchers. The research, begun in 1955, was published in a 1958 report, *Television and the Child: An Empirical Study of the Effects of Television on the Young*.[3] The American and Canadian study was conducted by Wilbur Schramm and his colleagues in communications at Stanford University. This project began in 1957 and was published in a 1961 report, *Television in the Lives of Our Children*.[4]

The British and American/Canadian surveys provided an important benchmark for understanding the broad and general effects of television on children. For example, Himmelweit and her colleagues noted that "we have found a number of instances where viewers and controls differed in their outlook; differences which did not exist before television came on the scene. There was a small but consistent influence of television on the way children thought generally about jobs, job values, success, and social surroundings."[5]

With regard to aggression, these correlational studies were less specific, as Himmelweit and her colleagues observed: "We did not find that the viewers were any more aggressive or maladjusted than the controls; television is unlikely to cause aggressive behavior, although it could precipitate it in those few children who are emotionally disturbed. On the other hand, there was little support for the view that programs of violence are beneficial; we found that they aroused aggression as often as they discharged it."[6]

The Schramm study's conclusions about television violence included the observation that those Canadian and American children with high exposure to television and low exposure to print were more aggressive than those with the reverse pattern. Thus, the early correlational studies or surveys identified some areas of concern about television violence and set the stage for more focused investigations. Finally, it should be noted that these 1950s studies of viewers and nonviewers took place when television was new in the United States, Canada, and England. Later studies—in the 1970s—would revisit these issues and this research strategy when television was being introduced into isolated communities in Australia and Canada.[7]

Moving beyond these 1950s surveys was another set of studies that emerged in the early 1960s. These were not surveys or correlational studies but experimental studies that addressed cause-and-effect relationships in the TV-violence-viewing/aggressive-behavior equation. These initial experiments were conducted by Albert Bandura at Stanford University, who studied preschool-age children, and Leonard Berkowitz at the University of Wisconsin, who worked with college-age youth. In both instances, the studies were experimental in design, which meant that subjects were randomly assigned to various viewing experiences and that therefore the results of this manipulated viewing could be used to address the issue of causal relationships between viewing and behavior. The early Bandura studies, such as "Transmission of Aggression through Imitation of Aggressive Models" or "Imitation of Film-Mediated Aggressive Models,"[8] were set within a social learning paradigm and were designed to identify the processes governing the ways that children learn by observing and imitating the behavior of others. In this context, therefore, the studies used stimulus films (videotape was not generally available) that were back-projected onto a simulated television screen, and the behavior of the children was observed and recorded in a playroom setting immediately following the viewing period. Despite the structured nature of these studies, Bandura's research was central to the debate about the influence of media violence. Moreover, the work of Berkowitz and his colleagues, such as "Effects of Film Violence on Inhibitions against Subsequent Aggression" or "Film Violence and the Cue Properties of Available Targets,"[9] studied the simulated aggressive behavior of youth and young adults following the viewing of segments of violent films, such as the Kirk Douglas boxing film, *The Champion.* The demonstration of increased willingness to use aggression against others following viewing further fueled the debate about the influence of media violence.

Concern about the influence of TV violence began as early as the start of this new medium. The first congressional hearings were held in the early 1950s.[10] At these early hearings, developmental psychologist Eleanor Maccoby and sociologist Paul Lazarsfeld presented testimony that relied on some early studies of violence in films, such as the 1930s report *Boys, Movies, and City Streets*, to outline a necessary program of research on the issue of TV violence and its effects on children.[11]

As the 1960s progressed, concern in the United States about violence in the streets and the assassinations of President John F. Kennedy, Martin Luther King Jr., and Robert Kennedy stimulated continuing interest in media violence. In response, several major government commissions and scientific and professional review committees were established, from the late 1960s through the 1990s, to summarize the research evidence and public policy issues regarding the role of television violence in salving or savaging young viewers.

The six principal commissions and review panels—the National Commission on the Causes and Prevention of Violence, the Surgeon General's Scientific Advisory Committee on Television and Social Behavior, the National Institute of Mental Health, the Television and Behavior Project, the Group for the Advancement of Psychiatry Child and Television Drama Review, and the American Psychological Association Task Force on Television and Society—have been central to setting the agenda for research and public discussion.[12]

In 1982, the National Institute of Mental Health (NIMH) published a ten-year follow-up of the 1972 surgeon general's study.

The two-volume report, collectively titled *Television and Behavior: Ten Years of Scientific Progress and Implications for the Eighties*, provided a reminder of the breadth and depth of knowledge that has accumulated on the issue of TV violence.[13] In this regard, the NIMH staff and consultants concluded:

> After 10 more years of research, the consensus among most of the research community is that violence on television does lead to aggressive behavior by children and teenagers who watch the programs. This conclusion is based on laboratory experiments and on field studies. Not all children become aggressive, of course, but the correlations between violence and aggression are positive. In magnitude, television violence is as strongly correlated with aggressive behavior as any other behavioral variable that has been measured.[14]

In 1986, the American Psychological Association (APA) put together a Task Force on Television and Society to review the research and professional concerns about the impact of television on children and adults. The nine psychologists assigned to this committee undertook reviews of relevant research, conducted interviews with television industry and public policy professionals, and discussed concerns with representatives of government regulatory agencies and public interest organizations. The final report, titled *Big World, Small Screen: The Role of Television in American Society*, included the following observation about television violence:

> American television has been violent for many years. Over the past 20 years, the rate of violence on prime time evening television has remained at about 5 to 6 incidents per hour, whereas the rate on children's Saturday morning programs is typically 20 to 25 acts per hour. There is clear evidence that television violence can cause aggressive behavior and can cultivate values favoring the use of aggression to resolve conflicts.[15]

The extent of concern—both social and scientific—is demonstrated by the fact that over the past half century, about 1,000 reports have been published on the issue of TV violence.[16] Of course, only a small percentage of these thousands of pages represents original studies or research reports, but there is an extensive body of research on the impact of TV violence. Nevertheless, the research history is best described in terms of the nature of the research approaches: correlational and experimental and their variants, cross-lagged panel studies and field studies.

CORRELATIONAL RESEARCH

The demonstration of a relationship between viewing and aggressive behavior is a logical precursor to studies of the causal role that TV violence may play in promoting aggressive behavior. In this regard, the early surveys of the impact of television on children, conducted by Himmelweit, Schramm, and colleagues addressed some of these concerns about violence.[17] Later research has been more focused on studying the correlations between TV violence viewing and aggression.

In typical correlational studies, such as those conducted for the surgeon general's research program, the researchers found consistent patterns of significant correlations between the number of hours of television viewed or the frequency of viewing violent programs and various measures of aggressive attitudes or behavior.[18] Also, another study found that heavy-TV-violence viewers were more likely to choose physical and verbal aggressive responses to solve hypothetical interpersonal conflict situations (i.e., 45 percent of the heavy-violence viewers chose physical/verbal aggressive responses vs. 21 percent of the low-violence viewers).[19] Similarly, a further study in this genre found that adolescents who reported enjoying TV violence were more likely to hold attitudes and values favorable to behaving aggressively in conflict situations.[20]

In another approach, a large database, the Cultural Indicators Project, has been used to explore the relationship between television portrayals and the viewer's fearful conception of the world. In a series of studies begun in the 1960s, George Gerbner and his colleagues at the University of Pennsylvania have tracked public perceptions of society in relation to the extent of the respondent's television viewing.[21] Of relevance to the violence issue, these researchers have identified differences in risk-of-victimization perceptions, described as the "mean world syndrome" effect, between light versus heavy viewers. The heavy viewers (those who usually watch television five or more hours per day) are much more fearful of the world around them than are light viewers (those who watch about two or fewer hours per day). When questioned about their perceptions of risk, heavy viewers are much more likely to overestimate (i.e., greater than the FBI crime reports for their locale would suggest) the chance that they will be the victim of crime in the ensuing six months, are more likely to have taken greater precautions by changing the security of their homes or restricting their travels at night, and are generally more fearful of the world. As Gerbner and his colleagues note: "we have found that long-term exposure to television, in which frequent violence is virtually inescapable, tends to cultivate the image of a relatively mean and dangerous world ... in which greater protection is needed, most people cannot be trusted, and most people are just looking out for themselves."[22]

Special-Case Correlational Research

Studies such as the early surveys clearly demonstrate that violence viewing and aggressive behavior are related, but they do not address the issue of cause and effect. There are, however, some special-case correlational studies in which "intimations of causation" can be derived from the fact that these studies were conducted over several time periods. There have been three major panel studies: one funded by CBS, one by NBC, and a third by the Surgeon General's Committee and the NIMH.[23] The CBS study was conducted in England with 1,565 youths who comprised a representative sample of thirteen- to seventeen-year-old males living in London. The boys were interviewed on several occasions concerning the extent of their exposure to a selection of violent television programs broadcast during the period 1959–71. The level and type of violence in these programs were rated by members of the BBC viewing panel. Thus, it was possible to obtain, for each boy, a measure of both the magnitude and type of exposure to televised violence (e.g., realistic, fictional, etc.). Furthermore, each boy's level of violent behavior was determined by his report of how often he had been involved in any of fifty-three categories of violence over the previous six months. The degree of seriousness of the acts reported by the boys ranged from only slightly violent aggravation, such as taunting, to more serious and very violent behavior such as "I tried to force a girl to have sexual intercourse with me"; "I bashed a boy's head against a wall"; I burned a boy on the chest with a cigarette while my mates held him down"; and "I threatened to kill my father." Approximately 50 percent of the 1,565 boys were not involved in any violent acts during the six-month period. However, of those who were involved in violence, 188 (12 percent) were involved in ten or more acts during the six-month period. When Belson compared the behavior of boys who had higher exposure to televised violence to those who had lower exposure (and had been matched on a wide variety of possible contributing factors), he found that the high-violence viewers were more involved in serious interpersonal violence.

The NBC study was conducted over a three-year period from May 1970 to December 1973 in two cities, Fort Worth and Minneapolis. Interviews were conducted with samples of second- to sixth-grade boys and girls and a special sample of teenage boys. In the elementary school sample, the information on television viewing and measures of aggression was collected in six time periods over the three years. The aggression measure consisted of peer ratings of aggressive behavior based on the work of Eron and his colleagues.[24] In the teenage sample there were only five waves of interviews over the three years, and the aggression measures were self-reported rather than peer-reported aggression. Although the initial analysis of the results did not establish a causal connection, re-analyses of these data have concluded that there are small but clear causal effects in the NBC data and that these effects become stronger when analyzed over longer time periods through successive waves of interviews.[25]

Finally, one of the longest-running panel studies, twenty-two years, was designed by Leonard Eron and his colleagues.[26] In the initial studies, conducted for the surgeon general's investigation of TV violence, the researchers were able to document the long-term effects of violence viewing by studying children over a ten-year period from age eight to age eighteen.[27] At these two time periods, the youngsters were interviewed about their program preferences, and information was collected from peer ratings of aggressive behavior. The violence levels of their preferred TV programs and other media and measures of aggression across these two time periods suggested that early television violence viewing was a factor in producing later aggressive behavior. In particular, the findings for 211 boys followed in this longitudinal study demonstrated that watching TV violence at age eight was significantly related to aggression at age eight ($r = .21$) and that the eight-year-old's TV violence preferences were significantly related to aggression at age eighteen ($r = .31$), but that TV violence preferences at age eighteen were not related to aggressive behavior at the earlier time period, age eight ($r = .01$). When other possible variables, such as parenting practices and discipline style, were controlled for, it was still clear that early media violence was a significant risk factor for later aggressive behavior. Furthermore, in a follow-up study performed when these young men were age thirty, the authors found a significant correlation ($r = .41$) between their levels of watching TV violence at age eight and their levels of serious interpersonal criminal behavior (e.g., assault, murder, child abuse, spouse abuse, rape) at age thirty.[28]

Thus it seems clear that a correlation between television violence and the watcher's aggression can be established from diverse studies. And some special cases of longitudinal correlational studies (described as cross-lagged panel studies) can lead to intimations of causation. However, the issue of causation is best assessed in experimental designs that allow for random assignment of subjects to various treatment conditions or, in the case of field studies, take advantage of naturally occurring variations in television-viewing experiences.

EXPERIMENTAL STUDIES

The potential role of television violence in the causation of aggressive behavior was, as noted earlier, among the first topics investigated by social scientists. The studies by Bandura and Berkowitz set the stage for later experimental studies in which causal influences of TV violence could be assessed by randomly assigning subjects to various viewing conditions.[29] These later studies employed both the structured, laboratory-based settings as well as more naturalistic settings in schools and communities.

One of the earlier studies in this genre assessed the effects of viewing segments of a violent television program, *The Untouchables*, on the aggressive behavior of five- to nine-year-old boys and girls.[30] In this study, the children viewed either *The Untouchables* or a neutral but active track race. Following viewing, the child was placed in a playroom setting in which he or she could help or hurt another child who was ostensibly playing a game in another room. The subject could help the other child by pressing a button that would make the game easier to play and allow the other child to win more points. Similarly, the subject could hurt the other child by pressing a button that would make the game very difficult to play and hence the player would lose points. The results indicated that youngsters who had viewed the violent program manifested a greater willingness to hurt the other child than youngsters who had watched the neutral program. Moreover, an elaboration of this study by Paul Ekman and colleagues included the recording of the facial expressions of these children while they were watching the television violence.[31] In this instance, the children whose facial expressions indicated interest or pleasure while watching TV violence were more willing to hurt the other child than were the youngsters whose facial expressions indicated disinterest or displeasure while watching TV violence. Thus, this set of studies identified some potential moderating variables in the TV-violence-viewing/aggressive-behavior equation.

Other early experiments by researchers, using physiological measures of arousal (e.g., galvanic skin response, heart rate, respiration changes) of participants while they were watching violent cartoons, found that children are emotionally responsive even to cartoon violence.[32] So too, other studies found that exposure to even one violent cartoon leads to increased aggression in the structured playroom settings.[33] Furthermore, studies by Drabman and his colleagues have shown that children who view violent television programs become desensitized to violence and are more willing to tolerate aggressive behavior in others.[34] Moreover, later studies with emotionally disturbed children have found that these youngsters may be more vulnerable to the influence of TV violence.[35] For example, Grimes and colleagues found that eight- to twelve-year-olds who were diagnosed as having attention-deficit/hyperactivity disorder, oppositional defiant disorder, or conduct disorder manifested less emotional concern for victims and were more willing to accept violence as justified than a matched group of children who did not have these disorders.

All of the studies described above were conducted in fairly structured laboratory or playroom settings, where displays of aggression, emotional arousal, or desensitization followed soon after viewing TV violence. Questions remained about what might happen in more naturalistic settings or in field studies of violence viewing and aggressive behavior. One early study that assessed these issues was the work of Aletha (Stein) Huston and Lynette (Friedrich) Cofer, in which they evaluated the impact of viewing aggressive versus prosocial television programs on the behavior of preschoolers in their normal childcare settings.[36] In this study, the preschoolers were assigned to view a diet of Batman and Superman cartoons, or *Mister Rogers' Neighborhood*, or neutral programming that contained neither aggressive nor prosocial material (e.g., special travel stories for preschoolers). The "diet" consisted of twelve half-hour episodes that were viewed one-half hour per day, three days per week, for four weeks. The researchers observed the children in the classroom and on the playground for three weeks before the start of the viewing period to establish a baseline for the amount of aggression or prosocial behavior; they continued to observe the children during the four weeks of viewing and for an additional two weeks. The results showed that children who were initially more aggressive and had then viewed the diet of Batman and Superman cartoons became more active in the classroom and on the playground, played more roughly with toys, and got into more aggressive encounters. Conversely, youngsters from lower-income families who had viewed the *Mister Rogers' Neighborhood* diet increased their prosocial helping behavior. This early field study suggested that viewing aggressive program content can lead to changes in aggressive behavior, while the opposite is also true for prosocial programming. Moreover, these changes were demonstrated in a relatively short viewing period (twelve half hours) and in the context of other viewing that took place outside the classroom setting.

Another approach to field studies involved the assessment of the effects of naturally occurring differences in the television exposure available to children in communities with or without television or communities with differing television content. In one set of studies the researchers were able to study the introduction of television in a rural community in Australia, in contrast to two similar communities that had experiences with television.[37] In a second set of studies, the research team studied the introduction of television in a rural Canadian community, in contrast to two similar communities with television experience.[38] The results of both the Australian and Canadian studies converge in showing that the introduction of television had a major influence on restructuring the social lives of children in these rural communities. Both studies found that television displaced other media use and involvement in various social activities—a finding not dissimilar to the earlier studies of children in England or the United States and Canada.[39] However, with regard to the effects of TV violence, these newer field studies provide stronger evidence of negative influence in differing but complementary ways. Murray and Kippax found changes in perceptions of the seriousness and prevalence of crime among children in the town exposed to higher levels of television violence, while Williams and Macbeth found increases in aggression among children following the introduction of television in the town.[40]

WHAT HAVE WE LEARNED?

Research conducted over the past fifty years leads to the conclusion that televised violence does affect viewers' attitudes, values, and behavior.[41] In general, there seem to be three main classes of effects—aggression, desensitization, and fear:

- Aggression. Viewing televised violence can lead to increases in aggressive behavior and/or changes in attitudes and values favoring the use of aggression to solve conflicts.

- Desensitization. Extensive violence viewing may lead to decreased sensitivity to violence and a greater willingness to tolerate increasing levels of violence in society.
- Fear. Extensive exposure to television violence may produce the "mean world syndrome" in which viewers overestimate their risk of victimization.

Although the body of research on the effects of viewing television violence is extensive and fairly coherent in demonstrating systematic patterns of influence, we know surprisingly little about the processes involved in the production of these effects. Although we know that viewing televised violence can lead to increases in aggressive behavior or fearfulness and changed attitudes and values about the role of violence in society, it would be helpful to know more about how these changes occur in viewers.

To set the context for the continuing research—within the broad framework of a social learning paradigm—we know that changes in behavior and thoughts can result from observing models in the world around us, be they parents, peers, or other role models, such as those provided by mass media. The processes involved in "modeling" or imitation and vicarious learning of overt behavior were addressed in social learning theories in the 1960s, but we need to expand our understanding of the neurological processes that might govern the translation of the observed models into thoughts and actions.[42]

With regard to aggression, we know that viewing television violence can be emotionally arousing, but we lack direct measures of cortical arousal or activation patterns in relation to violence viewing.[43] The pursuit of neurological patterns of cortical arousal in violence viewing would likely start with the amygdala because it has a well-established role in the control of physiological responses to emotionally arousing or threatening stimuli.[44] Indeed, a recent National Research Council report from the Panel on the Understanding and Control of Violent Behavior, concludes:

> All human behavior, including aggression and violence, is the outcome of complex processes in the brain. Violent behaviors may result from relatively permanent conditions or from temporary states.... Biological research on aggressive and violent behavior has given particular attention to the following in recent years: ... functioning of steroid hormones such as testosterone and glucocorticoids, especially their action on steroid receptors in the brain; ... neurophysiological (i.e., brain wave) abnormalities, particularly in the temporal lobe of the brain; brain dysfunctions that interfere with language processing or cognition.[45]

Thus, one suggestion for further research on the impact of media violence is to assess some of the neurological correlates of viewing televised violence. In particular, the use of videotaped violent scenes can serve as the ideal stimulus for assessing activation patterns in response to violence. These neurobiological studies hold the key to understanding the ways in which children might respond to seeing violence in entertainment, and this might also be the key to understanding the desensitization to violence, or what some might describe as a "drugging" effect on the developing child. To assess this possibility, we embarked on an initial study of children's brain activations while the youngsters viewed violent and nonviolent video program material. We reasoned that there may be similarities between the ways humans respond to threats of physical violence in the real world and the neurobiological response to so-called entertainment violence.

We began our study with some notions and expectations drawn from previous research suggesting that we might find the "threat recognition" system—involving the limbic system and right hemisphere of the brain—as an area that will be activated while viewing video violence.

It is very likely that the amygdala will be involved in processing violence, but the projections to the cortex are not clear. Hypotheses about violence viewing and brain activation need to start with research on physiological arousal and then be linked to cortical arousal.[46] In this regard, the work of Paul Ekman and Richard Davidson using EEG recordings while subjects viewed gruesome films (a leg amputation) indicates asymmetries in activation patterns in the anterior regions of the left and right hemispheres.[47] In particular, positive emotions are associated with left-sided anterior activation, while negative emotions are associated with right-sided activation.[48]

In our pilot study, we found that both violent and nonviolent viewing activated regions implicated in aspects of visual and auditory processing.[49] In contrast, however, viewing TV violence selectively recruited the right precuneus, right posterior cingulate, right amygdala, bilateral hippocampus and parahippocampus, bilateral pulvinar, right inferior parietal and prefrontal, and right premotor cortex. Thus, TV violence viewing appears to activate brain areas involved in arousal/attention, threat detection, episodic memory encoding and retrieval, and motor programming. These findings are displayed in figure 1, showing the significant contrasts between violence viewing and nonviolence viewing by brain lobe/region

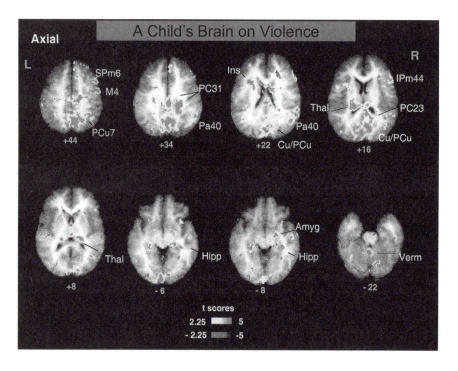

in the xyz stereotaxic atlas coordinates.[50] It can be seen that the Regions of Interest (ROI) of the composite activations of eight children, combined in adjusted Talairach space, include the amygdala, hippocampus, and posterior cingulate. These areas are important because they are likely indicators of the perception of threat and may include possible long-term memory storage of the threat event (these patterns in particular are similar to the memory storage of traumatic events by PTSD patients). These activation patterns demonstrate that video violence viewing selectively activates the right hemisphere and some bilateral areas, which collectively suggest significant emotional processing of video violence.

Our continuing research at Harvard Medical School, Children's Hospital, Boston, is designed to address these questions about violence viewing in a more robust study that employs a larger and more differentiated sample of children who have had differing experiences with violence (e.g., children who are identified as high or low in aggressive tendencies and children who have been victims of abuse). We will continue to use the methods and procedures that were demonstrated to be effective in the pilot study: we will conjoin measures of physiological arousal (e.g., GSR, heart rate) with neuroimaging techniques (e.g., functional Magnetic Resonance

Imaging, or fMRI) to track the emotional and neurological processes involved in viewing televised violence. We anticipate finding clear differences in the three groups of children, with the victims of violence—the abused youngsters—being most responsive to viewing media violence and the aggressive youngsters being the least responsive to the entertainment violence. This desensitization effect is the one that results from extensive violence viewing and acting out of the violence witnessed in the entertainment world of film, television, and video game violence.

Can we say that "drugging" children by immersion in entertainment violence is an accurate description of the effects of toxic media content? Perhaps it is too early to come to a definite conclusion on that issue. However, the "entertainment violence" that surrounds our children almost from birth and throughout their childhood is a potent toxic influence on our youth and the future of our society.

Part II
Medical Remodel

6

Child Psychiatry, Drugs, and the Corporation

MICHAEL BRODY

Banners with the message "Welcome to the American Psychiatric Association Convention" beckoned me into the imposing lobby of New York City's cavernous convention center. "Dissolving the Mind–Brain Barrier" was the theme of the 2004 annual meeting that brought together some 20,000 delegates from around the world. The convention is a magnet for global pharmaceutical corporations, whose colorful, larger-than-life displays dwarfed all others in the exhibit area. Their computers, plasma TVs, and attractive representatives commanded attention. Abbott, Bristol-Myers Squibb, Eli Lilly, Pfizer, Shire, and GlaxoSmithKline took the lion's share of the display area acreage.

"Sign in" beckoned the drug rep. "Have you tried our drug for bipolar disorder? It works with kids," he announced casually, in a manner better suited to selling toys or candy. "Here, take some literature on our study of fifty-six patients." On a big-screen TV, children were playing and riding bikes. A clinical trial with only fifty-six patients and images of happy children—was this scant evidence supposed to convince me to give a powerful psychiatric drug to a sick child? After I glanced back from the oversized screen, the drug rep handed me yet another pen.

Prior to 1990, psychotropic drugs were almost always considered treatments of last resort for children. But the last fifteen years have witnessed an explosion in the use of drugs to treat children's psychiatric disturbances. In 2002, in the United States, about 2.7 million prescriptions for antidepressants were written for children aged one to eleven, and more than 8 million for children aged twelve to seventeen years.[1] Meanwhile, 4–5 million children diagnosed with Attention Deficit Hyperactivity Disorder (ADHD) are on stimulants.[2] It is no longer uncommon for children to be on two or more psychiatric medications concurrently.

Some mental health professionals herald these developments as a victory for public health, citing them as evidence that childhood psychiatric diseases such as depression and learning disorders are being diagnosed more accurately and treated more effectively than in the past. But others like myself are deeply concerned that the dramatic increase in psychotropic drug use with children signals a profound insensitivity to the root causes of their suffering and developmental needs. To fully grasp the causes and consequences of the steep rise in the use of drugs to treat children, we must consider the power of the $200 billion a year pharmaceutical industry—the most generous and influential lobby group in American politics by a wide margin.[3] We also need to examine profit-driven managed care companies that generally insist on drug therapies from generalists rather than psychotherapy with specialists. But first of all, we must explore American psychiatry's fairly recent embrace of the biological (or medical) model of mental illness and the symbiotic relationship between psychiatry and the pharmaceutical industry that has resulted.

AMERICAN PSYCHIATRY AND THE MEDICAL MODEL

Historically, psychiatry has been the black sheep of the medical profession—a specialization that lacked credibility and respect. One reason was the veritable "confusion of tongues" that plagued the profession's early efforts to develop a uniform system for classifying mental disorders. In the 1890s, Emil Kraepelin finally imparted some clarity and rigor to the diagnostic process, but no therapeutic leverage followed from this.[4] To remedy that situation, in the 1920s American psychiatry embraced psychoanalysis, which became the dominant model of mental illness for several decades. With a few notable exceptions, however, psychoanalysis, with its characteristic emphasis on early childhood traumas, afforded little leverage against severe mental disorders.[5] Moreover, psychoanalysis is notoriously sectarian, and during the 1970s, infighting among various psychoanalytic factions and growing competition from psychologists and social workers contributed to the implosion of the medical/psychoanalytic "empire."[6] The biological or medical model of mental illness, which locates the source of psychological disturbance in faulty genes and brain chemistry, quickly filled the void, offering psychiatry a semblance of scientific legitimacy that psychoanalysis never really conferred.[7]

Miracle Drugs, Marketing, and the Medical Model

Other factors also contributed to the decline of psychoanalysis and psychiatry's embrace of the medical model. In the early 1950s, a potent group of psychotropic medications were discovered that were able to subdue the most florid symptoms of schizophrenia and bipolar disorder. Thorazine, Mellaril, and lithium enabled thousands of patients—who would have spent their remaining years in the back wards of hospitals—to reenter the community.[8] The promises of "talking cures" paled by comparison with the dramatic results achieved with these new "miracle drugs."

Chemical companies were quick to recognize the potential of this untapped market and wasted no time in forming alliances with psychiatrists to encourage the use of drug therapies. In his book *Blaming the Brain,* Elliot Valenstein points out that as soon as Thorazine was established as a treatment for schizophrenia, Smith, Klein and French—the company that produced it—launched an all-out media campaign that included legislative lobbying, speakers programs, medical conferences, and building alliances with hospital-based psychiatrists. As a result, only eight months after its release, *over 2 million patients* were taking Thorazine regularly.[9] The extraordinary success of this marketing campaign quickly became a template for all other new psychiatric drug launches in the United States.

Antipsychiatry and the *DSM*

Although it was intended to weaken or discredit psychiatry's burgeoning reliance on drugs, the "antipsychiatry" movement of the 1960s and 1970s actually reinforced it because it obligated psychiatrists to clarify and systematize their diagnostic procedures to justify extreme measures such as incarcerating psychotic patients and medicating them against their will.[10] The effort to refine and extend psychiatric diagnoses culminated in the development of the *DSM-III (Diagnostic and Statistical Manual of Mental Disorders,* 3rd ed.) in 1980, which described categories of psychiatric disturbance in a systematized and rigorous fashion, in keeping with the standards of other medical specialties. *DSM-III* quickly became the "bible" of modern psychiatry.

The *DSM*, now in its fourth edition (with the fifth one well under way), *does* make diagnosis more uniform and facilitates communication among mental health professionals, who now speak the same "language." At the same time, each new edition of the *DSM* presents a staggering array of new psychiatric conditions and changing criteria for old diagnoses, leading more people to be diagnosed with psychiatric disturbances, many of whom are then treated with psychotropic drugs. For example, with the fourth edition of the *DSM* in 1994, the number of symptoms that a child needed to exhibit in order to be diagnosed with ADHD was lowered from eight to six, resulting in a significant increase in the number of children being diagnosed and placed on stimulant medication.[11]

Parent Advocacy

The abandonment of psychoanalysis in favor of the medical model was also welcomed by many parents, who resented the "shame and blame" that psychoanalytic theory inflicted on them through its skewed emphasis on "bad parenting" as the source of their children's distress. And in due course, bona fide medical diagnoses also gave many children access to special education programs under the Individuals with Disabilities Act.[12]

Today, many parent-run advocacy groups such as CHADD— Children and Adolescents with Attention Deficit Disorder—are closely allied with and funded by pharmaceutical companies, which provide them with educational materials, help to launch campaigns to raise awareness about the illness in question, support their meetings and websites, and inevitably encourage members to seek and in some cases demand drug therapies for their children.[13]

THE RISE OF THE PHARMACEUTICAL INDUSTRY

In the 1960s new laws allowed chemical companies to take out patents on a compound rather than on the method of producing it or on the use to which a drug would be put, thus providing individual companies with never-before-imagined control over the potential use and sales of new drugs.[14] Then, in 1980, the Reagan administration passed a series of laws that removed most of the checks and balances provided by independent research and the Food and Drug Administration (FDA). This enabled what were formerly comparatively small enterprises—small subdivisions of larger chemical companies—to become giant multinational companies with formidable political clout.[15] According to Marcia Angell, former editor of the *New England Journal of Medicine*:

> The most important of these new laws was the *Bayh-Dole Act* which enabled universities and small businesses to patent discoveries emanating from research sponsored by the National Institutes of Health (NIH), the major distributor of tax dollars for medical research, and then to grant exclusive licenses to drug companies. Until then, taxpayer-financed discoveries were in the public domain, available to any company that wanted to use them.... The Reagan years and Bayh-Dole also transformed the ethos of medical schools and teaching hospitals. These nonprofit institutions started to see themselves as "partners" of industry, and they became just as enthusiastic as any entrepreneur about the opportunities to parlay their discoveries into financial gain.... One of the results has been a growing pro-industry bias in medical research—exactly where such bias doesn't belong....
>
> Starting in 1984, with legislation known as the *Hatch-Waxman Act*, Congress passed another series of laws that ... extended monopoly rights for brand-name drugs. Exclusivity is the lifeblood of the industry because it means that no other company may sell the same drug for a set period.... As their profits skyrocketed during the 1980s and 1990s, so did the political clout of drug companies. By 1990, the industry had assumed its present contours as a business with unprecedented control over its own fortunes. For example, if it didn't like something about the FDA, the federal agency that is supposed to regulate the industry, it could change it through direct pressure or through its friends in Congress.[16]

When did the FDA finally cave into pressure from the drug companies? Arguably, in 1992, when Congress passed the Prescription Drug User Fee Act, which authorized drug companies to pay user fees to the FDA. By 2002, the FDA was receiving $576,00 per new drug application, amounting to $260 million per year, which bankrolled about a thousand new FDA employees who have been added to hasten the passage of new drug applications. These industry-paid employees constitute more than half of the FDA staff involved in approving drugs.[17]

Drug Companies Control Their Own Research

Since the early 1980s, drug companies have been designing and funding their own clinical trials, which are then carried out by researchers at multiple sites. Few of the researchers engaged by these companies have access to the complete dataset and therefore cannot definitively interpret the results they get. Consequently, drug companies can and do make public only the results that support their "product." While selective reporting is already a hazard to public safety, researchers on company payrolls have been caught using fictional subjects or professional subjects who may be in more than one clinical trial at a given time.[18]

The ethical and scientific integrity of drug research has been further compromised by the extent to which pharmaceutical companies influence the content of articles in scientific journals and symposia at medical conferences, which are the primary vehicles through which physicians acquire information about which drugs are safe and effective. According to physician Richard Horton—editor of *Lancet*, the prestigious British medical journal—"even the most prestigious medical journals, supposedly the neutral arbiters of quality by virtue of their much-vaunted process of critical peer review, are owned by publishers and scientific societies that derive and demand huge earnings from advertising drug companies."[19] Communication or medical writing agencies, now ghostwrite up to 50 percent of the articles that appear in medical journals. Articles written by these agencies are generally commissioned by drug companies, which then find well-known (and well-paid) "researchers" to affix their names to the articles.[20]

According to psychiatrist David Healy, a respected researcher and former drug industry consultant, similar practices govern presentations at medical conferences: pharmaceutical agencies heavily fund and influence proceedings at major medical conferences by underwriting delegates' expenses and running prominently featured "satellite symposia."

> Speakers at these symposia are drawn from a small handful of figures who rotate from one company symposium to the next. They will frequently say uncritically congratulatory things about the drug produced by the symposium sponsor, making essentially the same statements about all drugs despite their manifest differences.... Big names become big names in this field because they are pushed forward by pharmaceutical company support; some of these people may have little scientific achievement to justify their inclusion on the

programs of major meetings.... These individuals, who may be too busy to do hands-on scientific work or even to see patients, and who may never have observed the effects of the drug they are talking about, will be the ones informing others about the drug in some exotic location, perhaps by delivering a message worked out by the pharmaceutical company beforehand. All that is really required of the big name is to remember the brand name of the drug and to stick to the script.[21]

The appraisal and reporting practices described by Healy are no longer egregious exceptions or oversights. They are standard practice. What makes them even more dangerous is that most American citizens assume that the mandate of the FDA is to serve as a consumer watchdog and to ensure that drugs entering the market "work." But that was never quite the case. Although the FDA *is* expected to ensure that drugs do not have dangerous side effects, it is *not* their mandate to prove that drugs are clinically effective. In fact, the FDA can approve a new drug as long as two clinical trials show that it does "something" different than a placebo, which is a far cry from showing that it is clinically effective for the illness it was designated to treat.[22] In the final analysis, it is doctors—who are charged with the right and responsibility to prescribe—who are our designated watchdogs. But without independent clinical research to guide their decisions, doctors no longer have a sound basis for making treatment decisions. All most of them have is "spin."

Direct Marketing to Consumers

In 1997, under pressure from drug companies and their friends in Congress, the FDA loosened the rules on direct-to-consumer advertising for prescription medications. As journalist Christine Gorman recalls, "soon the airwaves were saturated with pharmaceutical messages, complete with big-budget videos and catchy jingles. Side effects received scant play, and most viewers assumed that if the drugs were FDA approved, the risks were probably minimal. Patients bombarded their doctors with requests for the new drugs.... Demand for heavily promoted blockbuster drugs quickly soared and harried physicians often acquiesced."[23]

Direct-to-consumer advertising is riding the wave of "patient empowerment," in which patients access websites and chat rooms in order to find information and take charge of their own health. Although taking responsibility for one's own health is a positive step, health-related websites and chat rooms are often funded and infiltrated by the pharmaceutical industry, so in reality, more often than not consumers are accessing "sound bites" designed to sell product rather than genuine scientific information.[24]

Direct-to-consumer television advertising has had the desired effect. Indeed, by the year 2000, the pharmaceutical industry was spending $2.5 billion—over 60 percent of its advertising budget— addressing consumers directly.[25] (The European Union, which enjoys lower health care costs and a higher life expectancy than the United States, has banned prescription drug advertising.)[26]

MANAGED CARE: HEALTH CARE FOR PROFIT

The American Medical Association (AMA) was formed in the mid-nineteenth century to establish formal qualifications for physicians. From the mid-1800s through the 1950s, fee-for-service payment was the standard practice. By the 1950s, however, population expansion and advances in medical technology led to increased health care costs that were well beyond the reach of the average citizen. And so, insurance companies that dispersed the costs of health care across a large population were established. These health insurance companies preserved the fee-for-service system of independent practitioners—who were squarely in charge of clinical decisions—for another four decades.[27]

Managed Care Wrests Control from Physicians

In the early 1990s, however, during the Clinton administration, managed care corporations, whose sole mandate is profit, wrested control of the health care system from physicians. The managed care industry—the third largest in the United States—exercises considerable control over the laws that govern it, even when these laws are not in the public interest. For example, managed care companies increase profits by limiting patients' choices to a preselected group of physicians, contracting with them for specific services, and negotiating the lowest possible price. Indeed, very often hospitals and health care professionals are paid a flat fee, based on the average cost of care for a patient's diagnosis, regardless of how straightforward or complicated a given patient's course of treatment may be.[28] This "bargain basement" mentality deters many primary care physicians and pediatricians from referring their patients to specialists or taking the necessary time to form a humane and caring relationship and to explain or explore multiple paths to recovery or wellness.

Drug Therapies: A "Win-Win" for Big Pharma and Managed Care

Whatever else it may be, the market is essentially an *amoral* mechanism, so when profit becomes the guiding principle in our health care system, its primary target will be illnesses with large preexisting (or readily manufactured) markets. In other words, treatments that are profitable for "big pharma" and cost-effective for managed care will generally prevail. And certainly, recent drug therapies for "depressed" and "restless" children fit these criteria perfectly. Community outreach, parenting interventions, and psychotherapy cannot be patented and are labor and time intensive (in the short run). So it is no coincidence that in the early 1990s, as health maintenance organizations rose to dominance and the pharmaceutical industry reached the height of its power, nondrug interventions began to disappear from doctors' arsenal of treatments for distressed children.

Managed care companies also instituted peer reviews, monthly phone or mail monitoring, and other complex gatekeeping mechanisms to ensure that physicians complied with their policies and recommendations. Noncompliance with their directives could mean the loss of a lucrative—or essential—referral source. In-depth psychotherapy was frowned on, and as a result many psychiatrists turned to medication as the treatment of choice. Psychiatrists started seeing a high volume of patients—often several each hour—dispensing meds to appease the "managed care" companies, which had become their de facto employers, robbing them of the independence they formerly enjoyed.

Primary Care Physicians Take Center Stage

Of equal significance is the new role for primary care physicians. Although marginalized for many years by specialists, primary care doctors have now become very powerful because they control the flow of referrals. It is they who decide which procedures and tests are appropriate for their growing patient pool. Capitation, or one flat fee for the patient's health needs, is very different from fee for service, where each therapeutic intervention produces a charge. With capitation, the primary care physicians have an economic incentive to hold back on tests and procedures, because the money for tests that fall outside the HMO's area in essence comes out of their pockets.[29]

As a result of the expense of referring patients to a psychiatrist, it is tempting for primary care doctors and pediatricians to succumb to the pharmaceutical representatives' pitches and perks and simply dispense a pill. Not surprisingly, then, primary care physicians are targeted by drug companies because many willingly try new drugs after attending "continuing education" courses given over a weekend at a nice resort and underwritten by the drug company in question. Indeed, 75 percent of all prescriptions for antidepressants and 30 percent of antipsychotic meds are written by *nonspecialists*, who treat a higher volume of patients but have neither the time nor the training to do a thorough evaluation.[30]

The consequences for children are doubly disturbing, because the use of psychotropic drugs with children requires sophisticated, well-trained, and experienced specialists. These are powerful drugs that impact the child's developing brain. If this were not the case, the drugs would not be under prescription to begin with. Unfortunately, the ratio of psychiatrists to primary care physicians is now 1:7, and the field of child psychiatry is shrinking steadily.[31] A child psychiatrist can appreciate that severe depression may affect only 3–5 percent of children and adolescents.[32] Depression can also be a symptom that forms part of another illness such as schizophrenia or bipolar disorder, or a reaction to stress or trauma. The effectiveness of therapy and drugs is *specific for each condition*, and mental health professionals understand these nuances. Not every sad kid coming to see a primary care physician should get a pill. But a managed care system, aided and abetted by the pharmaceutical industry, encourages a "one size fits all" mentality.

Case Studies

The following clinical vignettes, culled from my practice, illustrate how children are inadequately treated when given a cursory exam by a nonspecialist.

Jen's parents brought her to see me when she was seven years old. She had been diagnosed with attention-deficit/hyperactivity disorder (ADHD) and prescribed Ritalin (by her pediatrician) three months earlier. Soon thereafter, she had difficulty falling asleep and began to lose weight. Thin to begin with, Jen appeared frail and sick. Her parents argued through the entire first meeting and revealed that Jen was the focus of a nasty divorce dispute over visitation rights. Jen's symptoms were more consistent with depression in reaction to her failed attempts to make peace between her parents than they were with ADHD. With a little encouragement, she began playing out her family's conflicts using my cloth puppets. Upon completing my evaluation, I continued psychotherapy with Jen; her parents began regular meetings with a family counselor, who served as a mediator on visitation and other issues related to Jen's development. Jen soon stopped taking Ritalin.

Jeffery came to see me at the recommendation of his school psychologist because he was disruptive in class and refused to leave the classroom for recess. Born two months prematurely, Jeffery, who was nine, was the third of three children. He spoke at thirteen months and walked at almost two years. His parents were high-level political appointees who spent limited time with their children. The only consistent time they spent together was on weekends at their second home near the beach. This house was also the setting for the near drowning of Jeffery's older sister when he was five. The sister suffered brain injury as a result of the incident and attends a private school for students with learning "issues." Jeff had difficulty sleeping and eating after his sister's accident, but the parents were reassured by his pediatrician that "this would pass." After several weeks, Jeff began to eat and sleep better but developed other symptoms. He became anxious and frightened of loud noises. He lost interest in other kids and had difficulty learning simple tasks like tying his shoes. His family doctor put him on an antidepressant and a long-acting stimulant.

On evaluation, it was clear that Jeff was regressed. He had difficulty making eye contact and spoke very little. His parents were ambivalent about him. Indeed, they did not seem to know their child and used their interview to discuss their guilty feelings about their brain injured daughter. While medication was indicated for Jeff, his parents needed guidance to relate more meaningfully to him and therapy to deal with several important familial losses. Drugs alone would not solve Jeff's problems.

Howard, an overweight ten-year-old boy, was brought to me because he was acting aggressively toward his mother and baby brother. Two months previously, Howard was prescribed an SSRI antidepressant by his family physician because of his apparent lack of motivation, enthusiasm, or interest in friends. While watching TV incessantly in his room, Howard demanded snacks; he left the house only to attend school, where he was failing and isolated. Soon after the start of medication, Howard did indeed come out of his room, but in an angry, aggressive, and uncontrolled manner, physically attacking both his brother and mom. My evaluation revealed that Howard was not the only family member with problems. His father was diagnosed with a bipolar disorder, and two grandparents were alcoholic. During subsequent visits Howard displayed hyperactivity and pressured speech. He was taken off all of his medications, calmed down, and then placed on a mood stabilizer for a bipolar disorder. He continues to do well.

And so we see the dangers of handing over treatment of distressed children to nonspecialists. In the first case, Jen was prescribed Ritalin when in fact she needed psychotherapy to help her cope with her parents' acrimonious divorce and another skilled therapist to diffuse and contain the acrimony between her warring parents. Jeffrey, by contrast, benefited greatly from psychotropic medication, but his family needed therapy and guidance as well. Finally, Howard was given the *wrong* medication, with very serious potential consequences that were narrowly averted.

SSRI ANTIDEPRESSANTS: A CAUTIONARY TALE

In December 2003, the British equivalent to the FDA—the British Medicines and Healthcare Products Regulatory Agency—set off a firestorm when it barred the use of all but one of the newer generation of antidepressant drugs for treating children. These drugs are the selective serotonin reuptake inhibitors (SSRIs), which increase the availability of the neurotransmitter serotonin in the brain. A year later, in October 2004, the FDA followed suit by ordering all pharmaceutical companies that manufacture antidepressants to place black-box warnings on the labels stating that they "increase the risk of suicidal thinking and behavior in children and adolescents." Black-box warnings are the toughest sanction short of banning the use of a drug. In addition, the agency directed the manufacturers to print and distribute medication guides with every antidepressant prescription to inform patients of the risks—a requirement made of fewer than thirty drugs currently on the market. The FDA also issued a statement recommending that patients given the pills be closely observed, cautioning that few antidepressants have proven effective against depression in children and teenagers.

Clinical Trials of SSRIs in Children

In spite of the FDA decision, some researchers and clinicians continue to argue that suicidal thoughts and behaviors are a symptom of depression and that therefore it is impossible to determine conclusively whether the SSRIs themselves or the illness is to blame. In 1991, however, Riddly King and his associates at the Yale Child Study Center reported several case studies of children who were not depressed but nonetheless became actively suicidal while taking SSRI antidepressants for their obsessive compulsive disorders. These findings have been echoed in several other case studies. Of equal concern, clinical trials of SSRIs with distressed children have almost uniformly failed to show positive results, yet prescriptions continued to climb through the 1990s—so much so that Seymour and Rhonda Fischer in a 1996 review article in the *Journal of Nervous and Mental Disease* were prompted to ask "whether the usual rules of science were somehow being suspended."[33] The trial results were uniformly negative, they pointed out, yet clinicians prescribed increasing amounts of antidepressants to children.

The answer to this conundrum is that distressed children show extremely high placebo response rates. In 1997, as a result of the "placebo washout phenomenon," Graham Emslies and colleagues excluded subjects showing a placebo response and then randomly assigned the remaining children to Prozac or placebo. In this instance, the children taking Prozac did do better, but not dramatically better. Nonetheless, David Healy, former secretary of the British Association for Psychopharmacology, concludes that "the finding does not legitimize widespread prescribing in this age group. Indeed, this trial demonstrated that many children—perhaps a majority—did no better on Prozac than they would have done simply seeing a sympathetic clinician."[34]

A select group of patients do appear to benefit from SSRI antidepressants. Indeed, some report feeling "better than well." Many others, however, do *not* benefit from SSRIs, and still others may be seriously harmed. Only when drug research is designed and conducted by disinterested scientists with no ties to drug companies, and all drug trials are in the public domain, will clinicians really know when and to whom psychotropic drugs should be prescribed. And only when the right to prescribe these drugs are limited to clinicians with specialized training in their use can we ensure the safety and well-being of our distressed children.

CURBING THE PHARMACEUTICAL AND MANAGED CARE INDUSTRIES

Fortunately, the 2004 FDA decision to put black-box warnings on antidepressants prescribed to children has resulted in a number of positive initiatives. Eliot Spitzer, New York's attorney general, launched a civil suit against the drug giant GlaxoSmithKline for committing fraud by concealing information about the antidepressant Paxil. According to the suit, the company conducted five trials but published the results of only one, whose mixed results it described as positive. The company sat on two major studies for up to four years, thus disguising the fact that Paxil was no more effective than a placebo in treating adolescent depression and might even provoke suicidal thoughts.[35] As a result of the suit, GlaxoSmithKline agreed to publish the results of all of its clinical trials.

Meanwhile the extent to which clinical drug trials are financed and controlled by the pharmaceutical industry has come under public scrutiny. Legislation was recently introduced in Congress that would mandate reporting of all clinical trials in a central government data base to which the public would have access. This legislation is endorsed by the Association of American Medical Colleges, the American Medical Association, the American Psychiatric Association, and the International Committee of Medical Journal Editors.[36]

The pharmaceutical industry, nonetheless, continues to exercise enormous influence over medical education, drug research, scientific journals, professional conferences and associations, and the FDA. When we add to this picture the fact that managed care companies have directed distressed children's care away from well-trained professionals and into the hands of generalists whose knowledge about psychiatric care often comes from weekend seminars sponsored by drug companies, we begin to appreciate the seriousness of the problem. Unless we curb the power of the pharmaceutical and managed care industries and draw attention to their profoundly unethical practices, which place corporate profits before safety and clinical efficacy, we will continue to do a grave disservice to our suffering children. Drug therapies have their place in the treatment of psychologically disturbed youngsters, but they will be used judiciously only when the following measures are taken:

- the FDA is fully funded by our tax dollars and no longer allowed to receive "user fees" from the pharmaceutical industry;

- clinical drug trials are designed, conducted, and disseminated by independent government agencies and academic institutions rather than for-profit drug companies;
- drug trials designed specifically to consider the sensitivity and vulnerability of the child's growing brain are required before psychotropic drugs can be used to treat children;
- a data bank is created for all pediatric psychopharmacology trials and placed in the public domain; this includes negative (including a drug's failure to show effect vs. a placebo) as well as positive results;
- pharmaceutical companies no longer have the legal right to subsidize medical schools, teaching hospitals, continuing medical education, professional meetings, and scientific journals;
- parenting education that focuses on fostering healthy psychological development is made widely available;
- consumer drug advertising is banned; and
- therapeutic choice is returned to clinicians and consumers rather than managed care corporate executives whose only guiding principle is profit.

AFTERWORD

The exhibit areas at The Child Meetings are almost empty of the pharmaceutical companies that used to promote their antidepressants for children. At one display a woman sits at a lone computer, available to answer any questions about the safety of her company's antidepressant for kids. There are no banners naming the product and no pens or pads. At another small space, two detail people speak anxiously of their drug as "part" of a whole package of what depressed kids need. The size of the booths representing psychostimulants, such as Ritalin, have grown since last year, filling the antidepressant void. Media exposure and the FDA's decisions about antidepressants for kids has affected "shelf space" at my organization's national meeting but not the content of the scientific proceedings. Data-driven papers about drugs and molecules still rule, presented by physicians who disclose long lists of financial and other affiliations to drug companies, while paradoxically claiming that "they have no conflicts of interest." There is still much work to be done.

7

The Development of Mentally Healthy Children

Stuart G. Shanker

The U.S. surgeon general declared 2005 to be the Year of the Healthy Child,[1] with the emphasis placed firmly on the importance of physical activity as a means of combating the growing epidemic of childhood obesity and promoting cardiovascular endurance, muscular strength, and flexibility. Also mentioned in passing is the importance of promoting children's mental health, although there is no clear indication of what this involves.

Some idea of how mental health is viewed in the surgeon general's office can be gleaned from a 1999 report on the subject. It is defined in terms of the absence of the childhood disorders cataloged in the *DSM-IV*. Significantly, mental illness is identified as the second most crippling "disease burden," on a list comprised of cardiovascular, malignant, and respiratory conditions, infectious and parasitic diseases, and alcohol and drug use.[2]

The contrast between the way physical and mental health are viewed is striking. Physical health is seen in both negative and positive terms, that is, as the absence of disease and the development of physical strengths and abilities. Mental health, however, is viewed only as the absence of disease, with no corresponding emphasis on the development of mental strengths and abilities. Indeed, as we have just seen, mental illness is actually located on the list of diseases from which the physically healthy child is free. Accordingly, a child is deemed to have returned to mental health when the "signs and symptoms" of such disorders have significantly diminished.[3]

This difference between the way *physical health* and *mental health* are viewed lies at the very heart of the debate over "drugging our children," for this disparity has led to a significant divergence in our attitudes toward medication in the treatment of physical versus mental disorders. Consider the case of a child with *familial hypercholesterolemia* (high cholesterol) who has been placed on a statin because a regimen of strict exercise and diet has failed to reduce the narrowing of his arteries. Even if his cholesterol level were successfully lowered, such a child would not be regarded as healthy if he could still not climb a flight of stairs, touch his toes, or do a partial push-up and sit-up. But consider the case of a child who has been placed on a stimulant to reduce his impulsive behavior. Should this behavior cease as a result of the medication, such a child would rarely be referred for further treatment (e.g., psychotherapy), for medication alone, in the case of a mental disorder, is widely seen to suffice if it serves to eradicate the child's troublesome symptoms.

To be sure, the thinking here is not that one is treating the symptoms per se but rather that the efficacy of the drug lies in its targeting the source of the disorder, as manifested by the course of these symptoms. Such a view of the origins of mental disorder amounts to what the philosopher Ludwig Wittgenstein described as a crude picture of "outward symptoms standing for inner processes."[4] That is, the view of mental illness that is operating here is one in which, like a physical disease, the source of the disorder is treated as an internal condition that can be corrected by biomedical intervention.

To appreciate simply that there is something deeply wrong with this way of thinking is no easy task, for this view of mental illness is buried deep in the Western psyche. In fact, it can be traced back to the philosophical revolution that took place in Cos in ancient Greece during the fifth century B.C.E. The changes ushered in by Hippocrates and the Hippocratic school determined not only the course of medicine over the next two and a half millennia but also the manner in which mental illness has been perceived and treated.[5] An important step, therefore, toward developing a positive concept of mental health and, correspondingly, of the treatment of mental disorders is to see how this philosophical framework has shaped and continues to shape our thinking about mental illness.

THE HIPPOCRATIC REVOLUTION AND THE
MEDICAL MODEL OF MENTAL ILLNESS

Hippocrates set out to remove illness from the realms of religion and magic and, instead, to establish medicine as the science of the causes, signs, and treatment of disease. As for mental illnesses, Hippocrates undertook to show that they—just like any other disease—were due to natural causes, not deities or sin, and as such they could only be cured physically, not through cleansings or incantations. Indeed, Hippocrates went a step further, insisting that there is no categorical distinction between mental and physical disease, and thus no difference between the kinds of therapies that should be administered to each.

When we speak of Hippocrates, we are no doubt referring to a group of thinkers, all of whom likely were doctors, who together contributed to the doctrine known as Hippocratic thought.[6] What is important, however, is that the texts present a systematic attempt to define health in general, including mental health, as the state that obtains when there is a proper balance between basic bodily humors (blood, phlegm, yellow bile, and black bile). Disease as such, including mental illness, results from an excess or deficiency in one of the humors.

This argument marks the introduction in Western thought of the medical model of mental illness. According to this outlook, one analyzes mental illness as one would analyze any physical disease. There are numerous examples of physiological explanations of mental aberrations and prescribed physiological treatments throughout the Hippocratic writings. For example, in *On Internal Diseases*, Hippocrates describes the onset of delirium as the result of bile flowing to the liver and then settling in the head, "especially at the temples." The patient begins to see "before his eyes creeping things and other animals of various sorts, and armed men fighting, and he himself thinks he is fighting in their midst." The prescribed treatment for such a state of delirium is to give the patient "five obols of black hellebore, and administer it in sweet wine."[7] Also noteworthy are Hippocrates' various remarks on melancholia. In the first treatises of the corpus *Hippocraticum*, melancholy is described as a permanent feature of a subject's character, caused by an excess of black bile, having physical as well as psychological effects (e.g., it was thought to cause hemorrhoids, dysentery, stomachache, and skin eruptions), and predisposing the subject to act and think in specific ways.

Undoubtedly the most famous of the Hippocratic texts on mental illness is his discussion of epilepsy in *On the Sacred Disease*. Here Hippocrates argues that "this disease forms and prevails from things which enter into and go out of the body, and it is not more divine than other diseases."[8] He goes on to explain that emotions, thoughts, and perception all originate in the brain and that "by this same organ we may become mad and delirious."[9] That is, madness as such emanates "from the brain, when it is not healthy, but is more hot, more cold, more moist, or more dry than natural." This "depravement" of the brain

> arises from phlegm and bile, either of which you may recognize in this manner: Those who are mad from phlegm are quiet, and do not cry out nor make a noise; but those from bile are vociferous, malignant, and will not be quiet, but are always doing something improper. If the madness be constant, these are the causes thereof. But if the terrors and fears assail, they are connected with derangement of the brain and derangement is owing to its being heated.[10]

As can be seen from these examples, the Hippocratic model is *medical* in a number of senses:

- it presupposes a physiological origin of mental illness and prescribes physical treatments;
- deviations in the "normal" or "natural" functioning of the organs are understood to cause mental aberrations; and
- it describes and catalogs observable symptoms.[11]

The influence this model would exert on scientific approaches to mental pathology over the next two millennia was largely the result of the writings of Galen (A.D. 131–ca. 201), who considerably refined and extended the Hippocratic model of mental functioning. Following in Hippocrates' footsteps, Galen developed a view of mental illness that was fundamentally physiological: all disease, including mental illness, was said to have a biological origin. Hence mental illness was treated with the same methods as were used to treat organic disease.[12] Mental disease, for Galen, was quite simply the opposite of mental health. All disease was caused by an imbalance in the humors, which was pathological when it impinged on the individual's ability to function.

In Galen's system, each humor is associated with a temperament, or what in modern terms might be called a basic personality type. Blood is associated with a sanguine temperament, black bile with a melancholic, yellow bile with choleric, and phlegm with phlegmatic. Each of the four temperaments is paired with an element: fire with yellow bile, water with phlegm, earth with black bile, and air with blood. Humors, temperaments, and elements are also associated with the qualities heat, moisture, dryness, and cold. For example, a sanguine temperament may be associated with the compound quality of "warm-moist" or the simple quality "warm."

Galen has been criticized through the ages for the crudeness of his physiological explanations for such phenomena as speech disturbances, alcoholism, convulsions, headaches, and delirium. Yet in some cases his neurobiological explanations of mental illness sound remarkably contemporary (such as his discussion of the role of brain lesions in pathological conditions). And although it would be a travesty to compare modern theories of the role of neurotransmitters in mental functioning to Galen's neurohumoral theory, still the claim that mental pathology can be explained in terms of excesses and deficiencies of neurotransmitters does indeed bear a striking resemblance to Galen's neurohumoral theory.

MODERN REDUCTIONISM

The most striking feature of the medical model introduced by the Hippocratic thinkers, which has informed Western thinking about mental health ever since, is the premise that, like physical diseases, mental disorders are diagnosed on the basis of observable symptoms. This assumption is particularly clear in the work of the German psychiatrist Emil Kraepelin, who attempted to develop a systematic taxonomy of mental disorders. The underlying assumption in Kraepelin's system is that in order to develop a successful treatment for a mental disorder one first has to classify it, and as is the case with physical disorders, one does so on the basis of observing the onset, course, and outcome of illness-specific symptoms and behaviors (as Kraepelin himself did in his classification of dementia praecox).[13]

The basic principle of Kraepelin's approach, therefore, is that a classification system of mental disorders must follow the same methodology as applies to the natural sciences. On this outlook, the limitations of what is observable and measurable define what is meaningful. Not only are there are no agreed-upon principles regarding the range and depth of human functioning and its mentally healthy and pathologic forms, but indeed in our modern bibles of psychiatry, the *DSM-IV* and *ICD-10* (*International Classification of Diseases*, 10th ed.), such principles are explicitly eschewed in the hope that the resulting works will be as "theory neutral" as possible in regard to studying the pathogenesis, etiology, and treatment of mental disorders.

The problem with this reductionist framework is not only that mental illness is treated as if it were simply a biological condition. More fundamentally, the problem is that there is no concept of mental health as such, other than the absence of mental illness. That is, there is no corresponding emphasis on the development of mental strengths and abilities, and accordingly, no understanding of the processes involved in the development of such strengths and abilities. This is the reason it is so widely assumed that mental health can be restored through psychopharmacology alone, for without a clear understanding of the range and depth of human functioning, the "cure" is reduced to suit the manner in which the condition is perceived.

UNDERSTANDING THE FULL COMPLEXITY OF MENTAL FUNCTIONING

In *The First Idea*, Stanley Greenspan and I presented a model that not only identifies the strengths and abilities that a mentally healthy child possesses at different ages but also explains how a child develops these capacities.[14] On the basis of our research and clinical studies, we identified a series of "emotional transformations" that a child goes through in the early years of life as the result of infant–caregiver emotional interactions. We refer to these stages as emotional transformations because of the primary role that emotions play in these interactions and because of the fact that the child's emotions go through a series of transformations, acquiring more and more cognitive, social, and communicative dimensions as a result of these caregiver–infant interactions.

A child's ability to progress through these stages depends to a considerable extent, of course, on a healthy central nervous system. However, we have found that no matter how robust a child's biological endowment, the presence of specific types of caregiver–infant interactions is decisive in the formation of these emotional transformations and the higher-level symbolic and mental capacities to which they lead.

The following five stages of emotional transformation culminate in the development of language.

Stages of Emotional Transformation from Infancy through Toddlerhood

Stage 1: Regulation and Interest in the World (Birth to Three Months)

In the first months of life, emotions enable the infant to connect emerging sensory and motor patterns. For example, a baby hears a human voice to her left but only coordinates the motor action of looking in that direction if the sound is pleasurable (i.e., not overwhelming or aversive). This important first step enables the infant to take an interest in the outside world and to begin patterns of self-regulation and sensory-motor coordination.

> Baby Jonah was brought in for consultation at only fourteen weeks because his parents were concerned about the absence of any social smile or cooing and his pronounced tendency to avert his gaze. Jonah had been born three weeks prematurely with a very low body weight. (His mother had smoked throughout her pregnancy.) It was obvious from the start that Jonah was suffering from a pronounced case of colic. None of the standard methods—rocking, swinging, swaddling, soothing sounds—helped to calm him down. Working on the assumption that he was suffering from an allergic reaction to his formula, he was switched to one of the special formulas with significantly reduced milk protein that are commercially available. Within five days his colic had improved to the point where he could now begin to take an interest in his surroundings. He started to spend longer and longer periods attending to his mother while she gently rocked him and sung softly. This important first step prepared him for the second stage of emotional transformation.

Stage 2: Engaging and Relating (Two to Five Months)

The second stage of emotional transformation enables synchronous and often rhythmic emotional interactions between the infant and primary caregiver. Positive and often joyful emotions enable the infant to coordinate looking, listening, and movement in patterned interactions with the primary caregiver. Here begins the first intimate social relationship that not only organizes all the senses and the motor system but positions the infant for the critical milestone of initiating intentional actions.

In Jonah's case it was clear that, in addition to his food sensitivities, he was highly sensitive to bright lights and loud noises. In order to avoid overloading him, his caregivers were careful to reduce his visual and aural stimuli. It was also clear that they were going to have to work especially hard to woo him into social interactions. Throughout the day they would take turns trying to engage his attention with funny faces and voices, always careful to avoid overwhelming him with their actions. Gradually he began to respond to their antics with a weak smile. By seventeen weeks he was not only sharing their broad smiles with broad smiles of his own, and responding to their playful overtures with shining eyes and joyful vocalizations, but he could even be observed to move his arms and legs in synchrony with the cadence of their voices.

Stage 3: Intentionality (Four to Nine Months)

Stage 3 is characterized by the shift from synchronous emotional engagement to reciprocal emotional gesturing between the infant and caregiver. These gestures involve gaze, facial expressions, vocalizations, and other types of bodily movements; they become part of a system of two-way intentionality and coregulation. During this stage, early social patterns are beginning to form. These patterns serve as a preliminary framework for the child's growing understanding of social causality and her emerging sense of self, as well as her ability to attend to and grasp her caregiver's feelings, moods, and intentions.

At twenty weeks Jonah made a significant leap in his development: left alone in his cot, he began to vocalize—not because he was hungry or wet but solely to get attention. As his mother approached he would begin to smile broadly. There immediately followed a loud bout of vocalizations that culminated in Jonah's first real laugh. He could now be observed to be working at his vocalizations, as he experimented with new sounds. Soon he was calling anyone in the house when he was ready for a play session. These were becoming longer and more intricate duets in which both partners took turns initiating and responding to each other's vocalizations, facial expressions, and gaze. Where in the beginning he could only sustain this kind of interaction for a couple of turns, he was able, by twenty-four weeks, to engage in these back-and-forth circles of communication for several minutes at a time.

Stage 4: Coregulated Social Problem-Solving (Eight to Eighteen Months)

During the fourth stage, reciprocal emotional exchanges become more complex, going from fleeting back-and-forth exchanges to a continuous flow of "coregulated emotional gesturing." This continuous flow of emotional interaction enables the toddler and her caregivers to engage in shared social problem-solving. These exchanges not only involve the child's emotional and social life but also orchestrate what she sees, hears, and does under the leadership of her emotional intent.

> Jonah began to flourish in every sense: physically, emotionally, socially, cognitively, and communicatively. By twelve months he was able to vocalize to get his father's attention, take him by the hand and lead him to the bookshelves, look up and point at his toy on the top shelf, and wait while his father fetched the toy for him. This sort of behavior demonstrated that he was coming to understand the elements of a pattern. These included his own emotional needs (what he wanted), the action patterns involved in finding the toy, the visual-spatial patterns involved in going from ground level to upper-shelf level where the toy was lying, the vocal pattern involved in attracting his father's attention, followed by a gleeful exclamation of triumph, and the social pattern involved in working together with his father toward a common goal. In other words, Jonah's growing pattern-recognition abilities involved seeing how the pieces fit together rather than being merely piecemeal behavior. Elaborate negotiations or play with others made it possible for Jonah to experience the world in larger integrated patterns.

Stage 5: Creating Symbols and Using Words and Ideas (Toddlerhood)

As a result of this sort of more complex social pattern recognition, the toddler starts to engage in more advanced forms of social imitation. Going beyond earlier patterns of copycat games, in which as an infant she could stick out her tongue when daddy did so, the toddler can now put on daddy's hat and pick up his briefcase before motioning to go out the door. As well, she is starting to repeat whole words and even phrases.

Once a toddler is capable of a continuous flow of emotional exchanges as part of shared social problem-solving, she can separate perceptions from fixed actions. Young infants tend to be locked into fixed perceptual-motor patterns, and as a consequence their emotional reactions are often global and catastrophic (all or nothing, or shutdown reactions). Complex emotional signaling enables the infant or toddler to begin to regulate her emotions. A continuous flow of back-and-forth emotional gesturing gradually replaces a fixed perceptual-motor action pattern (i.e., the infant moves from more instinctive to more socially flexible response patterns).

Perceptions, which were once tied to fixed actions, now gradually become "freed." A freestanding perception (an image) can then acquire "meaning" through the numerous emotional interactions that are associated with it. The image of mother goes from eliciting crying or global delight to integrating the multiple experiences an infant and toddler has with her mother. These freestanding images acquire more and more emotional meaning and serve to organize all the experiences that have been occurring during the first four stages of emotional transformation. These symbols continue to acquire further meaning through additional emotional and social interactions and go through a series of additional transformations, which we describe in detail in *The First Idea*.

> By fifteen months there was no longer any residue of Jonah's earlier challenges. He was now able to direct as well as share gaze and to engage in fairly complex social-problem interactions involving gaze, gesture, facial expressions, vocalizations, and body movements. Not only was he well advanced in the two-word stage of language development, in which he was able to put together words in distinctive patterns to convey his intended meaning, but he no longer demonstrated the sensitivities to light and noise that had been so pronounced when he was an infant. If anything, the amount of effort that his parents had put into wooing him into joyful interactions in those first months seemed to have produced a toddler with unusually developed attentional and social problem-solving skills. Most striking of all was the love and joy that he demonstrated when interacting with his parents.

ASSESSING THE MENTAL HEALTH OF A CHILD

As just outlined, the theory of emotional transformations holds that a series of critical emotional interactions early in life is responsible for the development of social, emotional, cognitive, and language abilities. The theory suggests that when these abilities do not develop, these critical early emotional interactions have not been mastered. Biological factors can make it difficult for a child to participate in these emotional interactions (as in autism), or as happens in institutional care, the caregivers themselves may not provide them. I exemplify these points through our clinical research with children diagnosed with autistic spectrum disorder (ASD).

Autistic Spectrum Disorder

To give just one example, Jane had been diagnosed with autism at the age of three. Her parents had immediately begun an intensive behavioral modification intervention program with her, but after one year very little progress had been made. She was hypersensitive to visual stimuli and had considerable difficulty in holding eye gaze or engaging in any kind of physical contact; she would spend hours perseverating and self-stimulating; she always had a vacant look on her face and demonstrated no facial expressions of emotion of any kind; and she would only make various grunts and inarticulate vocalizations. When her parents brought her in for a "floortime" session with Stanley Greenspan, Jane began to wander aimlessly around the room while her mother sat anxiously on the floor trying to coax her into an interaction and her father sat on a couch, both physically and emotionally removed from the scene. After observing this interaction pattern for a few minutes, Stanley gently began to coach the mother on how to be playfully obstructive so as to create an emotional interaction that would hold the child's attention. Within minutes the child was gleefully playing a game of peek-a-boo with both her parents, with shrieks of joy and laughter. She was able to sustain this interaction for around fifty back-and-forth exchanges before she lost interest and started to wander aimlessly again. She began to perseverate on opening and closing a door: an action that, through Stanley's coaching, was immediately turned into another interactive game, with the mother hiding behind the door. And so it went for another half hour, with Jane engaging with both of her parents in highly emotional interactions, leading to hugs and even kisses. At this point Stanley decided that this child was ready to take her first steps into language. Mother was instructed to leave the room and close the door purposely behind her. Jane rushed to the door and began banging on it, clearly insisting to be let out. But at this point Stanley had become utterly obtuse, wandering about the room trying unsuccessfully to understand which toy it was that she wanted. As she became increasingly frustrated, the little girl suddenly shouted "O," at which point Stanley immediately grasped her intention and said, "Oh, you want me to *open* the door." The child's language gains after this first session were astonishing, as was her social, emotional, and cognitive development.

When we studied children with autistic spectrum disorders and children with early emotional deprivation, we found that as predicted, they had not fully participated in and mastered a number of these critical early emotional interactions. Most important, we found that a subgroup of children with ASD whose biological challenges were not too great (but who nonetheless had a biological basis for not mastering these developmental capacities) were able, through an intervention program that focuses on basic emotional interactions in the context of the child's individual processing differences, to engage in these critical emotional interactions and progress to high levels of relating, symbolic thinking, and empathy.[15] A study of 200 children diagnosed with ASD who underwent this type of intervention bears out the significance of this approach. Outcomes were divided into three broad groups:

1. A "good to outstanding" group that included children who, after two or more years of intervention, evidenced joyful relating with a variety of emotional gestures; were able to engage in purposeful, organized, and sustained interactions and share attention in various social, cognitive, and motor-based tasks; could use language creatively and imaginatively and engage in coherent conversations; and no longer showed self-absorption, avoidance, self-stimulation, or perseveration.
2. A "medium outcome" group that included children who made significant gains in their ability to relate and communicate with gestures; could share attention and engage in social, cognitive, and motor problem solving; no longer evidenced self-absorption, avoidance of relating, self-stimulation, or perseveration; but still had significant problems developing their symbolic capacities.
3. A group that continued to have significant difficulties in both the presymbolic and the symbolic realms; had difficulty in attention and simple and complex sequences of gesturing; and continued to demonstrate a significant degree of self-absorption, avoidance, self-stimulation, and perseveration.

Of the 200 children, 116 (58 percent) were in the "good to outstanding" outcome group, 50 (25 percent) were in the "medium" outcome group, and 34 (17 percent) continued to have significant difficulties.

It is important to emphasize that this was not a representative population of children with ASD. The families who participated in this study were highly motivated, and their children may well have had some special strength. For the moment it is reasonable to hypothesize that a subgroup of children with ASD can make significant progress through such an intervention program, but only future clinical trial studies will be able to confirm this hypothesis.

CONCLUSION

Our developmental theory of emotional transformations highlights precisely what is wrong with the strictly negative view of mental health that underpins the narrow psychopharmacological attitude toward treatment discussed above. If one targets a child's symptoms alone, without any attempt to treat the underlying developmental challenges, one runs the risk of masking the problem, if not actually exacerbating it or creating a host of different problems. Consider, for example, the case of the child who has been placed on a stimulant to help control his impulsive behavior. Proponents of biomedical intervention will cite cases in which it can be shown that the child was thereby enabled to participate in a normal classroom setting and make rapid educational gains. But such children often demonstrate a deficit in their ability to engage in coregulated reciprocal interactions. If this deficit is the result of the fact that the child has difficulty in reading and responding to others' emotional cues (stage 3 in our developmental model), or more fundamentally, in his ability to engage in emotionally patterned interactions with others (stage 2), then drug therapy alone will do nothing to help him undergo the critical emotional interactions needed to progress to high levels of relating, symbolic thinking, and empathy.

We need to take the *full complexity of mental functioning* into account, therefore, when we assess a child's mental health. We need to observe not just the course of the child's symptoms but such factors as the development of his capacity to experience and express a wide range of both positive and negative emotions; his ability to understand himself—his thoughts, feelings, attitudes, and so forth—and others, and the quality of the friendships that he is capable of forging; his ability to engage in multicausal thinking about both social and physical phenomena, and to look at his own behavior in such complex terms; and his ability to look at the relative influence of multiple variables in both social and physical contexts, and to make social judgments based on internal standards.[16]

In other words, when we are assessing the mental health of a child, we need to establish not just whether he is free of the "signs and symptoms" of a DSM disorder, but, much more important, whether he possesses those age-appropriate mental strengths and abilities that will enable him to go on to become a flexible, reflective, and creative thinker: someone who will be able to form warm and caring relationships over the course of his lifetime; to cope successfully with the many stresses that he will encounter; and to confront and deal with the unique challenges that he and his generation will face. Until we have embraced a philosophical picture that stresses the positive and constructive aspects of mental health, our views about the role of biomedical intervention are destined to be as constricted, as is the reductionist view of mental functioning.

8

Diagnosis, Drugs, and Bipolar Disorder in Children[1]

Daniel Burston

Buddha said, "Life is suffering." And although life is usually much more than suffering, no one disputes that it is integral to the human condition. But although painful and disconcerting, suffering is not always a *bad* thing, especially when viewed in retrospect. Suffering provides us with potent incentives and challenges to grow and develop, to mature and to master fear and adversity. Yet nowadays, much of children's suffering is hidden from public view and addressed indirectly—often with drugs that obscure the true source of their difficulties and rob them of important opportunities for growth and development.

THE NATURE OF HUMAN SUFFERING

To suffer is to endure experiences and states of mind that are impressed or imposed on us by circumstances that run contrary to our needs and desires, without our prior knowledge or consent. Suffering takes many forms, but most of them are variations on the themes of *lack*, *loss*, and *conflict*.

Lack
Children may *lack* adequate nourishment, warmth, tactile stimulation, safety, security, or the kind of diligent parental involvement

and oversight that shields them from noxious experiences of one
sort or another. They may also lack an intact nervous system,
immune system, or the like. These deficits may be brief and transient, deep and abiding, or unpredictable and episodic.

Loss

Loss is different from mere lack, because it entails the removal
of a source of hope, comfort, or instruction that was formerly
a palpable presence. Children can suffer the loss of a beloved
parent, grandparent, friend, teacher, or cherished pet. They can
also experience the loss of their physical or neurological integrity, popularity, self-esteem, trust in others, faith in the future,
and so on. Whether these losses are irreversible depends in part
on temperament, creativity, resolve, and, above all, on the presence of environmental supports to help a child rally, regroup, and
move on.

Conflict

Children in distress often suffer from inner or interpersonal
conflicts as well. Interpersonal conflicts pit them against significant others, transforming relationships that ought to be a source of
psychic sustenance into a dreary or frightening source of tension,
misunderstanding, and in worst-case scenarios, emotional or
physical violence. Inner conflicts, which follow in the wake of interpersonal problems, are profoundly debilitating and potentially
paralyzing because they provoke irreconcilable desires, attitudes,
values, or beliefs and the inability to choose definitively between
them.

These three words—lack, loss, and conflict—cover the spectrum
of human suffering. When people of any age suffer from severe or
chronic deficits, profound loss, or painful inner or interpersonal
conflicts, the distress and disorientation they experience lead to
thoughts, feelings, and/or behaviors that make them candidates
for a psychiatric diagnosis.

SUFFERING REINTERPRETED AS MENTAL ILLNESS

Diagnosis is a word many of us simply take for granted. It is
something doctors do as a prelude to recommending a course of
treatment for a medical illness. Well, yes and no. The Greek word
gnosis means "knowledge"—usually knowledge of an immediate

and intuitive kind. The prefix *dia-*, which is also Greek, means "thorough," "comprehensive," or "encompassing." So by virtue of its etymological derivation, the word *diagnosis* ought to mean an encompassing knowledge or deep insight into the nature of a patient's malady. And if we are talking about children who are distressed or disturbed, it would presumably include an in-depth, empathic understanding of their developmental history and present familial and social circumstances, in addition to any medical problems they may be contending with. For Erik Erikson—author of *Childhood and Society*, and one of the most influential theorists in the field of child development—that is precisely what the term *diagnosis* meant.[2] Erikson was a psychoanalyst steeped in history and the humanities, who thought deeply about the human life cycle, and was not wedded to the classifications used by conventional psychiatrists.[3]

DIAGNOSIS ACCORDING TO THE MEDICAL MODEL

Until recently, theorists like Erikson helped to shape how the average psychiatrist thinks about children's emotional development.[4] That being so, the idea that a psychological crisis in childhood or adolescence might be a splendid opportunity to correct or deepen a child's development *without recourse to drugs* enjoyed considerable currency in the mental health professions. But since the publication of the third edition of the American Psychiatric Association's *Diagnostic and Statistical Manual* (*DSM-III*) in 1980, psychiatry began to divest itself of psychoanalytic habits of thought and practice, and as a result the word *diagnosis* has come to mean a narrow and "objective" classification of illness, based on the clinician's ability to identify and enumerate the various signs and symptoms of a disease. The word *disease* is pivotal here, since the underlying causes of the disorder are presumed to be traumas, deficits, or anomalies of a specifically *neurological* variety, even when interpersonal conflicts of one sort or another feature prominently in the patient's clinical profile and a clear-cut medical explanation for the alleged disorder has eluded researchers for more than a century (e.g., for diagnoses such as ADHD and depression). This one-sided emphasis on biological causation—often referred to as the "medical model"—renders the psychosocial determinants of a child's disturbed and disturbing behavior irrelevant or inaccessible to the clinician's gaze.

Proliferation of Diagnostic Categories

Many psychiatrists feel that the profession's rejection of psycho-analysis and return to the "medical model" represent a major advance in terms of objectivity. But there are dissenting voices as well. One source of their skepticism is the ceaseless proliferation of new categories of mental disorder.[5] In the U.S. census of 1840, only one category of mental disorder was in use, namely, insanity. In 1880, however, census officials listed seven categories of mental disorder, in keeping with prevailing psychiatric opinion. The *International Classification of Diseases*, published by the World Health Organization after the Second World War, listed ten categories of psychoses, nine psychoneuroses, and seven personality disorders, for a grand total of twenty-six categories.

Evidently, in the United States, these criteria did not suffice. We do things on a grander scale. Accordingly, the first edition of the American Psychiatric Association's *Diagnostic and Statistical Manual of Mental Disorder*, generally known as the *DSM*, published in 1952, contained 106 categories of mental disorder, while the second, published in 1968, had 182. The third edition, published in 1980, had 265, and the revised third edition (*DSM-IIIR*), published in 1987, had 292. The fourth edition, which appeared in 1993, has almost 400, and many new categories are currently under consideration for *DSM-V*.[6]

In other words, within 150 years, American psychiatry either discovered or (in some sense) manufactured almost 400 categories of mental disorder. And that total does not begin to reflect the potential number of variations to these diagnostic classifications wrought by the creation of the multi-axial diagnostic system for the *DSM-IIIR*. If all those specifications are taken into account, the diagnostic profiles available to clinicians number in the thousands. Sticking strictly to major categories, however, the average rate of increase in the last century and a half is twenty-five new categories of mental disorder per decade, with peak production occurring between 1962 and 1993, when each successive edition of the *DSM* produced an average of forty-eight new categories—almost double the rate of the preceding century. Even Allen Frances, who chaired the committee that produced the *DSM-IV*, recently expressed concern over "the wild growth and casual addition" of new mental disorders under the tenure of his predecessor, Robert Spitzer.[7]

Although the unchecked proliferation of psychiatric categories is disturbing in and of itself, it becomes all the more so when we consider that this trend has increased the ease and frequency with which we now label children mentally ill. An equally disturbing trend is that diagnostic categories—and the drugs used to treat them—that were formerly reserved for adolescents and adults are now being applied to children. Bipolar disorder is one such diagnosis.

BIPOLAR DISORDER IN CHILDHOOD

In contrast to the many new diagnostic categories that are currently listed in the *DSM*, bipolar disorder (BPD) antedates the giddy and headlong inflation of the *DSM* by many decades. The disorder was first described by German psychiatrist Emile Kraepelin in the 1890s. He characterized manic depression—as it was then called—by long bouts of profoundly debilitating depression, punctuated by bursts of frenzied activity, accompanied by sleeplessness, grandiosity, recklessness, incoherence, and giddy euphoria, which frequently escalates from odd or destructive behavior into frank psychosis. Depression punctuated by less florid symptoms of mania was termed hypomania, and mania that was not followed by obvious depressive symptoms was simply called mania.

Although the diagnostic criteria were revised several times, the epidemiological data on bipolar disorder were remarkably consistent until ten years ago; they furnished one of the best reasons to give credence to the medical model. The average age of onset for bipolar disorder was between fifteen and forty-four years. It affected both sexes equally and afflicted between 0.5 and 1.5 percent of the general population across the globe. This dogged consistency across time and place suggested strongly that it is subject to a very strong genetic influence, even as the authors of the *DSM* expanded their classification to include four discrete versions of BPD, each with its own unique profile.

In the last few years, however, psychiatrists are claiming that they can detect bipolar disorder in *children as young as two or three years old* and are medicating them accordingly.[8] In some instances, the child's symptoms conform (more or less) to the profile of BPD II. In others it is claimed that the child's mood swings are so rapid and frequent that they defy classification according to any of the existing *DSM* criteria.[9]

Although epidemiological data for pediatric bipolar disorder is still lacking, the Child and Adolescent Bipolar Foundation (CABF) nonetheless reports that the number of children diagnosed with BPD is rising dramatically, "as doctors begin to recognize the signs of the disorder in children." The CABF conservatively estimates that at "least three quarters of a million American children and teenagers—mostly undiagnosed—may currently suffer from bipolar disorder." In addition, the CABF claims that

> it is suspected that a significant number of children diagnosed in the United States with attention-deficit disorder with hyperactivity (ADHD), have early-onset bipolar disorder instead of, or along with, ADHD. Depression in children and teens is usually chronic and relapsing. According to several studies, a significant proportion of the 3.4 million children and adolescents with depression in the United States may actually be experiencing the early onset of bipolar disorder, but have not yet experienced the manic phase of the illness.[10]

Well, perhaps. But then again, the language on their website describing the vast number of "as yet undiagnosed" bipolar children creates the confident expectation that this is not a rare childhood illness, paving the way for a self-fulfilling prophecy. Similarly, in their chapter in *Bipolar Disorder in Childhood and Early Adolescence*, researchers Lewinsohn, Seeley, and Klein state that "while there are no community data on the prevalence of what has been called prepubertal, juvenile, and pediatric bipolar disorder, it may be relatively common in clinically referred children."[11] And so once again, despite the manifest absence of compelling evidence, psychiatric authors create *an expectation* in the reader that BPD is common in childhood.

Despite these uncertainties, pediatric bipolar disorder is becoming a very popular diagnosis and has been the subject of considerable media attention in recent years. Since the late 1990s, hundreds of research papers and several scholarly books have been published on the subject, whereas only ten years ago these were relatively uncommon. Meanwhile, cross-cultural comparisons reveal that prepubertal diagnoses of bipolar disorder are rare in Germany and the Netherlands but increasingly common in the United States, which is the only industrialized nation that does not provide universal health care and maternity leave, and in general has the weakest policies in support of children's welfare and environmental protection. Can this be coincidence? Moreover, research studies have indicated that the antidepressants and stimulants that are prescribed with such frequency in America may actually *exacerbate* the many behavioral disturbances that are labeled "early onset bipolar disorder."

For many mental health professionals, the proliferation of diagnoses of pediatric BPD is cause for concern. As a result, some modest steps have been taken to stem the tide. Guidelines that were recently issued jointly by the CABF and the American Academy of Child and Adolescent Psychiatry stipulate that children under the age of six should *not* be given this diagnosis under any circumstances.[12] In an editorial in the *Journal of the American Academy of Child and Adolescent Psychiatry* in which these guidelines were unveiled, John McLennan said: "Labeling severe tantrums in toddlers as major mental illness lacks face validity and undermines the credibility of our profession."[13]

Although these guidelines are a beginning, they do not eliminate all cause for concern because they are not mandatory or binding in any way. They are merely recommendations. They stress the importance of clarifying the frequency, intensity, number, and duration of symptoms but remind clinicians, for example, that "hot, hungry, stressed and/or tired children without psychopathology may become irritable." Likewise, clinicians are admonished that grandiose statements—such as "I am Superman!"—are not necessarily indicative of mental disorder, depending on the child's age.[14]

One problem with these guidelines is that everything here hinges on the description and enumeration of symptoms. Though clinicians are not actually forbidden from considering the possibility that symptoms often have a hidden meaning or that the children who behave in these ways are trying to *communicate* something in some desperate, disjointed fashion, these theoretical or interpretive options are not even mentioned in passing. The overarching presumption is that the child's symptoms are rooted in neurological losses or deficits, which are the true source of all of his inner and interpersonal ("behavioral") issues. Once a clinician makes that assumption, careful consideration of the developmental, social, and cultural contexts of children' lives is no longer integral, or even that relevant, to the diagnosis—as if profound psychic disturbance is merely a disease, like the flu or the measles. It is also of concern that McLellan and Kowatch are clearly concerned that many child psychiatrists have forgotten what it is like to be a hot or hungry child, or to feel that you are invincible (Superman).

But the most troubling thing of all about these guidelines is that they promote the practice of using multiple prescriptions—*polypharmacy*—to treat children and adolescents whose behavior is disturbing to adults. They recommend that if the first drug the psychiatrist prescribes does not work, after a certain interval of time, another should be tried, and another, and another, and so on, until the child is "stable." They never even hint at the possibility that the initial course of drug treatment might be ineffective because *the original diagnosis was actually incorrect and should be revised or discarded.* Rather, the clinician is charged with finding the right medication or combination of medications.

Furthermore, these recommendations fail to acknowledge much less account for the fact that there is no research evidence to date that proves polypharmacy is any more effective than *monotherapy*—or the use of a single pharmacological agent.[15]

In a recent article titled "How I Learned to Stop Worrying and Love the *DSM*," psychiatrist Philip M. Sinaikin recounts his clinical work with a seventeen-year-old female—whom we shall call Kate—hospitalized for depression, self-destructive behaviors, and vague suicidal thoughts, who received a diagnosis of bipolar disorder and placed on *three medications*—a mood stabilizer, an antidepressant, and an antipsychotic.[16] As a result of Kate's fragile emotional condition, it was decided that she should not return to school, despite the fact that she had earned a GPA of 3.5 and had a combined SAT score of 1,590—a remarkable achievement that prompted many colleges and universities to solicit applications from her *before* she graduated.

Careful questioning did not disclose any prior history of bipolar or even hypomanic behavior, and when asked why she was given this diagnosis, the patient replied that it was probably because she acknowledged having "mood swings" on a symptom checklist. When asked what was troubling her, Kate complained that she could not handle the stress of her senior project in high school and was distressed at the prospect of going away to college the following year. Further inquiry disclosed that she had no social life to speak of and had never been on a date.

Rather than accept Kate's diagnosis at face value, Dr. Sinaikin wisely revised the "story line" underlying her "case" to render Kate's distress intelligible to herself—and to others—by instilling a sense of agency and opportunity, rather than victimization, in his patient. Instead of narrating her difficulties in terms of a lifelong medical disability, he construed it developmentally as being due to a (temporary) lack of social skills and socioculturally as a lack of being valued for her academic achievements. In terms of our initial reflections, he interpreted Kate's suffering as the result of two types of lack, without attributing her problems to an underlying disease. He took her off the mood stabilizer and the antipsychotic medications, and urged her to return to school and apply for college. She promptly won a four-year scholarship and embarked on her undergraduate degree. Summing up this case, Dr. Sinaikin concluded:

> I am not arguing that psychiatric illness does not exist, nor am I op-posed to the use of psychotropic medication, but I do believe that di-agnostic labels and medications should be used judiciously and within the context of an appropriate narrative. Renarrativizing DSM story-lines can be exhausting work and sometimes meets with significant resistance, but overall, I believe it can be a successful and rewarding approach for the many clinicians who struggle with the reductionistic and impersonal DSM medical model that we are faced with today.

It is instructive that Dr. Sinaikin's approach to treatment—narrative therapy theory—does not privilege or dismiss the medical model but treats it simply as *one interpretive option among others*, includ-ing the existential, developmental, sociocultural, psychoanalytic, spiritual, and interpersonal perspectives, all of which have merit in his eyes.

Dr. Sinaikin also notes that narrative therapy theory is closely allied to (and inspired by) social constructivism, a philosophical movement that is predicated on the idea that

- realities are constructed and constituted through language;
- realities are maintained and organized through language; and
- there are no essential truths.

According to social constructivism, psychiatric labels are not neu-tral scientific terms that accurately describe an objectively existing disturbance. On the contrary, the disturbance itself is a social con-struction. By this account, diagnoses often become self-fulfilling prophesies, actively shaping the lives and destinies of those so la-beled in adverse ways. When deployed in this fashion, the *DSM* generates new narrative identities—or perhaps *pseudo-identities*—that patients then live out as existential truths. This is not the result of a disinterested scientific research, says Sinaikin, but of an (un-conscious) process of reification

> in which concepts, ideas and abstractions . . . are literally transformed into what appear to be objectively valid realities grounded in the im-mutable laws of nature. Thus, "rapid-cycling bipolar disorder" moves from the realm of the concept to concrete reality by the pro-cesses of reification, supported by the established institution of psy-chiatry and legitimized by what is presented as scientific research. From a social constructivist perspective, psychiatrists do not need to

prove whether bipolar disorder is a brain disease or whether someone has the disease, because those who are labeled and treated as
bipolar will, for all intents and purposes, be bipolar.

Dr. Sinaikin's constructivist philosophy is not merely a critical tool,
however. It is rooted in a strong sense of the clinician's obligation
to provide patients with narratives that increase their sense of
agency and self-authorship (nowadays termed "empowerment")
and diminish their (actual or potential) experience of vulnerability
and victimization at the hands of others. With these thoughts in
mind, Sinaikin invites us to imagine

> a 4-year-old rambunctious child presenting to the authority of the
> psychiatrist and emerging with the label of BPD (bipolar disorder).
> Not only would the child's sense of self form around that label, the
> surrounding reality will support and confirm it. Teachers, parents,
> school counselors, police officers will now respond to this child
> based on their understanding of how a person with BPD acts and
> should be handled.

Dr. Sinaikin's troubling scenario provokes reflection on the ill
effects of a thoughtless diagnosis for a child who is stressed or
poorly socialized but is still neurologically intact. Given the child's
youth and plasticity, whatever he or she currently lacks in terms of
appropriate attachment and parental care, clear rules and boundaries, and so on, can presumably be remedied in time to avert any
permanent ill effects—in principle, anyway. But without saying so
in quite so many words, Sinaikin implies that a misdiagnosis of
BPD forecloses on this possibility, robbing a child of his future.
Why? Because a child who believes that he or she suffers from a
lifelong disability acts accordingly and grows up with a brain burdened by toxic drugs.

Dr. Sinaikin's caution against an excessive or ideological reliance
on the medical model is welcome but hardly new. Ever since the
late 1950s, sociologists such as Erving Goffman and Thomas Scheff
have shown that a diagnosis of a severe mental disorder often con-
stitutes an induction ceremony whereby a child or adolescent is
launched on a career as a lifelong mental patient.[17] Very often, their
(real or alleged) disorder then becomes the core or the pivot of their
identity and the perfect excuse for ducking the challenges and responsibilities of a more mature existence.[18] In short, it is socially
and psychologically disfiguring, a license for immaturity, as well as
a potential hazard to the growing child's brain.

The question then becomes how prevalent or widespread are these instances of misdiagnosis? Very common, by some accounts. Psychiatrist Joseph Goldberg, of the Zucker Hillside Hospital in Glen Oaks, New York, states that nearly half of patients suffering from manic depression, or bipolar disorder, were abused as children. Needless to say, emotional, physical, and sexual abuse are all linked with dramatic mood swings and changes in behavior. In his own words, "our results suggest that a history of severe childhood abuse is to be found in approximately half of adults with bipolar disorder." Indeed, a third of his patients suffered from *multiple* forms of abuse. But in the kinds of cursory evaluations most such cases receive, these facts are suppressed, and if uncovered, they are either denied or minimized in the interests of "normalizing" the appearance of the family, because of the embarrassment, stigma, and potential legal entanglements and sanctions that might ensue if these matters were not "swept under the rug."

Child psychiatrist Mary Burke offers a somewhat different explanation for the dramatic increase of bipolar diagnoses among children. In her judgment, severely depressed mothers are emotionally and sometimes physically unavailable to their infants, which in turn can lead to "insecure attachment" and chronic anxiety. If these fretful, insecurely attached infants also have naturally sensitive temperaments, and are therefore more difficult to soothe than the average baby, their depressed mothers are more likely to perceive these traits as evidence of disturbance, leading them to retreat even further from their infants, causing even more rupture in the mother–infant attachment that is so critical for their infants' mental health. As their children's signals of distress mount— marked by tantrums, incessant crying, and irritability—the mothers, who are themselves overwhelmed by their own unmet emotional needs, may seek consultation with a psychiatrist, who validates their concerns that their children have a psychiatric illness. She also hypothesizes that in general children have difficulty regulating their moods in the face of chronic parental stress or ineptitude. If children's emotional lives become overwhelming and unmanageable to their parents, they are at a much higher risk of being labeled as bipolar.

Burke's remarks about the social and interpersonal roots of severe mood disregulation in infancy and childhood are consistent with a robust and rapidly growing research literature that stresses the importance of early attachment and attunement of parent to child as a guarantor of mood stability.[19] Significantly, references to this impressive body of work are conspicuously absent in the growing literature on pediatric bipolar disorder. That being so, it is important to emphasize that early losses, deficits, and/or conflicts between young children and their parents can render them emotionally overwhelmed, immature, and less able to regulate, express, or contain their feelings, which then erupt in ways that resemble bipolar disorder.

STEMMING THE TIDE OF MISDIAGNOSES

Bipolar disorder is widely understood to be a genetically linked, neurological illness. And no one who suffers from it, or anyone close to them, doubts its reality or potentially devastating effects. Given that this is so, it is alarming that so many children are being labeled as bipolar when their symptoms (1) usually do not fit the typical clinical profiles for this disorder and (2) can often be understood as the result of neglect or abuse. Why is this happening? Sinaikin suggests that many psychiatrists are so strongly committed to the medical model that they simply will not entertain alternative interpretations—or "narratives." That is undoubtedly true. But while this pervasive reluctance to reckon with other possibilities is usually justified on scientific—or *pseudo-scientific*—grounds, there are also many *nonscientific* reasons why this is so. Given the prevailing regime of managed care and the powerful influence of the pharmaceutical industry, many psychiatrists simply lack the time, the training, or the practical incentive to do a thorough psychosocial evaluation of the child and family or to provide psychotherapy or family therapy, if that is called for. And if they are courageous and conscientious enough to go this route, they may court disapproval and ostracism by their colleagues and forfeit the substantial financial "perks" that come from prescribing drugs in a routine and injudicious manner.

Another nonscientific factor that influences the judgment of psychiatrists is parental or familial pressure. Many families are experiencing a great deal of stress because funding for programs that support parents and communities has been slashed in recent years.[20] In addition, the number and quantity of pollutants that demonstrably undermine brain development and are being released into the environment have increased dramatically.[21] Moreover, efforts to reform the public school system through the No Child Left Behind Act often ignore children's developmental needs, while the media, which exert a powerful impact on children's minds, grow more violent and toxic by the day.[22] In the present cultural climate, it is intrinsically difficult to raise one's children to a wholesome maturity, and many stressed-out, beleaguered parents whose faltering efforts don't succeed may *prefer* to imagine that their children suffer from a neurological disorder rather than to ponder the Herculean task of reforming a system that has failed them, or admitting to any personal failure on their part to nourish, protect, or guide their offspring properly. Moreover, many parents are encouraged in this direction by mental health professionals and are often misinformed about the potential side effects of the medications prescribed to their children.[23]

On reflection, it is sometimes the case that in delivering a diagnosis of pediatric BPD, a child psychiatrist may collude with parents in their efforts to avert their attention from these deeply disconcerting scenarios. But although the diagnosis may afford some short-term relief, it then becomes part of the problem. Americans are experiencing a series of concurrent and overlapping crises with respect to parenting, education, and environmental sustainability— crises that are expressed in increasing numbers of distressed and disruptive youngsters, whose behavior disappoints and antagonizes adult caretakers, both in and outside of the home. Rather than tackling these systemic issues through the creation of new laws and policies that protect children and support parents, we "treat" children on a case by case basis, under the auspices of the medical model. In other words, we search for individually calibrated chemical solutions to what are really predominantly *social* problems. This expedient appeals to our individualistic American mind-set and our longstanding cultural romance with the idea of a quick chemical "fix" to our problems. But on deeper reflection, this approach is deeply irrational and holds the potential to backfire dangerously.

"BEEN THERE, DONE THAT"

Pervasive social pressures to deliver a diagnosis of pediatric BPD for deeply disturbed children must constantly be born in mind, because it will not be the first time that something like this has happened. Those who are versed in the history of psychiatry have an eerie sense of déjà vu about these recent developments. For example, in the 1950s American psychiatrists started to use the diagnosis of schizophrenia in a reckless, cavalier fashion. In fact, they were three to four times more likely to label someone schizophrenic than their British counterparts—which caused no end of trans-Atlantic controversy, with careful British psychiatrists scolding their profligate American cousins.[24]

These facts are well known. What is less well known is that the alleged "epidemic" of schizophrenia in the United States furnished the pretext necessary for psychiatrists to try out a new class of drugs—called phenothiazines—on this bumper crop of newly diagnosed patients.[25] Robert Whitaker, author of *Mad in America*, points out that in the late nineteenth century, when they were first invented, phenothiazines were used chiefly as industrial dyes; later, in the 1930s, they were used as an insecticide or an agent to kill parasites in swine. At that time, no one imagined that they had any medicinal value. When the market for them vanished, new applications were sought, and the discovery that they could function as "chemical straightjackets" created a bonanza for drug companies.[26]

Who else benefited from this dramatic market expansion? Certainly not patients! A recent study by the World Health Organization indicates that the average person's chances of complete recovery from schizophrenia is much higher in countries that are too poor to provide their populations with these medications. By contrast, someone who starts on phenothiazines—or other, "atypical" antipsychotics—stands an 80 percent chance of undergoing repeated breakdowns and hospitalizations, the infamous "revolving door syndrome." These data—whose integrity has stood up to repeated criticism and scrutiny from the mental health professions—would prompt any rational person to conclude that, in the average case, taking phenothiazines is more likely to hinder than help a psychotic person recover, at least in the long run.[27]

While the introduction of phenothiazines in the 1950s furnishes an ominous parallel to our present predicament, there are some notable differences between the 1950s and the present that render the plight of children even more worrisome. When American psychiatry diagnosed schizophrenics by the bushel in the 1950s, *pharmacological remedies were still considered the treatment of last resort*. If all else failed, medications were tried. Nowadays, however, pharmacological remedies are widely considered to be the first—and best— treatment option, a fact that is reflected in the policy statements of the Bush administration as well as the psychiatric and drug lobbies.[28] Indeed, if the FDA's behavior is any indication, the prevailing attitude in the mental health industry (and society at large) seems to be that a new pharmacological agent is presumed "innocent" (harmless) until proven otherwise. The Greek word *pharmakos* means "poison" as well as "medicine," and the presumption that a newly synthesized compound is "innocent" or harmless is a gross injustice to consumers, especially when the "consumers" are children, who unlike their adult counterparts never seek these treatments voluntarily and lack the skills to evaluate and the power to refuse such harmful medications. In the process, we are normalizing the use of powerful psychotropic agents in young children, whose brains are still fragile and unformed.

On a societal level, we might compare the increasingly routine drugging of children with the normalization of doping in professional sports. In both instances, drugging is used to increase performance, or to compensate for perceived weaknesses, and is becoming standard practice. The difference, of course, is that athletes are usually adults who give their (more or less) informed consent when they are drugged. It is a Faustian bargain, because in the long run they harm themselves by doping. But in the short run they derive considerable social and financial rewards in exchange for playing along. Finally, what they do is illegal and, although extremely prevalent, is still opposed by large sections of the sporting community, who are calling for more screening, tougher sanctions—and rightly so.

But unlike athletes, young children cannot weigh the risks and benefits of taking drugs and are powerless to refuse them. Moreover, very few people are actively opposed to the present state of affairs, and the use of excessive and inappropriate medication is perfectly legal. In instances like these—which are increasing steadily—only *others* profit. The child who is wrongly medicated is a hapless victim in an elaborate charade of abuse, neglect, and quasi-scientific labeling on the part of family, teachers, and mental health professionals.

In cases of (real or alleged) pediatric BPD, the treatment of choice is sometimes a mood stabilizer such as lithium, but more often than not the newer "atypical" antipsychotics are used in conjunction with mood stabilizers. The toxic side effects of lithium are well known, but those of the atypical antipsychotics were hidden behind a dense fog of industry hype until relatively recently.[29] The only certain benefits that accrue from their routine usage are to the drug companies that manufacture and sell them at an obscene profit— with the support of the state and federal governments. For though the rhetoric of psychiatry emphasizes the subtlety and complexity of clinical judgment, the need to tailor the treatment to the needs of the individual patient, and so on, the fact remains that the federal government has encouraged Texas, Pennsylvania, Ohio, and other states to legislate specific treatment protocols for specific diagnoses—protocols that stipulate precisely which drugs are to be used and in what circumstances. And although these protocols—called medical algorithms—purport to be "evidence based" or supported by "expert consensus," the "experts" who compose such panels are invariably industry insiders who are paid handsome sums for spinning the evidence favorably for big pharma and ignoring the abundant evidence of these same drugs' potential to do harm.[30]

And so we face the inevitable question: are the "early detection techniques" promulgated by the CABF, the American Academy of Child and Adolescent Psychiatry, and the many clinicians who diagnose and treat even earlier and more aggressively than their guidelines mandate based on sound scientific research? Or are they a supple and ingenious strategy to open up new markets for drug companies? When all the evidence is weighed carefully, it points strongly to the latter conclusion. Indeed, future generations may look back on the early twenty-first century as an era when the chemical colonization of childhood really began in earnest—though whether they view these developments in positive or negative terms is impossible to foresee. In any case, things have now reached such a pitch that many psychiatrists who are still wedded to the medical model, but are wary or opposed to these trends, are now afraid to speak out for fear of reprisals of one sort or another. They have reason to be fearful. Careers have been ruined or lost for this kind of candor. Dr. David Healy's recent hiring and abrupt divestiture at the University of Toronto's Department of Psychiatry is a disturbing case in point—although he was fired because he spoke out against the indiscriminate use of SSRIs, especially for teens, rather than the drugs that are prescribed for pediatric BPD.[31] Closer to home, Dr. Stephan Kruszewski, a Harvard-trained psychiatrist in Harrisburg, Pennsylvania, was fired from Pennsylvania's Department of Public Welfare for speaking out against government-sanctioned polypharmacy and the deepening collusion between government, psychiatry, and big pharma, which is mandated by the Pennsylvania Medical Algorithm Project.[32]

Furthermore, Medical Algorithm Projects for children and teens, which started in Texas under then governor George W. Bush,[33] are now sweeping the country and will soon be subject to federal oversight, which seeks to ensure that all Americans, young and old, get early and frequent "mental health" screenings and then be treated according to "algorithms" that mandate the use of drugs. While this new federal initiative is rationalized in terms of preventive mental health, the ones who really benefit will be the big pharmaceutical firms and the politicians (in both parties) who eagerly abet their activities. The consequent loss of liberty—both for children and their physicians, who will be constrained by the courts to medicate, regardless of whether they deem it necessary or desirable— will be drastic and perhaps, indeed, irreversible, unless vigorous steps are taken to raise public awareness of the issue.[34]

THE POLITICS OF DIAGNOSIS

In many instances, a psychiatric diagnosis for pediatric bipolar disorder and a host of other conditions masks, rather than reveals, the real roots of a child's suffering. So what do we do? Dispense with diagnosis altogether? Continue with business as usual? Reintroduce the psychoanalytic ideas and practices that psychiatry abandoned in the diagnostic arena? Let me address these proposals one at a time.

Dispense with Diagnosis?

When considering how to diagnose children who have symptoms that resemble bipolar disorder, we have much to learn from pediatrician Mel Levine's approach to treating learning disabilities. Levine has demonstrated that learning disabilities that allegedly result from underlying neurological abnormalities are remedied more effectively when they are framed as *different styles of learning*, each of which entails its own specific strengths and weaknesses, *rather than as medical diseases*. After all, the medical approach to mental illness presupposes a model of a "normal" brain that, from an empirical standpoint, is no more than a heuristic fiction. And even if there are neurological components or underpinnings to a specific learning problem, says Levine, an inordinate emphasis on them makes those so labeled feel not up to doing as well as others, or as well as they could and should do. In short, it becomes a self-attribution that becomes a self-fulfilling prophecy.[35]

Levine describes himself as an existentialist rather than a constructivist, but if we disregard the philosophical nuances and focus on commonalities, he obviously shares Sinaikin's ethical concern with providing patients with an overall assessment of their own

skills and situation that stimulates their optimism and sense of personal agency, rather than a global sense of inadequacy that promotes passivity and lowered self-esteem. Unfortunately, however,
when it comes to more severe behavioral problems, the call to abol-
ish diagnosis altogether is impractical. Whether pediatric bipolar
disorder per se really exists or not, there are many children who
suffer from brain disorders that stem from profound emotional
deprivation in infancy and/or from exposure to toxic pollutants
such as lead and mercury that are known to compromise brain development.[36] When that is so, simply developing new story lines to
help children organize their identities and build self-esteem (à la
Sinaikin and/or Levine) is not an adequate response.

Business as Usual?

So perhaps we should stick to "business as usual" and continue
to revise, refine, and expand the *DSM*. But as I pointed out earlier,
the *DSM* is already intolerably bloated; we need to think about how
to *shrink* the *DSM* without loosing the proverbial baby with the
bathwater. But to do that effectively, we must be able to discrimi-
nate between what is "baby" and what is "bathwater." To that end,
we should declare an immediate and binding moratorium on the
adoption of *any* new categories, including pediatric BPD, and reflect at length about the contexts in which different diagnostic categories emerged historically. Furthermore, clinicians who have
benefited financially from a long professional association with large
pharmaceutical companies should be excluded from the committees that review and revise existing criteria. Otherwise, we'll just
repeat and intensify the errors of the past.

Reintroduce the Psychoanalytic Model?

Should we go back to the days when psychoanalysis dominated
psychiatric thinking? In some ways, this proposal is quite appealing.
For one thing, analytically oriented clinicians are instructed early in
their training that as treatment proceeds and the patient improves, it
is prudent to revisit, revise, or completely discard their original diagnosis. Indeed, training analysts generally insist that a full and accurate diagnosis—that is, a deep and encompassing knowledge of
the patient's inner and interpersonal worlds—is generally somewhat elusive until the final phase of treatment, when the roots of the
patient's deepest and earliest developmental disturbances finally

surface for interpretation and reflection. Consequently, the idea of changing a patient's diagnosis two or three times in the course of treatment is not novel or aversive to the seasoned analyst.

By contrast, when treating a patient within the medical model, the psychiatrist generally arrives at a "correct" diagnosis *before* treatment begins and then tends to "lock in" to that diagnosis. Furthermore, under managed care, psychiatrists are often under enormous institutional and financial pressure to render a diagnosis swiftly—and they often do so in a matter of minutes. But once you have surveyed the world of mental disorder through psychoanalytic lenses, the idea that a thorough and accurate diagnostic appraisal can be based on check lists, or the mechanical enumeration of clinical symptoms and signs in the interval of less than an hour, seems superficial at best.

Yet despite the benefits of an approach to assessment that does not focus exclusively on symptoms or valorize drug treatment alone, problems remain because today there exist not one but dozens of schools of psychoanalysis, each of which favors different developmental theories and different diagnostic criteria. Theoretical differences between the various schools are notoriously impervious to arguments based on empirical research, prompting critics to liken it to a kind of secular religion, complete with dogma, schisms, and so on.[37] But while we cannot embrace psychoanalysis wholeheartedly, perhaps we cannot reject it completely either because it reminds us that (1) symptoms may have unconscious or inarticulate meanings in addition to neurobiological causes, and (2) if clinicians' efforts to be objective are not balanced by a strong attunement to their own needs and feelings, and to those of their patients, clinicians will fail their patients in some crucial respects. Ideally then, we must distill what is best in psychoanalytic practice and reconfigure the economic and institutional arrangements that shape and constrain the delivery of mental health services so that diagnosis can be practiced in a thorough and humane way.

CONCLUSION

When young patients' suffering is chiefly the result of interpersonal and/or cultural deficits, losses, or traumas, the summary invocation of the medical model to sanction reckless pharmacological interventions is not merely one way of understanding or addressing the patient, as Dr. Sinaikin suggests. In a real and disturbing sense, it is a way of *not* understanding patients—a way of averting attention from the social, interpersonal, and environmental dimensions of their suffering. Such an approach to diagnosis sanctions a callous indifference to the circumstances that provoke and sustain the patient's problematic behavior and is therefore more likely to hinder than assist them in converting their experience into an opportunity for reevaluating and redefining themselves and furthering their personal development.

The solution to the current crisis in child psychiatry is not to jettison the disease model of mental disorder completely. There are some instances in which it is valid. But clinicians should also remember that being rocked by grief, livid with rage, paralyzed with anxiety, or confused, disoriented, and prone to mood swings are perfectly normal and intelligible responses for people in extremis—and that children, especially, require more latitude in this regard than our culture tends to permit them. But even for healthy adults, intense emotional reactions such as these are ever-present possibilities of human experience rather than diseases per se. When the social and cultural circumstances that cause a child's suffering are ignored, he or she can easily become a candidate for diagnoses that render the child's prospects for a full and genuine recovery dim and the likelihood for acquiring an iatrogenic disorder later in adolescence or early adulthood high.

What is the alternative? In an ideal world, routine diagnostic assessments would never be conducted in a frantic hurry, nor would they result in summary assessments that are parsed in the pseudo-objective terminology of the medical model to facilitate the "efficient" handling of insurance claims. It is not enough that clinicians "assess" their young patients' behavior and enumerate the signs and symptoms that conform to specific diagnostic profiles. Their whole personality—including their feelings, imagination, and ethical sensibilities—must be engaged in the encounter, and they must seek to discern, address, and evoke the singularity of their patients. And when clinicians are not absolutely sure of what ails the patient—which is quite often, if we are honest—they would not hesitate to say so for fear that any uncertainty on their part would preclude getting treatment under way. In fact, clinicians would be somewhat tentative and deliberately austere in terms of their reliance on diagnostic categories but rich in empathy and rich in their descriptions of their patients' personal history and enveloping social context. If we want to stop drugging our children needlessly and wrestle the DSM down to a manageable size, we must change how we conduct "business as usual."

Part III
Pathologies of Normalcy

9

The Rise of Ritalin

Triumph and Tragedy of the Medical Model in Children's Mental Health

LAWRENCE DILLER

Ritalin and I know each other well. We go back over a quarter century of my prescribing this drug to children diagnosed with Attention Deficit Hyperactivity Disorder (ADHD). My relationship with Ritalin has forced me to examine my role as a physician in my community and country. In the early 1990s I became uncomfortable with the steep rise in requests to prescribe Ritalin to children in my practice, which is located in an affluent mostly white suburban community of the San Francisco Bay Area. In addition to the typical pre-1990s ADHD patient—an elementary school–aged boy—by the early 1990s, many of my new patients included toddlers, preschoolers, girls, and teens.

EXPLOSION OF ADHD DIAGNOSES AND RITALIN USE IN THE 1990s

Toddlers and Preschoolers on Ritalin

Four-year-old Joey was in preschool/daycare from 7:30 a.m. until 5:30 p.m. as both his parents worked and had lengthy commutes. Joey wouldn't sit for circle time during the academic portions of his morning. He'd fidget, squirm, wander away, even ignoring the teachers' verbal redirections and warnings. When confronted he'd lose his temper and then wind up on the time-out chair. He'd also find himself on the chair some afternoons when he became too aggressive with his playmates outside, where there was less supervision. Joey's preschool teacher wondered aloud to his parents if Joey needed a medical checkup, which they took as her suggestion for an ADHD evaluation. His parents also worried that Joey wouldn't be allowed to continue at the preschool unless he was checked and his behavior improved.

Some parents have come to my office with children *as young as two* with the same questions, "Does my child have ADHD?" "Does he need Ritalin?"

Girls and Teens on Ritalin

Sarah, age eleven, daydreamed in her class. She freely admitted it. She was an honest, thoughtful child in the sixth grade. Much of her school work was below grade level and homework routinely took two to three hours to complete. Her parents reported that at home, if Sarah was given two or three directions even on nonacademic chores, she'd only get the first or second task done. When checked, Sarah would be playing with toys (she still liked dolls at eleven). She didn't directly defy her parents or teacher. Her parents had been reading and checking websites about ADHD. They wondered if she had the nonhyperactive inattentive form. Maybe she too needed Ritalin.

Jonah was thirteen and in the eighth grade at his Christian private school. He wasn't completing his work in school and had trouble turning in all his homework assignments. Even more problematic was his tendency to occasionally challenge a teacher's public criticism of him in class. The school was well known for its high academic and behavioral standards. It also had a local reputation for higher rates of children taking medication. Jonah's parents bristled when the assistant headmaster suggested that they might want to get Jonah "checked out." Jonah's father, the CEO of a major corporation, insisted to me that his boy's behavior was nearly identical to his own of thirty years ago. "Now look what I've achieved without any medication," his father told me on first meeting me about his son.

Although presenting as candidates for possible ADHD and medication, none of the three—Joey, Sarah, or Jonah—was as disabled or impaired as children of a previous generation whom I had considered for ADHD. What was going on? I discovered that my experience was not a local one but was taking place across America.[1] More and more, parents wondered if their children had ADHD and should be taking Ritalin. Indeed, the parents wondered if they too had this condition of poor focus, lack of attention, and distractibility with or without hyperactivity.[2] They wanted to know if they should also take this wonder drug that seemed so miraculously to improve their children's behavior and performance, especially at school.

I was curious about this explosion of ADHD and the use of Ritalin in America. In particular I was concerned about my role as a behavioral-developmental pediatrician who was prescribing all this medication. I began a personal odyssey and ethical exploration which culminated in a book I wrote titled *Running on Ritalin: A Physician Reflects on Children, Society, and Performance on a Pill*, which was published in 1998. I never imagined when I began it that this journey would propel me into national media, the halls of the U.S. Congress, and to international shores where this same drug, Ritalin, is now also making headlines.

HISTORY OF STIMULANT DRUG USE IN AMERICA

Ritalin—unless otherwise specified—is used throughout this chapter to stand for the class of drugs known as the stimulants (the best known also include Dexedrine, Adderall, and Concerta). Stimulants have always been popular in the United States, whether a hundred years ago when cocaine was part of the original Coca-Cola or today, as reflected in the methamphetamine ("crack") epidemic.[3] The stimulants are so named because they raise the heart rate and blood pressure, improve alertness and athletic prowess, decrease the need for food or sleep, and of course, increase concentration.[4]

Stimulants have been integral to traditions in ancient cultures in the form of coca leaves chewed daily by the Andes Indians or *qat* used ubiquitously by Arabian tribesmen.[5] However, the synthesis of artificial stimulants such as amphetamine and cocaine in Europe in the late nineteenth century ushered in a degree of intensity, use, and abuse not present in preindustrial societies.[6] The explosion since the early 1990s in the use of pharmaceutical stimulants such as Ritalin, Adderall, and Concerta in the United States represents only the latest example of America's love affair with stimulant drugs.[7]

Doctor-Prescribed Stimulant Abuse Epidemics

The abuse potential of stimulant drugs was first acknowledged in the United States in the 1930s; as a result, stimulants were placed under government regulation. Some like cocaine were banned entirely. Amphetamine remained available but only with a doctor's prescription.[8] In spite of these precautions, there have been three waves of doctor-prescribed stimulant abuse epidemics since World War II, occurring at fifteen- to twenty-year intervals.

The First Wave

The first wave of stimulant abuse occurred during the Second World War, following the discovery that the German general Rommel was supplying his North Afrikan Corps with amphetamine. The Allies, to keep up, gave their troops the drug, and many of these soldiers returned from the war addicted to speed.[9]

The Second Wave

The early 1960s ushered in the era of the notorious "Dr. Feel-Goods," who prescribed amphetamine (even intravenously) for a variety of ill-defined maladies. Several notables, including President Kennedy and Marilyn Monroe, received such treatment. A number of physicians were eventually sent to prison for this behavior.

The Third Wave

The third major pharmaceutical stimulant epidemic in the United States involved amphetamine in the form of Dexedrine, which was given to women for dieting in the late 1970s and early 1980s. The positive effects were short lasting, and many women became addicted through their doctors' prescriptions.[10]

The Current Fourth Wave

The great rise in Ritalin prescriptions to adults for ADHD in the late 1990s seems uncannily right on schedule for putting the nation at risk for yet another stimulant abuse epidemic.

Stimulant Prescriptions For Children

Stimulants were first reported to help children control their hyperactivity (the old name for ADHD) in 1937.[11] The use of these drugs for hyperactivity was relatively rare until Ritalin was introduced in the United States in the early 1960s.[12] Except for a brief decline due to adverse publicity in the early 1970s, the use of Ritalin slowly climbed for thirty years.

Beginning in 1991, however, the rates of Ritalin use soared. Production of methylphenidate (the active ingredient in Ritalin) in the United States rose by over 700 percent during the 1990s.[13] Amphetamine use for ADHD, heavily marketed by the maker of Adderall, *climbed by an incredible 2,000 percent* during the same time period. (Adderall actually surpassed Ritalin as the most commonly prescribed brand name stimulant in 1998, but since then both short-acting stimulant drugs have lost heavy market shares to the newer long-acting stimulant drugs such as Concerta.)[14] In the year 2004 alone, about 31,000 kilograms of legal stimulants were manufactured in the United States.[15]

Today in the United States, 4–5 million children—about 5 percent of the total child population—take stimulant drugs. Their use remains more common among boys—three times as many boys take Ritalin.[16] Incidence peaks at about age eleven, when about *one in ten white school-age boys take Ritalin*. African American youth are only half as likely to use Ritalin, even when we control for socioeconomic class. Rates vary widely from community to community and state to state. For example, Hawaii perennially uses per capita about one-fifth the amount of Ritalin as that used by the leading states, which are mostly in the southeastern United States.[17]

According to World Health Organization (WHO) statistics, the United States consumes about 80 percent of the world's stimulants. France, by contrast, leads the world in per capita use of Valium-type tranquilizers (mostly for the elderly), causing the UN International Narcotics Control Board to proclaim, in one of its annual reports, that "America likes 'uppers' and Europe prefers 'downers.'"[18]

Proponents of Ritalin attribute the steep rise in its use to more public awareness of ADHD and "better diagnosis and treatment." But the reasons for America's increasing use of Ritalin are likely far more cultural and economic than scientific. It is possible but unlikely that U.S. youth are wilder than those of other countries. What is more likely is that American doctors, and now the culture at large, prefer to view and treat problems of children's behavior and school performance as reflections of biological and biochemical factors rather than as reactions to an unsupportive, demanding environment or as internal emotional factors within the children themselves. Systems of medical care (health insurance and reimbursement to physicians) and drug companies' power over research and advertising also strongly influence decisions about children's behavior in America.

BIOLOGY OF ADHD AND RITALIN: FRAUGHT WITH UNCERTAINTY

The ADHD diagnosis is far and away the leading reason invoked for using Ritalin in this country. What exactly does Ritalin do and how does it work? The exact answer is not known. However, all stimulants are thought to affect the neurotransmitter dopamine. The stimulants block reuptake at the dopaminergic synaptic receptor sites, leading to an increase in the levels of dopamine between the nerve cells. These effects seem concentrated in the parts of the brain that have been associated with impulse inhibition (also called neurocognitive executive function)—the prefrontal cortex and locus cerruleus.[19]

According to the *Diagnostic and Statistical Manual*, 4th edition (*DSM-IV*)—the psychiatric diagnostic reference manual used ubiquitously by clinicians across North America—one doesn't "have" ADHD; instead one meets the criteria for the diagnosis by demonstrating six of eleven behaviors in either of two categories, hyperactivity/impulsivity or inattention. Although it is not stated explicitly in the *DSM-IV*, "having" ADHD has come to mean having a biologically based genetically predetermined brain disorder mediated by a "chemical imbalance."

However, despite advances in neurochemistry and neuroimaging (MRI, PET, and SPECT scans) and our knowledge about stimulant medication, *there remains no diagnostic "test" for ADHD, nor is there any coherent theory to explain the effects of stimulant medication on reducing the symptoms of ADHD.* There are simply too many false positives and negatives, and there remains no biological or anatomical test that can reliably predict the effects of the medication on behavior.[20]

Yet medical researchers, supported by the drug industry, disseminate the message—through professional education meetings, parent self-help groups such as CHADD (Children and Adults with Attention Deficit Disorders), and television and magazine ads—that ADHD is a biological/genetic/neurochemically based condition. Prodigious efforts and a great deal of money have been spent trying to "prove" the biological basis of ADHD. Anatomic and functional brain scans using the latest PET or MRI technology, delineation of elaborate pedigrees, and detailed genetic mapping are regularly presented to scientific audiences and then trumpeted in the mass media as "evidence" of the physical nature of ADHD. Yet none of these sophisticated tests is able to determine with certainty who has ADHD, which remains a clinical decision.

Of course there are biological/genetic contributions to behavior. However, today's theorists almost singularly promote biological and brain-based contributions to the exclusion of other key factors. I believe this is in reaction to more than fifty years of a Freudian psychiatric model that ignored biology and blamed the mother. The pedigrees of carefully screened, very disabled children with ADHD *do* suggest a strong genetic component, but *all* behavior is in part biologically based and mediated by temperament or personality. The behavior of the average ADHD candidate is also strongly influenced by psychosocial factors, including family, school, and neighborhood.

Although the biological search for a "marker" or definitive test for ADHD is very popular these days, commanding a good deal of academic interest and research funds, the marker, unfortunately, will never be found—at least for the purposes of distinguishing borderline cases. Such cases are comparable to the problem of determining children with borderline short stature: a better, more accurate tape measure does not really help in determining which of those children are candidates for growth hormone. Rather, factors within the family or culture will influence the decision to treat or not, based on the degree of impairment the borderline small size confers. In analogous fashion, a positive biological "test" for ADHD will not substantially alter a decision to treat the borderline ADHD child. Yet millions of government dollars are being spent to develop such a test.

Research on the Efficacy of Ritalin for Treating ADHD

Short-Term Outcomes

There are thousands of studies examining the short-term effects (weeks and months) of Ritalin on thousands of children (mostly school-age boys, ages six through thirteen). The evidence is clear. In the short term, Ritalin improves concentration, academic grades, compliance, and relations with family and peers, and it decreases hyperactivity.[21]

Jeffrey was six years old in the first grade. He had always been an active, lively child. Although his overall intelligence was normal, he struggled with phonics, his sight word vocabulary was poor, and he was having difficulty learning to read. At times Jeffrey would impulsively shout out wrong answers or leave his seat to look out the window when in class. In the playground his enthusiasm often led to his being too affectionate with the other children. He would hug or grab them spontaneously. Some of the children began to avoid Jeffrey. In the office setting, Jeffrey struggled to stay seated while talking to the doctor. He didn't wait his turn in conversation with his family. His parents attempted many times to control their son's activity with only intermittent success. Attempts to help the parents gain better control over their son were only moderately helpful, and his teacher was not comfortable using behavioral approaches (tangible rewards and punishments). Jeffrey's learning problems were not sufficient to qualify him for special education at his school. After three months of attempting nondrug interventions, a methylphenidate product that lasted six to eight hours was instituted in the mornings. Jeffrey's self-control improved dramatically. His handwriting was greatly improved while his reading improved somewhat. He was no longer a behavior problem at school. Jeffrey, his parents, and teacher were very pleased with the results of the medication.

Long-Term Outcomes

Despite some short-term gains, there is no definitive evidence that taking Ritalin as a child improves long-term outcome nor that it is entirely safe. In fact, controlled studies from the 1970s in America indicated that ADHD children who took Ritalin were less likely to finish high school and to avoid substance abuse and juvenile delinquency compared to those who also received family counseling and special education. It should be noted, however, that even though subjects were matched for their severity of ADHD, these studies have been criticized for lack of randomization and the possibility of "severity bias"—that is, the more severely afflicted ADHD children might have been more likely taking medication, and thus their poorer outcomes reflected their condition, not the treatment.[22]

In America, Ritalin has become so much the standard of treatment for children's problems of behavior and performance that no research study could withhold the drug for any length of time to determine its value or harm. The longest randomized study to date continued for fourteen months and showed that Ritalin was actually more helpful than psychosocial interventions for relieving the specific symptoms of ADHD. But a combined approach of drug and nondrug interventions better addressed many of the non-ADHD problems (learning, conduct, and anxiety problems) common to these children and led to greater parental satisfaction compared to either Ritalin or psychosocial approaches alone. However, at the two-year follow-up, the advantages afforded the medication groups appeared to be decreasing.[23]

Long-Term Success: ADHD Is Only One of Several Risk Factors

I recently had the opportunity to hear about two patients I had treated since age seven who are now in their early twenties. I had not seen either boy in at least six years.

Bobby and Kevin were two of the most hyperactive, impulsive children I had ever met. Both children were treated with stimulant medication for almost ten years. And both made a personal decision to stop taking medication in their late teens. Bobby's parents had worked diligently on their parenting skills so that even when Bobby was not taking medication during weekends and summers he did rather well. Kevin's parents, however, were never able to be consistent enough to meet the demands of his behavior. They also had chronic marital problems and separated when he was eighteen. Bobby has fine artistic skills that were not adequately appreciated in middle and high school, but he finally found his niche at an arts college, and he has recently been recruited by a major computer animation film company. Although he still struggles to get organized occasionally, he has many friends, and his parents no longer feel that his personality poses a problem.

Although he is very bright, Kevin required a special high school for disturbed children to complete his education. He experienced intermittent episodes of anxiety and rage. After high school he moved in with his father and was employed irregularly. At age twenty-two he abruptly left his father's home to live with his girlfriend. After several months she asked him to leave, and in a fit of rage he stabbed her with a screwdriver. He is currently incarcerated and awaiting trial.

Although Bobby and Kevin met the criteria for severe ADHD as children, by their early twenties their paths had diverged considerably. Bobby became successful in relating to others and Kevin struggled. It's not clear whether Bobby has a greater endowment of "interpersonal" or "emotional" intelligence or whether over time he matured as a result of his many positive life experiences, which included superior and consistent parenting in a loving, stable home. I tend to favor the latter theory. The stories of these two boys are meant to highlight that *ADHD behaviors are risk factors which alone are not the key to poor outcomes. Rather, other aspects of behavior having to do ultimately with relating to others are more central to poor outcomes.*

The Myth of the Paradoxical Effect

One of the enduring myths of Ritalin use is its alleged "paradoxical" effect of "calming" the hyperactive child. This belief has led to the erroneous conclusion that the brains of ADHD children are "wired differently," causing them to react differently to stimulants. Therefore when a child appears "calmer" while on a "stimulant," this manifestation is presented as infallible diagnostic evidence that he or she has ADHD. Nothing could be farther from the truth.

Low doses of stimulant drugs *affect everyone in the same way*: children and adults, ADHD or not, will have better focus on tasks they find boring or difficult.[24] The drug's apparent "calming" effect on hyperactive children is in actuality a reflection of their greater ability to stick with tasks far longer on the drug than off. The medication makes them more methodical, and this steadiness *appears* as calming.[25]

While the universal enhancing effects of the stimulants were generally known for a long time, the National Institute of Mental Health (NIMH) formally studied their effects on adult human volunteers without ADHD and subsequently on children with *and* without the ADHD diagnosis in the late 1970s. This research proved beyond a doubt that stimulants work on everyone in the same manner. Normal adults experienced an improvement in their ability to focus on boring tasks. ADHD children experienced an improvement in their performance up to the levels of their normal peers, while the normal children experienced an enhancement in their abilities to "supranormal" levels.[26]

Ritalin Is Not a "Free Lunch": Side Effects

If Ritalin works on everyone in the same way, to enhance performance, why shouldn't everyone use it? First and foremost, taking stimulant drugs is not a "free lunch." There are adverse effects. Ironically, however, Ritalin is actually safer for children than for adults. The stimulant's main side effects are a short-term decrease in appetite (remember Dexedrine's use as a diet aid in the 1970s) while the drug is in the system and more difficulty falling asleep at night (which is why Ritalin can't be used in the evening to control children's behavior at home). Most children tolerate the medication quite well: between 70 and 80 percent respond favorably to their prescriptions.[27] Recent studies have renewed concerns about Ritalin's effect on slowing children's physical growth (about one-half inch per year), but questions remain whether ultimate height or weight is decreased.[28] Another side effect, motor tics, is often mentioned, but the connection between them and the medication is questionable.

Potential for Abuse and Addiction

The real risk in taking Ritalin is the danger of abuse and addiction, which paradoxically is much more real for teenagers and adults than for preadolescent children.[29] Children themselves do not have ready access to Ritalin, nor do they like the higher doses often associated with abuse. Typically, children complain of feeling "nervous" or "weird" when given high doses of Ritalin. Teens and adults, on the other hand, *can* self-medicate, and when taking higher doses of medication they often report feeling "powerful" and "grand."[30] And indeed, there are increasing reports about Ritalin abuse on high school and college campuses.[31]

The route and manner of administration make an enormous difference in the abuse potential of Ritalin. On college and high school campuses, reports of crushing and snorting Ritalin intranasally are common, and on rare occasions the medication is liquefied and injected intravenously. Both methods greatly increase the rapidity of delivery of the drug to the brain, which leads to a "high" or euphoria very similar to that of cocaine or methamphetamine.[32]

Perhaps the biggest worry that parents have in giving their children Ritalin for ADHD is the concern that medical treatment with a stimulant in childhood will predispose or sensitize them for subsequent drug abuse in their teens or adulthood. Evidence from the laboratory with animals and human volunteers is strong that sensitization does occur.[33] However, whether sensitization makes any difference in the real world is another question. Here, the evidence is contradictory. One prospective twenty-year study that followed children to young adulthood demonstrated increased rates of stimulant abuse and cigarette smoking in ADHD children who were treated with stimulants compared to similarly afflicted children who did not receive medication.[34] However, a major retrospective meta-analysis of several long-term studies came to exactly the opposite conclusion. ADHD children treated with stimulants had lower rates of subsequent abuse—they were apparently "protected" by having taken medication as children.[35]

As a doctor who continues to prescribe Ritalin, I take another position supported by yet a third major study and my own twenty-eight years of prescribing the drug to children. This study suggests that stimulants are neither sensitizing nor protective, but that factors in the family and neighborhood are much more powerful predictors of subsequent drug abuse.[36] It should be noted that all these studies are similarly flawed by their methodologies, which employed rigorous control groups but were not randomized.

A "final" answer on the future drug abuse potential of those taking Ritalin is unlikely to come from the United States. Here the medical standard of care for ADHD so completely embraces medication that it does not provide opportunity for a long-term randomized study that would include a nonmedicated cohort. Perhaps the definitive answer on the sensitization/protection question will come from ongoing European studies of ADHD, where a "culture of medication" continues to be challenged. In summary then, the *abuse potential of Ritalin among teens and adults is very real and warrants our concern*. In the case of children, nearly seventy years of clinical documentation suggests that it is unlikely that something "terribly dangerous" about using the drug will be discovered. In truth, the main challenges to our ubiquitous use of stimulants in children are moral rather than medical.

RITALIN USE: A MORAL OR A MEDICAL CHOICE?

If Ritalin is so safe and well tolerated in children, then why the concern about its widespread and ever-growing use in America? While few would dispute the power of Ritalin to improve performance in children, Ritalin is not the moral equivalent of or substitute for caring and consistently available parents and teachers.

Are We Treating "Chemical Imbalances" or "Living Imbalances"?

The psychologist at ten-year-old Natalie's school conference triumphantly announced that Natalie's academic performance was so improved that she no longer qualified for special education services. I was pleased for Natalie but also uncomfortable. I along with everyone else at the meeting (teacher, parents, and psychologist) knew that I had recently doubled Natalie's Concerta dose. With the higher dose, she was working harder and her effort was more sustained. Everyone knew that Natalie still had problems reading, yet the medication allowed her to persevere to perform at near grade level.

Was medication a legitimate long-term substitute for more personalized intervention for this child? I have my doubts, and long-term data are equivocal at best. But I knew that in our current climate, Natalie would no longer legally qualify for any further extra help at her school. Let me be more specific about my moral uneasiness with Natalie's "triumph." Even as questions remain about the long-term effectiveness of Ritalin compared to psychosocial interventions for ADHD children, the means to that long-term outcome are not equivalent. The following satiric "modest proposal" modeled after one offered by Jonathan Swift should make the differences clear:[37]

> With about 4 million American children taking Ritalin today, classroom size averages about twenty-nine pupils per class. In my modest proposal I suggest that we increase the number of children taking Ritalin to 7.5 million and increase classroom size to forty children per class, in the process saving a great deal of money.

When I've made this proposal in public, I get snickers and nervous laughter in response. Yet this is precisely what is happening in America today. As educational demands have increased to meet the expectations of an increasingly demanding and fast-paced technological world, supports to children, their families, and schools have correspondingly decreased, creating a "living imbalance" rather than the alleged "chemical imbalance" of ADHD—and leading to a huge growth in the use of Ritalin.

"Curing" the Absentminded Professor

Nine-year-old Fred was so named by me because he reminded me so much of the actor Fred MacMurray, who played the lead role in the 1960s Walt Disney comedy, *The Absentminded Professor*. Both Freds were sweet, bumbling characters who could completely immerse themselves in a subject to the exclusion of many other important responsibilities. The movie Fred was so preoccupied with his discovery of flubber, an antigravity substance, that he even forgot to attend his own wedding.

My Fred was obsessed with the medieval period of history. He was so preoccupied with this special interest that he often had difficulty completing his homework. My Fred was in the third grade of a prestigious private school and getting only Bs and Cs in his classes because he would daydream in class and not turn in all his homework. Much was expected of little Fred by his graduate-level-degree parents and his school because his IQ test had placed him in the superior range of intelligence. Even before he came to my office, his under-performance had already been "diagnosed" as ADHD, the nonhyperactive, inattentive only variety.

Although I tried to encourage Fred's parents and teachers to offer more structure and to be more accepting of Fred's performance and personality, he wound up taking Adderall. Now Fred gets straight As. He and everyone concerned were pleased.

I was happy for Fred but also uncomfortable. I wondered if we have lost our tolerance for the absentminded professor and his potential contributions to our society and culture. When it comes to children in our country, I believe we have.

Ritalin: A "Cognitive Steroid" for Supranormal Performance

The surge in the use of Ritalin in America now goes beyond the treatment of ADHD and has moved into the realm of enhancement of the normal. As discussed, Ritalin has the same effect on everyone, child or adult, ADHD or not. The NIMH experiments of the late 1970s and early 1980s are the modern-day proof that Ritalin will raise the performance of normal individuals to supranormal levels on tasks that are boring or difficult.

The case for Ritalin as a performance-enhancing drug is strengthened by evidence of its pattern of use in America. Except in extreme cases of hyperactivity and behavior problems, most children take their medication only on school days. Weekends, holidays, and summer vacations are exempted. Cynics ask how a "disorder" can only affect someone Monday through Friday. Parents (and the treating physicians) will answer that their children really don't need the medication on non–school days when the demands are less.

A disturbing trend highlights the natural consequence of such thinking and practice. Recently, parents have been asking doctors if they would medicate their child (usually an adolescent boy) for exam preparation and test taking. The parents typically agree that their son's ADHD is relatively mild and that for the most part he can cope without medication. The boy is not fond of routinely taking his Ritalin. He says that it (understandably) decreases his sociability. However, he finds the medication very helpful before and during exam time.

What is unsettling about this trend? The comparison with sports doping is inviting. Whether it is baseball players in America or cyclists in France, in sports we value not only the athlete's home-run record or speed on the Tour, but the effort involved in reaching that achievement. Taking steroids or amphetamines cheapens that effort. The other major objection is the pressure it places on other athletes to take performance-enhancing drugs in order to remain competitive.

Parents Feel Pressure to Give Their Children a Competitive Edge

This "free will under pressure" is already evident in the classrooms of America. Families of children in special education feel the pressure to medicate their children most acutely (recall Natalie). But American parents throughout the educational system regularly report feeling pressured by teachers and schools to medicate their under-performing children. In response, the U.S. Congress has passed a law prohibiting schools from making class attendance conditional on children taking a psychiatric drug.[38] On the other hand, growing reports of high school and college students using legally or illegally obtained Ritalin for exam taking raises the specter of random urine testing of students before national entrance exams like the SAT.

Adult Use of Ritalin for Performance Enhancement

The growing awareness of the universal enhancing effects of Ritalin, its acceptability, and availability make it highly attractive for adult use. The diagnosis of adult ADHD has exploded since the mid-1990s in America.[39] Also, by promoting a medical disorder—ADHD—as an explanation for adult under-performance, drug companies create a demand for Ritalin. It seems that only Ritalin's abuse potential restrains more widespread use. Indeed, advertisements to doctors and patients for the first new nonstimulant drug in the United States for ADHD, atomoxetine or Strattera, emphasize its non-abusability.[40] However, most word-of-mouth reports on Strattera suggest that it isn't as effective or as well tolerated as Ritalin.

While most teens and adults can manage Ritalin safely, the history of stimulant use and abuse in America strongly suggests that a core group will go on to abuse this drug and ultimately other illegal stimulants. If history is any guide, America is well on its way to its next doctor-prescribed stimulant abuse epidemic since World War II—this one under the guise of treating ADHD.

When Should Doctors Prescribe Ritalin?

Ritalin remains a prescription drug in the United States, reserved ostensibly for the treatment of ADHD. But the problem over who should or should not receive Ritalin is compounded by the fact that *the diagnosis of ADHD has no "gold standard"—no reliable biological or psychological test*. Two evaluating doctors may agree that a child "has" ADHD, but epidemiological evidence in the United States indicates very wide variations in Ritalin use, which strongly suggest that nonmedical cultural and economic factors are at play in who does and does not get Ritalin.

Furthermore, attempts to determine who has or does not have ADHD are doomed to failure because of a fundamental misconception or intentional misunderstanding of the nature of behavior problems in children. Problems with attention, overactivity, and impulsivity present as a spectrum ranging from very focused to extremely unfocused. Ability or inability to pay attention or restrain impulse is a dimensional issue, yet ADHD as defined by the *DSM* is categorical. Either you have it or you don't.

The real key to the ADHD diagnosis and the justification for prescribing Ritalin is the concept of impairment. How disabling are the behaviors of impulsivity, distractibility, and hyperactivity to the individual child? At the extremes of behavior it is easy to make that determination, but the vast majority of children treated with medication in the United States fall within a penumbra of diagnosis. Before the 1990s, a child would have to show symptoms in the doctor's office or be unable to focus on virtually all tasks. Now children who behave appropriately during an evaluation and concentrate well on nonacademic tasks may still be candidates for the ADHD diagnosis and medication if behavior and performance are wanting in the school or homework environments.

Even children like Fred, with average school performance, are now considered "impaired" if psychological IQ testing reveals above average or superior potential. Thus an uninspired student with Bs and Cs might be given Ritalin to achieve As, especially if his parents are high achievers (post-college graduates) themselves. Performance is a product of talent times temperament, in this case, motivation. As of this moment we have no drug to enhance talent, but in performance-obsessed America we now regularly employ a universal performance enhancer of motivation, Ritalin.

Tampering with Human Nature

At this very moment I'm sure drug scientists somewhere are still working vigorously to try to discover a nonaddictive drug as effective as Ritalin to improve performance and concentration. The economic and market implications of such a product go well beyond the treatment of child or adult ADHD. Who wouldn't want a drug that could improve one's ability to stay focused? Yet in developing such a product we tamper with the very values and qualities we consider human.

Recall Natalie or Bobby. One had learning problems and daydreamed. The other had severe hyperactivity and impulsivity. But both were very sweet children. Natalie in particular was held in high regard by her friends and teachers for her thoughtfulness and sensitivity. Bobbie was all boy. Regularly off medication he could go too far, especially in school, but he had many buddies who routinely laughed at his antics and silliness. Bobby for all his activity and impulsivity was not an angry or cruel child, and his friends appreciated him even as he drove his teacher and parents to distraction.

When we encourage a drug that can enhance one aspect of human nature—in this case, concentration—we inevitably diminish the importance of other human attributes we hold dear. Where does the use of drugs that improve focus leave the cultivation of human love and empathy? In the United States, publicity for interventions such as special education and family counseling for ADHD get short shrift compared to the daily barrage of TV and print commercials for "brain-based" treatments like Ritalin or Strattera. Unless we devise a stock-holding company for the promotion of teaching and love, these values are already "losing out" in America today.

Finally, one could ask if treating minimally impaired children with ADHD is ultimately desirable, even if safety and effectiveness were assured. Some of our most enduring and valuable qualities come from our learning to cope with our weaknesses. So many of the leading contributors to our culture, science, and government started out as poor students. In my opinion, many children in the United States who are diagnosed with ADHD are simply octagonal-pegged personalities whose differing talents are being squeezed into the same square educational holes. Undeniably, Ritalin can sand their rough edges away so they fit in more easily, but is this desirable?

To be sure, a case can be made for treating the extreme cases of ADHD with medication. These children would struggle in virtually any environment or culture worldwide. I estimate that these kinds of severely impaired children represent only about *one-tenth* of the children treated with stimulants in this country. Indeed, I myself continue to prescribe Ritalin regularly to children like Sarah, Natalie, or Fred who I feel are minimally disadvantaged. After I attempt to address the child's school and family life as best I can, I am willing to offer medication to help the child cope. I have no "specific" or "exact" criteria for ADHD. I've already explained why on a clinical level no precise criteria make sense. I admit that I regularly treat children with Ritalin who do not have a serious psychiatric disorder, in my opinion.

It boils down to the negative experiences of children like Natalie, Fred, or Bobby—experiences that affect their self-esteem. Sadly, at this moment in our history, we regularly diagnose minimally impaired children with a psychiatric disorder and give them medications in order to bolster or protect their self-image. Rather than accepting the differences in these children and creating environments that will adapt to their needs, we determine that they have a "chemical" imbalance and alter their brain's environment with a drug. In the end I am a realist who appreciates that society is unlikely to change in the near future. I play a role in this cultural process, especially when I decide to medicate a child with mild ADHD symptoms. But at the same time, in order that I avoid complicity with values and factors I feel are harmful to children and their families, I persistently raise questions about a society that creates a "living" imbalance for these children.

A World without Tom Sawyer, Huckleberry Finn, and Pippi Longstocking

Everyday I see another Tom Sawyer or Pippi Longstocking brought to my office for an evaluation by their parents who expect treatment with Ritalin. And I wonder about Tom's friend, Huckleberry Finn. If he too was brought to me and wound up on Ritalin, he'd probably be more successful at school. I imagine him sitting in the class paying attention to the headmaster, Mr. Dobbins, instead of daydreaming about life on the river. And I wonder with Huck and all his friends sitting at their desks, who would be left to help Jim, the runaway slave, escape from his master.

In America, I'm afraid that we've become a nation "running on Ritalin." In the process, we are in danger of losing sight of the value of the diversity of human nature that has made our culture rich (both literally and metaphorically). Drugs like Ritalin, in the end, reflect the predominant values of our country—performance at any cost. America's challenge in the twenty-first century is to find a better balance between the efficiencies and amorality of its market place. Until we do, performance-enhancing drugs like Ritalin will reign supreme.

10

Why Medications Are Not Enough

Looking More Deeply at Depression and Anxiety in Children

Mary Burke

Over the years, as a child and adolescent psychiatrist, I have become increasingly concerned about the growing use of SSRI antidepressants to treat depressed and anxious children. (SSRIs, or the selective serotonin reuptake inhibitors, include the brand name drugs Prozac, Paxil, Zoloft, Lexapro, and Celexa, as well as the related medicine Effexor.) Childhood anxiety and depression most commonly occur in the context of stressors that include loss or disturbance in parent–child relations.[1] Unfortunately, current trends in American culture—including escalating economic demands, the fracturing of communities, and the barrage of electronic media— leave parents distracted and overwhelmed. As parents become less available to help their children negotiate life's obstacles, children become predictably anxious and sad, deprived of the nurturing that can help them thrive in a perilous era. However, in our search for a medicine to "cure" children's unhappiness, we have both ignored its causes and neglected the practice of psychotherapy— which endeavors to understand the impact of stress on the individual. Furthermore, since the fall of 2003, information has continued to mount that throws into some doubt the efficacy and safety of these medicines in children. As I discuss in this chapter, the solution is not simply to find a safer, better pill. Our job is twofold: to vigorously address the causes of children's suffering and to restore the practice of psychotherapy with parents and children, thereby strengthening the relationships that help children flourish.

IS CHILDHOOD DEPRESSION JUST A "CHEMICAL IMBALANCE"?

- Sixteen-year-old Gina slouches on my couch. "I'm depressed," she tells me, "Give me some Zoloft; all the kids in my class take Zoloft."
- Eighteen-year-old Brad mentions that he has started taking a friend's Prozac because he has a "chemical imbalance."

These days teenagers swap antidepressant drugs with the same abandon with which they swap homework answers, and the image of children with "chemically disordered brains" has taken firm hold in the American mind. We commonly accept that depression is an illness caused by a deficit in the brain chemical serotonin. We therefore believe that depression should be cured by the use of an antidepressant, just as pneumonia is cured by an antibiotic.[2] Indeed, a class of drugs called SSRIs, which elevate serotonin levels in the brain, have become the standard of care for children with symptoms of depression and anxiety. Parents ask for the drugs by name, pediatricians prescribe them freely, and many insurance companies only reimburse the costs of psychiatric care if drugs are the primary therapy.

Despite these prevailing beliefs, however, childhood depression and anxiety are not best understood as "diseases" that can be "cured" with a pill. The interaction of the child's biology and the environment is far more complex. Rather, children are likely to become depressed and anxious in response to very real stressors. In particular, children are deeply distressed when their relationships with their parents are disturbed or disrupted[3]—an increasingly common occurrence in contemporary family life. Parents in the United States are bereft of support from the wider culture, which in turn makes it more difficult for them to provide their children with the consistent and reliable care that is so critical for their well-being. And so we must ask ourselves whether the growing population of depressed children have a "biological illness" or whether our children are struggling to cope with overwhelming adversity.

Despite the fact that childhood depression has been marketed as a biological illness, it is not the equivalent of adult depression.[4] While chronic stress and genetic vulnerability can cause recurrent depression in adults—who may benefit from the use of antidepressant medication—the evidence in children is contradictory.[5] Some of the more salient differences in the clinical profiles of depressed children and adults include the following:

- In contrast to adult patients, children are about as likely to respond to a placebo as they are to SSRIs.[6]
- Children who are labeled depressed frequently exhibit symptoms that are indistinguishable from general unhappiness or anxiety. These symptoms include separation anxiety, phobias, somatic complaints, and behavior problems. *In fact, in children we find that depression occurs more often in the presence of additional emotional or behavioral problems than it does in isolation.*[7]
- Children with depression do not have the same hormonal and sleep-cycle changes that depressed adults typically exhibit.[8]

In my clinical work with families who have a depressed child, I describe depression as an emotional state that is commonly associated with loss, chronic subordination, and enforced helplessness. Before I even consider a medication, I enlist parents' help in identifying stressors in their child's life and invite them to collaborate with me to help the child overcome them.

The current conceptualization in psychiatry (and American culture as a whole) that depression and anxiety in children are caused by faulty brain chemistry is relatively recent. Before 1980, child psychiatrists were more likely to use principles of psychotherapy to conceptualize their young patients' suffering, and as recently as 1990, individual and family therapies were more common than drug therapies. But between 1991 and 1995, antidepressant drug use for children aged two to four doubled,[9] even though there has never been FDA approval for use of these powerful drugs in this age range, when brain development is rapid and critical. By 1995, SSRI prescriptions for children and teens were running a close second to stimulant prescriptions (such as Ritalin).[10] In 2002, 40 percent of all Paxil prescriptions in the United States were for children, and 2.4 percent of all American children were taking SSRIs.[11] We now spend more as a nation on psychotropic drugs for children than we do on any other class of pediatric medications, including antibiotics.[12]

THE PHARMACEUTICAL AND MANAGED CARE INDUSTRIES AND THE RISE OF PSYCHOTROPIC DRUG USE

As discussed at greater length in chapter 6, the synergistic actions of the pharmaceutical and managed care industries ushered in the "biological era" in mental health care. In the early 1980s, the Reagan administration facilitated the exponential growth of the pharmaceutical industry by weakening the stringent checks and balances that were provided by independent drug research and the FDA. By the end of the decade, the drug industry had become the most profitable and powerful one in the United States, with near total control over the design and dissemination of research about its products.[13]

Then, in the early 1990s, President Clinton's health care reform initiative empowered managed care companies to radically alter the health care delivery system in the United States. For the first time in the history of medicine, clinical authority shifted from physicians to corporations whose mandate is profit rather than patient care.[14] HMOs make their profits on the concept of efficiency: the most rapid decline in symptoms for the least amount of effort expended. Unfortunately, this violates one of the principle healing factors in both psychotherapy and child development: the attuned, thoughtful relationship between individuals over extended periods of time.[15]

Many HMOs will not reimburse for psychiatric services if the physician does not provide a "medical diagnosis," which includes "depression" or an "anxiety disorder." This diagnosis puts psychiatrists in the position of having to employ the narrow "disease model," discussed at the beginning of this chapter, in order to get paid. What is more, psychiatrists will often get paid at a lesser rate, if at all, for working with the family of a mentally ill child, regardless of the diagnosis; that is, all family therapy, or psychotherapy without a medication, is paid at a substantially lesser rate than treatment with a medication. In effect, the HMOs have the financial power to dictate how a psychiatrist conceptualizes a child's disturbance and plans treatment. Treatment without a medication is not considered medical treatment.

What is fascinating is that current practice, as demanded by HMOs, is based on such a scarcity of data. By 1999, when the use of SSRIs in the pediatric population was still climbing, leading researchers pointed out the limitations of the data on psychiatric medications in children, noting that their use had far outstripped our understanding of their long-term effects as well as efficacy.[16] Scientists expressed similar concerns again in 2003.[17]

SSRIs, the FDA, and American Psychiatry

In October 2004, the FDA ordered pharmaceutical companies to place black-box warnings on the package inserts of all antidepressants, which state that these drugs are known to increase the risk of suicidality in children.[18] For several years before this ruling, my clinical experience with children had left me feeling increasingly concerned about the pediatric use of SSRIs. It has long been recognized that children are much more likely to become activated or "hypomanic" than are adults when taking an SSRI.[19] Young children on these medicines may become agitated and disorganized. Furthermore, although clinicians have talked anecdotally about the fact that many patients complain of feeling "flat" on these medicines, it is only recently that clinicians have recognized the extent to which patients complain of a loss of normal feelings, including normal sadness, anger, and anxiety.[20] I have seen older children and teens engage in risky or antisocial behavior while taking these medicines because they just "didn't care."[21]

Review (meta-analytic) studies published at the time of and after the FDA ruling have confirmed that "behavioral activation"—including hypomania, akathisia or motor restlessness, and agitation—are common side effects of SSRIs in children.[22] These studies also point out that SSRIs are not as effective as commonly believed in treating childhood depression.[23] Of very serious concern is that academic journals such as the *Journal of the American Academy of Child and Adolescent Psychiatry* had a policy of not publishing so-called negative studies (studies that fail to find a benefit) and that company-funded research is biased in favor of the drug under study.[24] Both practices have made it hard for clinicians to accurately understand drugs' risks and benefits. (These studies also indicate that Prozac *is* effective in treating childhood anxiety disorders, especially obsessive compulsive disorder, although the risks of side effects remain the same.)

The most disturbing information that has surfaced is that SSRIs increase the risk of suicidal thoughts and behavior in children. GlaxoSmithKline, the maker of Paxil, was sued for fraud by the State of New York for suppressing its own data on suicidal risk. It settled by agreeing to make all studies public.[25] It appears that the FDA knew about this risk as far back as 1996 but failed to act on it. The FDA even suppressed its own internal study conducted in 2003–2004, which supported a link between pediatric SSRI use and suicidality.[26] In addition, a recent review of British trials of SSRI use with children confirmed the link between suicidality and all SSRIs except Prozac. The researchers concluded that medicine should not be used as a first-line treatment for depression in childhood, and only in conjunction with psychotherapy. Then, and only then,

Prozac was deemed potentially useful.[27] Several cases of teens who killed themselves and/or others while taking an SSRI have been widely publicized in the media. None of these children appeared to be receiving intensive individual or family psychotherapy, which until recently had been the standard of care for depressed youth.[28]

In the wake of the FDA ruling, the American psychiatric community, as represented by the American Psychiatric Association (APA) and the American Academy of Child and Adolescent Psychiatry (AACAP), has added to the confusion that so many child psychiatrists are feeling. On the one hand, the journal of the AACAP has published some comprehensive review articles about the use of medications with children that counsel caution until more complete research is available.[29] At the same time, both the APA and the AACAP have issued a number of statements and news releases that urge clinicians to continue to use SSRIs for childhood depression because it is a "real illness" requiring medication. For example, in a recent news release, the APA stated that "antidepressants save lives ... we believe the biggest threat to a depressed child's well-being is to receive no care at all."[30] The implication of this statement is that psychotherapy is not a legitimate treatment option. The AACAP has been even more explicit, stating in its "talking points" on SSRIs that "pediatric depression is a real illness, with neurobiologic underpinnings," and that the "risk–benefit ratio" in the use of Prozac for treating depressed children is "acceptable." The paper goes on to state that it is unnecessary for treating psychiatrists to even see, on a weekly basis, children who are taking SSRIs; a phone check-in with parents is deemed sufficient.[31]

These statements reinforce the notion that childhood depression is a neurological disease—akin to epilepsy—that can be medicated away. This approach neglects the central role that interpersonal, social, and cultural factors play in shaping children's psychological well-being.

LOVING RELATIONSHIPS WITH CAREGIVERS NESTED IN A SUPPORTIVE COMMUNITY: KEY TO CHILDREN'S MENTAL HEALTH

In contrast to the narrow medical model psychiatry has embraced in recent years, an impressive literature on infant and child development—fifty years in the making—reveals the emotional intensity of children's inner lives and the critical role of loving relationships for healthy psychological development.[32] The renowned pediatrician and child psychoanalyst W. D. Winnicott once said, "there is no such thing as a baby," meaning that babies live only in the context of their caregivers. Similarly, it is meaningless to talk about children's mental health outside of the context of their caregiving relationships and the social and community supports that surround them.

Another extensive body of literature has established that the architecture and chemical balance of the brain, as well as genetic expression, are not hardwired but highly sensitive to environmental influence,[33] as discussed in chapters 2 and 3. (Two excellent syntheses of this research are *The Developing Mind* and *Neurons to Neighborhoods*.) [34] Therefore, even if a child has a genetic predisposition toward a brain-based disease, which in turn places her at risk for a psychiatric disturbance, interpersonal and wider environmental factors can serve a protective function or push her toward illness.[35] Biological factors contributing to mental illness should never be examined in isolation from environmental factors.

Psychiatrist Michael Rutter, a leading researcher on the interaction of genetic risk and environmental factors, summarizes decades of research by stating that there are two broad types of environmental risks to children: the first is a "lack of ongoing, harmonious, selective, committed relationships," and the second is a lack of social cohesion in the wider community.[36] Zero-to-Three, one of the leading research, treatment and advocacy centers for infants and young children, strongly advocates that we must address the factors that undermine maternal health—including poverty and domestic violence—in order to reduce children's mental illness.[37] This underscores that the mother–child unit supported by the wider community is the locus for children's psychological functioning, as opposed to the child in isolation.

Despite the extent to which healthy development is dependent on consistent and loving parent–child relationships embedded in supportive communities, American culture is failing to support parents' efforts to care for their children. Instead, children must cope with

- long hours in group childcare, necessitated by increasing demands of the workplace;[38]
- limited opportunities for exploration in open spaces;
- a barrage of media and marketing;
- weakening bonds with elders in the community;
- school environments that generate anxiety but increasingly fail to inspire;[39]

- soaring exposure to neighborhood violence, and images of violence on omnipresent screens;[40]
- a parental divorce rate—with all its attendant disruptions—of 50 percent; and
- unhealthy food and a growing obesity epidemic.[41]

Our media-saturated, work-driven, performance-oriented culture undermines the physical and emotional proximity between parents and children that is of such critical importance for psychological development. As a result, parents often feel less intimate and familiar with their own children. When children are hungry for connection with their parents and support from their communities, while coping with many age-inappropriate experiences, they present more emotional and behavioral challenges. But when parents feel alienated from their own children, they are also more overwhelmed and fearful of their children's bad, unusual, or unhappy behavior. Lacking the skills to manage their children's episodes of rage, sadness, or wildness, parents may react punitively or passively, thereby exacerbating their children's neediness and tendency to act out. As this vicious cycle escalates, it becomes easier for parents to believe that their children have a "disease" that can be "cured" with a drug. Moreover, children often see themselves as their parents see them, and they will instinctively live up to their parents' beliefs.[42] Like canaries in a coal mine, our children are trying to tell us that we are starving them of the "emotional oxygen" they need to thrive.

INDISCRIMINATE USE OF SSRIs OBSCURES CHILDREN'S LEGITIMATE COMMUNICATIONS OF DISTRESS

Children's tears and anguish are often legitimate responses to events in their lives. When we are too hasty to pathologize these responses and to dull them with drugs, children lose their only means of communicating essential information to adults entrusted with their care: parents, teachers, and therapists. The following case studies illustrate the potential hazards of blunting children's distress with medication.

Xavier

Xavier is a thin, sad, lonely eight-year-old boy whose parents have just initiated divorce proceedings. At the request of his parents, his therapist referred him to me for an evaluation for antidepressant medication. Xavier has a poor appetite and sleeps excessively. He often fantasizes that it would be nice to be dead, although he has no suicidal plans. Xavier routinely feigns illness in order to avoid going to school, precipitating daily arguments with his mother, who has to get to work. He has low self-esteem and feels that he is to blame for his parents' separation.

Xavier's father is a functioning alcoholic who has just moved out of the house. The quality of his visits with Xavier depend on whether or not he has been drinking. When he is sober, he can be loving and appropriate, but when he is drunk he is overly emotional—either aggressive or sentimental. Xavier's mother is full of anger about her impending divorce but cannot bring herself to talk about it. Because she herself is so overwhelmed, she has been leaving Xavier at his school's after-care program until the early evening, where he is the victim of bullying.

Xavier's therapist sees him weekly—all that is allowed by his insurance. She is occasionally able to convince his parents to attend with him but has found them resistant and unreliable. His parents feel that he is overreacting to their divorce and that an antidepressant would decrease his sadness.

What should the goals of treatment be for Xavier? Is it reasonable to expect an eight-year-old to be "high functioning" under such adverse circumstances: his parents' separation, an alcoholic father, an angry noncommunicative mother, victimization at the hands of bullies? As Harvard professor George Vaillant has pointed out, "mentally healthy responses to stress, analogous to pus and cough, are often misinterpreted as pathological." His words are particularly relevant to children who lack the developmental maturity to use healthy, adult defense mechanisms in the wake of traumatic life events. Instead, protest and negative behaviors are the norm; but when these are ignored or misunderstood, they may eventually give way to "disabling anxiety and/or depression."[43]

Xavier is using the only strategies available to him to communicate his distress to his parents. Would he feel less suicidal if they were responding, for example, by assuring him that he is not the cause of their separation, by spending more rather than less time with him during this period of transition, by talking to school authorities about his being bullied? If a pill blunts his feelings and he no longer feigns illness to win time with his mother or to avoid the school bullies, then he has been effectively silenced, and the adults in his life are free to continue ignoring his vital needs.

Yolanda

Yolanda is a fifteen-year-old girl, living in a residential treatment program, who was the victim of severe neglect and sexual abuse in early childhood. She was referred to me for an evaluation for medication because she is tearful, refuses to go to school, and suffers from panic attacks. She has resumed cutting her forearms, a habit she had relinquished several months earlier. When she was placed in her residential facility a year ago, she had a history of drug and alcohol abuse, shoplifting, oppositional behavior, and some symptoms of post-traumatic stress disorder.

Yolanda had been benefiting considerably from the programs offered at her residential setting, which included individual therapy twice a week as well as a drama group and an arts-based therapy group. She attended a school on-site, along with other girls in treatment. Unfortunately, as a result of recent funding cuts at the state and federal level she will no longer see her therapist, and all counseling will be provided by her county-assigned social worker, who already has a caseload of fifty children. In addition, her on-site school has been eliminated, and Yolanda will have to go to the public school in her old neighborhood, where she is terrified of gang members. Her neighborhood school recently lost two students who were killed in shootings.

Yolanda's social worker wants Yolanda to take medication to diminish her anxiety and depression while transitioning back to her old school. Yolanda, however, insists that the fear that she feels about returning to her neighborhood school is legitimate. "If you'd been through what I've been through, you'd be depressed too," she says.

Yolanda is furious at the sudden loss of all of the relationships that have been so helpful to her and is essentially going "on strike." She has reverted to her oppositional behavior and is threatening to run away from a program that feels inadequate and punitive. From Yolanda's perspective, her "symptoms" have a protective and communicative function. By refusing to go to her new school, she is keeping herself safe. Her tears and cutting relieve her psychic pain and alert those around her that she needs help: from her therapist to help resolve her early childhood traumas, from teachers who can educate her in a setting in which she can learn without fear, and from caregivers who can nurture her. These are eminently reasonable and age-appropriate expectations.

Another teenage patient whom I worked with in a residential treatment facility had been taking SSRIs for about a month when she announced that she was going to stop doing so because she couldn't cry when she needed to or feel sad for her friends when they were in distress. It is a great irony that a juvenile offender was able to articulate with such clarity a vital point that has been largely ignored by psychiatry: *children need to experience a full range of feelings, including sadness, in order to feel whole and as a catalyst for ethical development.* When SSRIs blunt children's feelings of anxiety, fear, and sorrow, then they lose a powerful source of information and motivation that helps them to stay out of trouble, to work hard to improve their lives, and to form loving relationships.

SSRIs Cannot "Cure" Relationship Disorders or Replace Psychotherapy

Two well-documented effects of SSRIs when used with adults are a decrease in interpersonal sensitivity and impulsive anger; in other words, they can help depressed or anxious adults to "mellow out."[44] In the early enthusiasm for SSRI use with children, a study was published noting the value of SSRIs to treat children with "obsessive difficult temperament."[45] I believe that without explicitly acknowledging it, clinicians have tried to replicate this "mellowing" effect with intense, demanding, and moody children—whose temperaments are sometimes referred to as "difficult" in the mental health literature. A leading figure in the field of temperament research objected to this practice, noting the perils of creating a diagnosis for "difficult" children. He also raised the serious ethical risk of promoting the idea that "aversive temperament traits can and should be managed with medication."[46]

My own clinical experience has led me to believe that it is common for clinicians to diagnose children who are angry, intense, and "difficult" as anxious or depressed, which often leads to treatment with SSRIs. Although a given temperament should never be labeled as pathological, a mismatch in temperamental styles between parent and child can sometimes contribute to the development of a relationship disturbance—a significant disturbance in the mother–child relationship, which manifests itself in symptoms of mood instability in the young child.[47] Although severe "attachment disorders" are more easily recognized because they exist in clear-cut cases of abuse, neglect, or disruption such as foster care placement, more subtle disturbances of attachment—often referred to as "relationship disturbances"—are not as readily diagnosed because they involve less dramatic circumstances. The current structure of family life in America increases the risk of relationship disorders because it undermines intimacy between parents and children in so many ways, such as exposure to a parade of different caregivers or inappropriate daily routines that are innately stressful for infants and children. Neither attachment disorders nor relationship disturbances in older children can be corrected with a pill. Rather, they require patient therapeutic intervention, as illustrated in the following cases of Wendy and Veronica.

Wendy

Wendy is a six-year-old who was referred to me by her social worker for treatment of her severe tantrums. She is being raised by her grandmother, after being removed from the custody of her drug-addicted parents two years previously. Her grandmother had kept her distance from her daughter and her granddaughter prior to this because she was disgusted by her daughter's drug-fueled lifestyle. Grandmother describes herself as old-fashioned and has little patience for Wendy's out-of-control behavior, which includes overreacting to her efforts to set limits, with screaming, tears, and minor property damage. Wendy cannot sleep alone at night and insists on sleeping at the foot of her grandmother's bed. She cries every morning before school, where she is often in trouble for failing to comply with the teacher's requests.

When I interviewed Wendy on her own, she revealed severe symptoms of anxiety, including obsessive fears of insects and rats, compulsive rituals of counting in her head and needing to "even up," and a phobia of dirt, leading to excessive hand washing. She is afraid of the dark and has frequent nightmares. Although she herself discloses little about her life with her parents, the child protective report that ended in her removal cited squalid living conditions, lack of food, and the presence of drugs and paraphernalia. Wendy's parents have made no effort to contact her since her removal, and she misses them. Her grandmother is so angry with her daughter that she cannot bring herself to talk to Wendy about her. Although she says that she is committed to Wendy, she also has health troubles and is afraid that she cannot take care of her if the child persists in this behavior. She believes that Wendy is damaged like her mother.

Wendy is eligible for remedial services in her public school, but this has amounted to her being placed in a class with extremely disruptive children and inexperienced teachers, so that the classroom often resembles a combat zone. Her school-appointed therapist is an inexperienced student intern whose work with Wendy is about to end as summer vacation draws near. Over the course of the summer,

Wendy's health insurance will only pay for monthly, twenty-minute visits to a psychiatrist. Wendy's social worker hopes that if Wendy is on medication, her grandmother will be more able to "cope" with her and will continue as her guardian.

Wendy's government-funded, managed care health plan parcels out her treatment: to a chaotic school, an inexperienced and transient therapist, an overworked social worker, and a hog-tied psychiatrist. This fragmented care prevents Wendy and grandmother from forming an effective relationship with any one mental health professional.[48] What Wendy and her grandmother need is a therapist who can guide them toward a loving, long-term relationship. Grandmother needs strategies that will help her to parent Wendy effectively, so that Wendy will be less stressed and consequently less overwhelming in her behavior.[49] Wendy's grandmother also needs to understand how her anger toward her daughter is negatively coloring her attitude toward her granddaughter. Wendy needs the opportunity to work through her traumatic past, including painful feelings of abandonment that are causing her so much anger and anxiety.[50]

It might even be the case that treatment with Prozac could help to diminish Wendy's many symptoms of anxiety and facilitate therapy. However, with access to a psychiatrist limited to twenty minutes once a month, there are substantial risks. For example, if Wendy experienced any "behavioral activation" or agitation as a result of her medication, the psychiatrist would not be able to recognize it in a timely fashion, and her grandmother might be unable to keep her safe, or might relinquish custody of her altogether, sending her back into the foster care system. Even without the risk of side effects, a medication alone cannot help Wendy to overcome the neglect and abandonment suffered at the hands of her parents or enable her to form a deep attachment to her grandmother, which is critical to getting her derailed development back on track.

Veronica

Four-year-old Veronica was assessed at an interdisciplinary clinic because she is aggressive at preschool and at home, biting and kicking when she doesn't get her way. According to her mother, she has "trouble with transitions," is easily frustrated, and has difficulty sustaining attention.[51] Her mother is convinced that she has a learning difficulty. In addition, she becomes agitated in the evening, running frenetically around her house until late at night. Several months earlier, her pediatrician started her on a course of SSRIs to treat her anxiety.

Veronica lives with her mother and maternal grandparents, because her father died soon after she was born. Her mother describes herself as feeling both very angry at and excessively dependent on her own parents, and she responds to them with passivity. She feels overwhelmed by Veronica and helpless to intervene effectively. Veronica, apart from her preschool, has little routine in her life, eating meals at fast-food restaurants on her way home from preschool, watching television by herself for several hours each day, and having no consistent shared activities with her mother or grandparents. When visiting Veronica's preschool, the therapist observed that it was very large, consisting of one huge room with different "play areas." Thirty-five children move between areas at a signal from the teachers. Veronica has difficulty staying in her requisite area and is often intrusive with the other children. The large, highly stimulating site is clearly overstimulating to Veronica, exacerbating her reactivity.

A series of play evaluations of Veronica and her mother shows that Veronica's mother is unable to interact with her daughter in any kind of positive or spontaneous way: she cannot play with her, or contain her unruly behavior, or even talk with her in a developmentally appropriate way. She directs most of her attention to the therapist and criticizes Veronica in her presence. Veronica is provocative with her mother, but when her mother leaves the room she can be induced to settle down and play cooperatively after much effort on the therapist's part. All the while, Veronica checks the waiting room frequently for her mother's presence. She is intense in her reactions with the therapist and demands her full attention, with loud protests when she turns it briefly away from her. She frequently tests the consistency of the rules and boundaries of the playroom.

The poor "fit" between Veronica and her mother is severe enough to be a relationship disturbance. Veronica and her mother visibly experience repeated failures of understanding and empathy with each other, a process that both stems from and reinforces conscious and unconscious distortions in their perceptions and experience of each other, often a consequence of the mother's own childhood. Mary Main's landmark work has shown that mothers who do not have an opportunity to talk about their own unhappy childhoods will predictably repeat them with their own children,[52] and this appears to be the case with Veronica and her mother As a result, Veronica's world is confusing and overwhelming, and she has no adult with whom she can experience intimacy, comfort, or shared feeling. In addition, the therapist suspected that some of Veronica's agitated behavior was a result of the SSRI she was taking. If treatment with Veronica is to be successful, it will clearly have to involve her mother, and perhaps the extended family.[53]

Near the conclusion of *Listening to Prozac*, psychiatrist Peter Kramer states:

"The belief—espoused not infrequently by health-care cost-cutters in the 'managed care' industry—that medication can obviate psychotherapy conceals, I believe, a cynical willingness to let people suffer. If medication does interfere with self-examination, it may be in this concrete and practical way—that it serves as a pretext for denying patients psychotherapy."[54] If this is a troubling concept in the treatment of adults, it is all the more deeply troubling in the treatment of children, who are still living in their formative environments.

CONCLUSION

Where does this leave us? The investigation into the SSRIs continues to unfold, even at the time of this writing. Interested parties have staked out positions. At one extreme are critics of child psychiatry, who condemn psychotropic drug prescriptions for children and recommend that their use with children be prohibited by law. At the other extreme are members of the psychiatric establishment, who deny that there are any concerns at all.[55]

Focusing narrowly on the benefits and risks of using psychotropic drugs to treat children distracts us, however, from the bigger picture: childhood mental illness is on the rise. According to the surgeon general's 2000 report, "growing numbers of children are suffering needlessly because their emotional, behavioral, and developmental needs are not being met by those very institutions which were explicitly created to take care of them. It is time that we as a Nation took seriously the task of *preventing* mental health problems and *treating* mental illnesses in youth" (emphasis mine).[56] The surgeon general's recommendations of broad social action necessary to stem the tide of children's mental illness imply that children's emotional disturbances cannot be described by the clean cause-and-effect conditions of the molecular sciences. Instead, they must be viewed within the context of all the factors—relational, social, socioeconomic, cultural, and biological—that impinge on children.

I close with a story, paraphrased with permission:

A group of friends gathered on a riverbank for a picnic. However, they soon saw a drowning child struggling to stay afloat. One member of the party jumped in to rescue him. No sooner was the child saved when a second child came struggling by. The rescuer pulled this child out of the river too. When a third child came struggling by, the rescuer ran up the riverbank. "Where are you going?" shouted his friends. "You rescue that child," he answered, "I'm going to find out who is throwing the children into the river!"[57] Let us borrow this powerful metaphor. The rescuer who pulls the children one by one out of the river, thereby preventing them from drowning, embodies the goals of the child psychiatrist, whose interventions are directed at individual children. The SSRIs are being offered as a "cost-effective" life preserver. Unfortunately, not all children have been able to grab the ring, and even worse, the ring is sometimes defective! Although someone needs to keep pulling children out of the river, our efforts must also be directed toward defining and preventing the forces that are placing so many children in danger.

11

Global Girls, Consumer Culture, and Eating Disorders

Margo D. Maine

Eating disorders were once considered to be the purview of up-wardly mobile, Caucasian adolescent girls in technologically ad-vanced nations such as the United States and western Europe.[1] However, as a result of globalization, these conditions now affect every stratum of American culture and at least forty countries worldwide. Girls and women with eating disorders such as an-orexia nervosa, bulimia nervosa, body image despair, and severe dieting can now be found in places as unlikely as Nigeria, India, China, South Korea, South Africa, the former Soviet Union, and Mexico.[2]

Although many factors contribute to eating disorders, their in-creasing incidence and changing demographics strongly suggest that sociocultural influences *must* be considered in all efforts to understand, treat, and prevent them. However, with the current focus on *genetics* as a key contributor, sociocultural factors—in par-ticular those related to globalization—are not being adequately addressed.

Multinational corporations have made girls and young women all over the world targets for their marketing messages. As a result, American girls, Soviet girls, Fijian girls, Mexican girls, and others now experience their lives more similarly than ever before.[3] They are "global girls," with unprecedented global pressures, and no role models to help them navigate this new territory of psychosocial experience. This broader view elucidates the limitations of a traditional medical model in conceptualizing, treating, and preventing eating disorders; it is the focus of this chapter.

THE EVOLUTION OF THE GLOBAL GIRL

Although everyone is experiencing the effects of globalization, adolescents may be feeling its impact more acutely. Teens more readily pursue and accept influences from outside the family, but at the same time they have not yet consolidated their values or their sense of self with which to evaluate new experiences.[4] Although young people are often considered to be more resilient and flexible than adults, a lack of internal self-regulatory mechanisms and of external role models who have mastered similar stressors make their adjustment to global culture extremely challenging. Furthermore, developing a personal identity and sense of self—a central task of adolescence—is particularly arduous when the culture constantly conveys the importance of wanting external products and encourages them to "look for self-love in all the wrong places."

Gender research has shown that girls in particular are sensitive to social messages and demands.[5] As the content, number, and forcefulness of these messages intensify, girls' lives, already brimming with challenge and complexity, become all the more daunting. As our world becomes more interdependent, personal and local influences from the family, community, and religious institutions gradually weaken. And so even as the global girl's universe expands, her personal resources remain considerably smaller.

Expert advice on how to act and what to be is more available than ever before to girls, but little of this advice comes from people who actually know them, let alone care, about them. These expert sources include fashion magazines, entertainment idols, and Internet sites or chat rooms, all of which may be promoting products and images instead of values and wisdom. There are even pro-anorexia and pro-bulimia websites (also known as pro-Ana or pro-Mia), which glorify eating disorders as lifestyle choices rather than the culture-bound illnesses they are.

GENDER AND GLOBALIZATION

While the cultural transformations wrought by globalization have been stressful for everyone, they may be impacting females disproportionately and in ways that increase their risk for body image and eating disorders. Increasingly complex and fast-growing economies and rapid technological growth have created a powerful global consumer culture, with new expectations about female appearance and definitions of beauty as well as dramatic revisions in women's social role.

With greater access to education, increased involvement in the workplace, and the accompanying gender equity issues, the lives of girls and women in diverse countries are in an unsettling process of transformation. In addition, globalization is exporting the sedentary Western lifestyle and diet, which is filled with processed foods that are higher in calories and fat—a recipe for obesity. And so, as has been the case in the United States for some time, the body reality and the beauty ideal are in conflict for global girls.[6]

Globalization even affects the onset of puberty because the modern Western diet and lifestyle stimulate earlier menarche. Whereas two centuries ago, the average age at menarche was between fifteen and sixteen years, in the United States today, girls are likely to enter puberty at twelve to thirteen years of age.[7] Global girls are also increasingly exposed to Western media with its barrage of sexual imagery and to a clothing industry that produces provocative, revealing garments for tots and teens alike. With the early onset of puberty and exposure to Western media and clothing styles, global girls are becoming precociously sexualized before they are emotionally ready. At the same time, ironically, they are marketing targets for feminine hygiene products that wash away any real signs of sexuality. The subliminal message is that the natural female body must be controlled or disguised, creating an excruciating level of self-consciousness—fertile ground for the development of disordered eating and body image despair.

THE NEW NORMATIVE DISCONTENT

Contemporary culture's objectification of the female body and glorification of slimness create inordinate pressure for girls and women to aspire to be thin and "beautiful." As a result, discontent with self-image has become *normative*. At a point in history when opportunities for women are greater and their lives are more complicated and demanding than ever before, global culture creates additional stress, instructing them to obsess about their bodies, to limit their food intake, and to manage any uncertainty or anxiety by controlling their appetite and appearance. They share the global "language of fat," wherein all difficult or negative emotions are translated into just "feeling fat."[8] While urged to want more and to be more, global girls are simultaneously instructed to eat less and take up less space. These mixed messages can be difficult to decode.

Extreme control and manipulation of the body is a hot commodity in global consumer culture. Western culture inculcates the myth that the body is the answer to all angst. Dieting is the promised quick fix for self-doubt, identity confusion, and anxiety. Body hatred and desperation to lose weight or to otherwise change their appearance are now expected experiences for global girls and seen as nothing more than a rite of passage. The industries of body change have become powerful lobbies against self-acceptance.

While body despair may be bad news for the health of global girls, it is good news for the consumer economy. The dieting industry alone is responsible for $50 billion in revenue per year.[9] It sells a multitude of products, including foods, diet pills, diet programs, and books. A search for diet books on a popular Internet bookstore lists 108,864 titles.[10] This barrage of dieting aids and advice serves as a catalyst for eating disorders and makes efforts to recover a daunting challenge.

If eating disorders have become the norm for girls as a result of specific cultural conditions, then a medical model of treatment that focuses on individual pathology is clearly not optimal. Physician and author Christiane Northrup eloquently expresses that "the state of a woman's health is indeed completely tied up with the culture in which she lives and her position in it."[11]

THE GLOBAL BODY IMAGE

Body image is the deeply personal experience of one's own body. It is not what each of us sees in the mirror but rather our own interpretation of what we see, an interpretation shaped by many factors and generally not something of which we are fully conscious. Early life experiences, such as how others treated our body or talked about it, our physical problems or limitations, and our social environment—all these contribute to body image. Global media now disseminate Western cultural attitudes and standards, which have a powerful influence over the body image of global girls.

Today's tweens and teens have no perspective on the changes in the body ideal over time. A brief history of the beauties of yesteryear can put things in perspective. Marilyn Monroe, the dream girl of the 1950s and early 1960s, would now likely be considered a plus-size figure. The first runway models all weighed 155 pounds or more, and the first Miss America, crowned in 1922, weighed 140 pounds at 5'7". A half century later, beauty was fifty pounds leaner, with Twiggy weighing in at 91 pounds and 5'6".[12] Meeting the criteria for anorexia nervosa, the deadly eating disorder, became necessary to be considered model material.

The diagnosis of anorexia nervosa requires a weight of less than 85 percent of the expected weight for a given height and age.[13] Twiggy's weight was approximately 70 percent of the ideal, which is the standard used to consider implementing tube feeding when treating serious eating disorders. Barbie's reported "ideal" weight is 76 percent of the expected. Although today the average American woman is 5'4" and 140 pounds, the average fashion model is 5'11" and 117 pounds, or 75 percent of the "normal" body weight for that height.[14]

Girls may be surrounded by average women's bodies in their families, schools, and communities, but they quickly see that only the very thin and very "beautiful" Caucasian women are idealized. Despite the diversity of skin color that exists in our global village, light skin, and a very Western look is the hottest global image around. Any woman of color who is seen in a fashion layout or in prime time tends to be whitewashed, making ethnic and racial pride an unreal expectation for global girls.

The contemporary definition of beauty continues to shrink. Many already thin female stars have felt pressure to be thinner, transforming their bodies through extreme dieting, exercise regimens, and plastic surgery. These efforts are chronicled in popular magazines regularly. Despite increased awareness that the bodies of most of our stars today are crafted and not natural, they are still seen as icons to emulate rather than as women who are suffering from body image despair, self-doubt, or potentially deadly eating disorders.

Global girls are taught to want a particular body type—one with big breasts and a boy's washboard stomach. As a result, the number one wish of girls aged eleven to seventeen is to lose weight.[15] Over a two-year period in the late 1990s, plastic surgery for teens increased by nearly 50 percent and continues to increase each year.[16] One poll found that 25 percent of teen-aged girls in the United States had already considered cosmetic plastic surgery, even before their bodies matured.[17] In Eastern countries, the most popular plastic surgery procedure is "upper lid Westernization," in which an Asian eye is reshaped to look Caucasian.[18] By promoting one standard of beauty, globalization shortchanges all cultures, making the potential to appreciate diversity and uniqueness an impossible dream. Globalized consumer culture creates an unhealthy and unrealistic fixation on external appearance and an endless appetite for the right purchase, be it clothing or body transformation, but at the cost of psychological growth.

GLOBAL GIRLS AND CONSUMER CULTURE

For several decades, the United States has been reliant on a consumer-based economy, which is dependent on marketing efforts to convince people that they desperately need what they simply desire. Historically women have been the target for the marketers of consumerism because of their traditional role as the caretaker of home and family. Exposed to relentless, sophisticated, and well-crafted advertising campaigns, Western women were long ago convinced that buying the latest product is the litmus test for their ability to love and care for their families.

In the post–World War II environment of the 1950s, the focus of consumerism was on homemaking; by the 1960s, however, it broadened to include buying the right look or body in order to be a successful woman who was deserving of male attention. During the affluent years of the late twentieth century, the industries of fashion, media, and mass marketing developed and expanded rapidly, in the process creating rigid and universal standards for beauty and appearance. The twenty-first century ushered in the era of globalization, with unique and endless opportunities to foster women's consumerism.

A primary goal of globalization is to expand markets and trade, which allows contemporary consumer culture to flourish. To assure profits, more people must want, so marketing and product development have consistently lowered the age of their target audiences. In the new and globalized twenty-first century, global girls are fair game.

Universal peer pressure is one of the most troubling by-products of globalization. Nowadays, market researchers focus on "global teens," hoping to capitalize on the shared desires and insecurities of adolescents from different places and cultures and to develop global brands for items such as soft drinks, clothing, snack foods, and beauty aids.[19] Global girls have a clear calling: to confuse true hunger, desire, and need with accumulating external possessions and crafting the "perfect," or most trendy, image. They get the message that to be wanted and valued by others, they must want and get the right things, and in return they will be successful, desired, and valued. Consumer culture constantly communicates this notion, and global girls, lacking any real alternative, have bought it. But they have bought far too much—not just the material goods but also the vacuous values at the core of mindless consumerism, which lead to problems like eating disorders.

BE ALL YOU CAN BUY

Global girls are taught to purchase before they are taught to read. Today's toddlers readily recognize corporate logos. By kindergarten, many girls already think about appearance, body image, and fashion. Advertisers use Disney characters and other child-oriented images to promote a wide range of products, including cologne, clothing, and cosmetics. Encouraging young girls to want things they cannot find inside themselves or in relationships makes them vulnerable to self-doubt, body image despair, and the inner emptiness that can lead to disordered eating and life-threatening eating disorders.

For many global girls, the gateway drug into the culture of consumerism and inner emptiness is the Barbie doll, which lures millions of girls each year into their lifelong role as consumers. If you ask a little girl what she likes about Barbie, the answer is uniformly "the clothes" or "the stuff." Barbie is about how you look, what you wear, and what you have—all image, no substance. By three years of age, most American girls own their first Barbie and are well on their way into her world of consumerism, clothes, and "beauty."

Each new Barbie is more coveted than the last: Calvin Klein Barbie comes with CK logos, Shopper Barbie has a charge card, Talking Barbie says things like "Math class is tough," and Slumber Party Barbie comes with a scale permanently set at 110 pounds and a book titled *How to Lose Weight*, which instructs "Don't eat." Barbie's autobiography describes her as a "full figure" at 5'9" tall and 110 pounds, a weight that would put her at medical risk and unlikely to function normally or have her period.[20] Her measurements of 39-18-33, with a permanently deformed child's size-3 foot,[21] are not a realistic introduction to the world of women's bodies. New lines of dolls specially developed to capture slightly older girls who may have tired of Barbie have an updated image with pouty lips and a sexier, more hip attitude. Now global girls from completely different cultures, ethnicities, and body types can all aspire to the same un-real images. And they do.

Tweens, a recent marketing frontier—generally defined as eight-to twelve-year-olds—are particularly attractive to corporate America. In fact, 80 percent of companies that market globally have developed campaigns specific to tweens.[22] Girls in this age group are too old to be kids but are not yet teens; they are desperate to be liked, to define themselves, to "grow up" and be taken seriously. Teen magazines pull them in and consolidate their consumerism. With celebrities on the cover and pricy clothes inside, these maga-zines are more like catalogs pushing the unaffordable but the desir-able, convincing elementary school children that they need to be sexy and trendy to be successful and that designer brands are the answer to insecurity.

The largely unregulated and rapidly growing advertising indus-try spends over $15 billion each year marketing to children alone.[23] As a result, the average American child sees more than 40,000 tele-vision ads annually.[24] It is an investment that has paid off: children now influence the spending of more than $600 billion, including $28 billion of their own money.[25] Teenage girls spend more than $9 billion per year on makeup alone.[26] Marketers capture their minds along with their money and intend to never let go. Consumer culture instructs global girls to "Be All that You Can Buy." And it succeeds.

The relentless exposure to messages promising everything—from beauty and popularity to peace of mind, self-confidence, and fulfilling relationships—turns children, especially girls, into insa-tiable consumers. The quick fix of a purchase robs them of self-determination, self-awareness, and self-esteem. Encouraged to look outside of themselves for comfort, values, and direction, global girls easily fall prey to advertising messages that foster addictions. In fact, the diet, tobacco, and alcohol industries target women of all ages, but especially girls and teens, capitalizing on the body im-age issues, weight concerns, and beauty ideals that make them so vulnerable.[27]

THE MEDIA AND "ME"

The mass media impose impossible standards that keep women of all ages unsure, uneasy, "in their place," and wishing to be some-one other than who they are. As a result, global girls are encour-aged to develop a false self that expresses their sense of self and their femininity through their appearance rather than their feelings, actions, and relationships. To become their ideal false self, global girls must constantly change themselves, buying product after product or diet after diet, seeking self-satisfaction but being doomed to fail.

Teenage girls are especially vulnerable to media manipulation for several reasons. Adolescence is always a critical time in identity formation. The central task for adolescents is to figure out who they are and what they want to become. And in the process they become keenly aware of cultural standards and ideals. Adolescence is a time of peak exposure to the media and its messages in all forms, while simultaneously they are spending less time with their families. As a result, media messages have the potential to exert an immense psychological impact on adolescent identity formation.

The greater a girl's exposure to media, the more likely she is to diet and be dissatisfied with her body, her appearance, and herself, which places her at serious risk for eating disorders, depression, and anxiety. Adolescent girls who attempt suicide *often report that weight and body image contributed significantly to their despair.*

A systematic review of magazine articles reveals an inordinate emphasis on women's bodies as compared to men's and the not very subtle message that for men many things may be important, whereas for women only the body counts. Girls are constantly portrayed in silly positions, sometimes off balance, often passively observing others, while boys are portrayed as active, powerful, and in control. Today women are more sexualized and objectified in magazine ads than they were even a decade ago. Female body exposure has increased, with almost 53 percent of black women models and 62 percent of white women models scantily clad as compared to only 25 percent of male models. More than 17 percent of ads show women in lower-status positions, such as on their knees or the floor. Black women in particular are placed in sexualized, predatory poses, often wearing animal prints.[28]

As a female's exposure to these media images of beauty escalates, so does her likelihood of developing an eating disorder. Women undergraduates report more stress, depression, guilt, shame, insecurity, and body dissatisfaction immediately after viewing ultrathin models, and 70 percent of college women report feeling worse about themselves after reading magazines.[29] Unfortunately, global girls of all ages are constantly exposed to these images and messages, while they rarely hear that they (or someone who looks like them) are beautiful just as they are. Men and boys are also influenced by the distorted portrayal of femaleness in the media, and they begin to experience girls and women in their lives as less attractive than their magazine counterparts.

Television, one of the most influential forms of mass media, rarely depicts women as powerful or prestigious. On those rare occasions when a woman is depicted as such, the empowered female character is also stunningly beautiful and exquisitely thin, fostering an image of perfection that few can meet. And so it is no surprise that watching soap operas, movies, and music videos is associated with greater body dissatisfaction and a desire for thinness. Images of thinness on the television screen alternate with tantalizing food advertisements for high-fat, low-nutrient fast food, creating conflicting messages and wants.[30] As a result, global girls feel all the more confused about their natural bodies, basic hunger, and desires.

A dramatic example of the impact of globalization and media images on attitudes and behaviors surrounding food and women's bodies occurred in Fiji after television was introduced. Strong Fijian traditions and values were overturned with startling speed. In Fijian culture, large female bodies were valued for their strength, and women were esteemed for their contribution to the family and community life. Food was celebrated, integrated into culturally rich traditions, and imbued with special meaning. As recently as 1995, eating disorders were basically nonexistent in Fiji. But after less than three years of limited exposure to Western network television shows, they were rampant. By 1998, 11 percent of Fijian girls and women practiced self-induced vomiting, 29 percent were at risk for an eating disorder, 69 percent had dieted to lose weight, and 74 percent felt "too fat." Watching popular female images on television had created a desire for the kind of life these stars seemed to have, and these new global girls became committed to changing their bodies to get it.[31] The Fiji experience demonstrates how global influences can overturn strong local cultural traditions and values in nearly no time. This is not good news for global girls.

CONCLUSION

Western society is in the midst of a cultural crisis that globalization now exports all over the world. Consumer culture values global girls *only* as potential consumers; it is a culture that instills want and desire, promotes a profitable economic system, and at the same time discourages female self-acceptance, emotional awareness, self-esteem, and positive body image. It is no wonder that disordered eating and body image despair are now normative experiences and that serious and life-threatening eating disorders continue to rise and appear across the globe, in girls and women of all ages, ethnicities, races, and socioeconomic strata. As Caroline Knapp eloquently expresses, "culture is written on the body ... encoded on it. Fat, thin, sculpted, adorned, starved, stuffed, the female body is a kind of text which, properly deconstructed, may tell us a lot about how women are seen in the culture and what they grapple with."[32]

Global girls are alive at a time of great opportunity, but they are uniformly told to buy more and be less, leaving them empty inside and constantly looking for the external quick fix that will fill them up. It may be a lost pound or a found purchase, all to solve the dilemma of how to be taken seriously and valued by others. In this environment, eating disorders will only flourish. No prevention program, treatment approach, or drug can address this problem, except for isolated and very fortunate individuals.

The culture-bound nature of these biopsychosocial disorders must be acknowledged and addressed. We must understand the multiple negative impacts of the new globalized consumer economy and make a commitment to save the lives and health of girls and women. Global girls should be able to want more than what our consumer culture offers them. While their appetites have been supersized, their bodies have been downsized and they are taught to question and deny their true hungers—for food, for self-fulfillment, and for life itself. Wanting can be hazardous to a global girl's health. Let us want more for them.

APPENDIX

Facts about Eating Disorders

Eating disorders, while certainly present in previous eras, have increased dramatically in recent decades. Now the American Psychiatric Association estimates that between .5 and 3.7 percent of young women in the United States will have anorexia nervosa at some point during their lifetime and between 1.1 and 4.2 percent will have bulimia nervosa. Of those suffering, 90 percent are women.[33] At least one-third of those treated in eating disorder clinics are diagnosed as Eating Disorder Not Otherwise Specified (EDNOS), a category that shares some but not all of the features of anorexia and bulimia.[34] Fewer data are available on these cases, despite their prevalence. See Table I for diagnostic criteria (*DSM-IV*).

Among psychiatric conditions, anorexia nervosa has the highest morbidity, with an estimated 10 percent mortality rate at ten years of symptom duration and 20 percent at a twenty-year follow-up.[35] Anorexia is the leading cause of death for young women aged fifteen to twenty-four years; the women in this group have a general mortality rate 12-fold greater than expected and a suicide rate 75-fold greater.[36] Less is known about the mortality associated with bulimia nervosa, due both to the potential long-lasting medical

Table I   Diagnostic Criteria for Eating Disorders

Anorexia nervosa
- refusal to maintain body weight at/above a minimally normal weight for height and age
- weight loss to 85 percent of the expected body weight for height/age or failure to gain weight during growth period resulting in weight less than 85 percent of expected
- intense fear of gaining weight despite being underweight
- disturbance in how weight/shape are experienced and undue influence of weight/shape on self-evaluation
- denial of seriousness of low weight
- amenorrhea (missed three or more cycles or only has period when receiving hormonal treatment)

Types: Restricting or Binge-Eating Purging Type

Bulimia Nervosa
- recurrent periods of binge eating (eating an abnormally large amount of food in a discrete period of time and feeling unable to stop or to control the amount eaten)
- recurrent inappropriate compensatory behavior to avoid weight gain, such as self-induced vomiting, misuse of laxatives, diuretics, enemas or other medications, fasting, excessive exercise
- the binge-purge cycles occur, on average, twice a week for three months or longer
- self-evaluation is unduly influenced by weight/shape
- behavior does not occur exclusively in periods of anorexia nervosa

Types: Purging (uses self-induced vomiting or laxatives, diuretics, enemas) or Non-Purging (uses other compensatory behaviors such as fasting or exercise)

Eating Disorder Not Otherwise Specified
- atypical anorexia—key signs of anorexia are present but does not meet all criteria (still menstruates or has not had significant weight loss)
- atypical bulimia—all criteria are met except frequency or duration of symptoms
- use of inappropriate compensatory behaviors after eating normal amounts of food
- binge-eating disorder—recurrent binging without purging repeatedly chewing and spitting out food without swallowing

consequences and to diagnostic limitations. For example, as many as half of those with anorexia will develop bulimic symptoms but will still be diagnosed with anorexia.[37] Even less is known about those women diagnosed as EDNOS, although their symptoms and treatment needs may be just as serious.

Subclinical Eating Disorders

Subclinical eating disorders are an additional threat to the health of global girls. This term is used to describe those who may be sporadically symptomatic or whose symptoms do not quite meet the criteria for a full-blown clinical eating disorder. Some of these will later emerge into full anorexia or bulimia.

Although estimates of the incidence of subclinical eating disorders are inconsistent, two comprehensive studies provide compelling data regarding the common use of pathogenic weight control techniques in teenagers whose bodies are still developing and growing. A study of more than 80,000 ninth and twelfth graders in the United States found that 56 percent of ninth grade females and 28 percent of males are engaged in unsafe dieting practices. In the twelfth grade, 57 percent of females and 31 percent of males practice dangerous dieting, including skipping meals, ingesting diet pills or laxatives, inducing vomiting, smoking cigarettes (for the purpose of affecting their weight and food intake), and binge eating. Hispanic and Native American students had the highest rates. The good news from this study is that positive self-esteem, emotional well-being, school achievement, and family connectedness serve to protect teens from these dangerous diet practices.[38]

The Centers for Disease Control report epidemic rates of weight loss attempts among high school students.[39] For example, in its extensive study of teenage diet-related behaviors in the past month, the CDC reports that 46 percent are trying to lose weight, 44 percent are actively dieting, and 60 percent are exercising to lose or avoid gaining weight. The breakdown by gender shows that although both sexes are troubled by weight concerns, girls are engaging in dangerous dieting much more than boys are. The CDC asked teenage girls about their dieting "in the past month." The results can be found in Table II.

Dieting is an equal opportunity activity for girls that is now taking hold of all cultures, ethnic groups, and classes throughout the United States. Body image despair and disordered eating are no

Table II Unhealthy Weight Loss Techniques in Adolescent Girls

	White	Black	Hispanic
Exercising to lose weight	72.5%	53.4%	66.2%
Dieting	63.1%	40.2%	56.5%
Fasting	19.7%	15.2%	23.1%
Diet Pills	13.6%	7.5%	13.5%
Purging	8.2%	4.2%	10.8%

longer upper-middle-class Caucasian issues; instead, they are now homogenized into all segments of American culture. The sad truth is that few adolescent females living in the United States like their bodies. A survey of 2,600 teen girls reported that 38 percent think about weight constantly, 68 percent want to flatten their stomachs, 74 percent work out two to three times per week, and 84 percent envy other girls' bodies.[40] In fact, 70 percent of normal-weight girls feel fat and are dieting, 13 percent of fifteen-year-old girls diet at least ten times a year, 90 percent of high school junior and senior girls diet regularly, although only 10–15 percent are overweight, and 50–60 percent of college women are currently dieting.[41]

These obsessions with weight, appearance, and body image are a tremendous waste of energy, imagination, and time. Younger and younger girls share these concerns, and the age at which clinical eating disorders now appear mirrors this trend.[42] Research as long ago as the early 1990s reports the startling facts about the downward trend in the ages of girls experiencing body angst. One study reports that 42 percent of first, second, and third grade girls want to lose weight.[43] Another finds that 51 percent of nine- and ten-year-old girls feel better about themselves when they are dieting; 81 percent of ten-year-olds are afraid of being fat; and 9 percent of nine-year-olds have vomited to lose weight.[44] And finally, a longitudinal study reports that 4 percent of middle school girls vomited to lose weight and fewer than 1 percent used diet pills in the 1980s, but by the 1990s more than 11 percent vomited and more than 6 percent used diet pills.[45]

With the help of globalization, Western culture is exporting these problems around the world, endangering the health of all global girls. The Fiji experience shows how quickly a culture can be transformed from a safe haven for women's strength and size to one that makes them doubt their basic biological need to eat.

Notes

CHAPTER 1

1. The National Advisory Mental Health Council Workgroup on Child and Adolescent Mental Health Intervention Development and Deployment. (2001). *Blueprint for Change: Research on Child and Adolescent Mental Health.* Washington, DC, p. 1.

2. Psychotropic drugs treat psychiatric disturbance by altering brain chemistry.

3. Zito, J. M., et al. (2003). Psychotropic practice patterns for youth: A 10-year perspective. *Archives of Pediatric and Adolescent Medicine, 157* (1); and Zito, J. M., D. J. Safer, S. dos Reis, J. F. Gardener, M. Boles, and F. Lynch. (2000). Trends in the prescribing of psychotropic medications to preschoolers. *JAMA, 283*, 1025–1030.

4. Sullivan, M. (2004, April 1). FDA wants new warnings on 10 antidepressants. *Clinical Psychiatry News*, 8; and Safer, D. J., et al. (1996). Increased methylphenidate usage for attention deficit disorder in the 1990s. *Pediatrics, 98*, 1084–1088.

5. Zito, J. M., and D. J. Safer. (2005). Recent child pharmacoepidemiological findings. *Journal of Child and Adolescent Psychopharmacology, 15* (1), 5–9.

6. Zito, J. M. (2005). New data evaluates prescribing patterns in children and adolescents, *Brown University Child and Adolescent Psychopharmacology Update, 7* (4), 1, 5–7.

7. The character of Anne is based on author L. M. Montgomery's own childhood.

8. Kluger, J. (2002, August 19). Young and bipolar. *Time*, cover story. ADHD is the acronym for attention-deficit/hyperactivity disorder.

9. Kowatch, R. et al. (2005). Treatment guidelines for child and adolescent bipolar disorder. *Journal of the American Academy of Child and Adolescent Psychiatry, 44* (3), 213–235.

10. Ibid., 231.

11. Whitaker, R. (2002). *Mad in America*. New York: Basic Books.

12. Healy, D. (2003). *Let Them Eat Prozac*. Toronto: James Lorimer and Co., pp. 12–13.

13. Whitaker, *Mad in America*.

14. Ibid., 277, 279.

15. Ibid., 280–281.

16. Walters, R. (2005, May/June). Medicating Aliah. *Mother Jones*, 281

17. Whitaker, *Mad in America*, 281.

18. Walters, Medicating Aliah, 52.

19. Whitaker, *Mad in America*.

20. Kowatch et al., Treatment guidelines, 213–235. In these treatment guidelines, the authors rank their medication recommendations according to how rigorously the drugs have been tested and whether they have ever been tested for use with children in randomized, controlled clinical trials. Drugs that were tested for use with children received an A rating. None of the atypical antipsychotics that the authors recommended received this rating. The phrase "rigorously tested" refers to randomized, controlled clinical trials.

21. McClellan, J. (2005). Commentary: Treatment guidelines for child and adolescent bipolar disorder. *Journal of the American Academy of Child and Adolescent Psychiatry, 44* (3).

22. Kowatch et al., Treatment guidelines.

23. Seven out of nine donors listed are pharmaceutical companies: www.cabf.org/CABF People/Organizational Donors and Foundations.

24. Kowatch's affiliations to pharmaceutical companies are listed in a disclosure at the end of his March 2005 article, "Treatment guidelines."

25. See www.dshs.state.tx.us/mhprograms/TMAP.shtm.

26. Walters, Medicating Aliah.

27. See www.dshs.state.tx.us/mhprograms/CMAP.shtm.

28. Walters, Medicating Aliah.

29. Ibid., 86–87.

30. U.S. Census Bureau. (2002). *Statistical Abstracts of the United States*, 123rd ed. Washington, DC.

31. Children's Defense Fund. (2003). *The State of America's Children: Yearbook 2003*. Washington, DC.

32. Colman, R. (In Press). Measuring Genuine Progress. In R. Cavoukian and S. Olfman (Eds.), *The Power of Child Honoring: How To Turn This World Around*.

33. Sharna Olfman (Ed.). (2005). *Childhood Lost*. Westport, CT: Praeger.

34. Burston, D., and S. Olfman. (1996). Freud, Fromm and the pathology of normalcy: Clinical, social and historical perspectives. In M. Cortina and M. Maccoby (Eds.), *A Prophetic Analyst: Reclaiming Fromm's Legacy* (pp. 301–324). North Vale, NJ: Jason Aronson.

35. PULSE (2005, April 21), 1 in 5 Teens Abuses Prescription Drugs. http://radio.weblogs.com/0108660; Hartocollis, A. (2005, February 13). High school chemistry class. *New York Times*.

36. Cicero, D., et al. (2003). Antidepressant exposure in bipolar children. *Psychiatry: Interpersonal and Biological Processes, 66* (4), 317–322; DelBello, M. P., et al. (2001). Prior stimulant treatment for adolescents with bipolar disorder: Association with age at onset. *Bipolar Disorders, 3* (2), 53–57; Reichart, C. G., and W. A. Nolen. (2004). Earlier onset bipolar disorder in children by antidepressants or stimulants? An hypothesis. *Journal of Affective Disorders, 78* (1), 81–84.

CHAPTER 2

1. Bronfenbrenner, U. (1988). Strengthening family systems. In E. F. Zigler and M. Frank (Eds.), *The Parental Leave Crisis: Toward a National Policy* (pp. 143–160). New Haven, CT: Yale University Press.

2. Schore, A. (2003). *Affect Disregulation and Disorders of the Self*. New York: Norton.

3. Karen, R. (1998). *Becoming Attached: First Relationships and How They Shape Our Capacity to Love*. New York: Oxford University Press.

4. Ibid., 3. (Emphasis added.)

5. Small, M. (2004). The natural history of children. In S. Olfman (Ed.), *Childhood Lost: How American Culture Is Failing Our Kids* (pp. 3–18). Westport, CT: Praeger.

6. Ibid., 12.

7. Karen, *Becoming Attached*, 3; Small, Natural history of children.

8. Stern, D. (1985). *The Interpersonal World of the Infant*. New York: Basic Books.

9. Rice, R. S. (1997). Neurophysiological development in premature infants following stimulation. *Developmental Psychology, 13*, 69–76; White, J. L., and R. Labarba. (1976). The effects of tactile and kinesthetic stimulation on neonatal development in the premature infant. *Developmental Psychobiology, 9* (6), 569–577.

10. McKenna, J. J., S. S. Mosko, C. Richard, S. Drummond, L. Hunt, M. B. Cetel, and J. Arpaia. (1994). Experimental studies of infant–parent co-sleeping: Mutual physiological and behavioral influences and their relevance to SIDS (Sudden Infant Death Syndrome). *Early Human Development, 38*, 187–201.

11. Angier, N. (1994, May 24). Mother's milk found to be potent cocktail of hormones. *New York Times*, B5.

12. Gerhardt, S. (2004). *Why Love Matters: How Affection Shapes a Baby's Brain*. New York: Brunner-Routledge, 24–25.

13. Schore, *Affect Disregulation*.

14. Gerhardt, *Why Love Matters*.

15. Ibid.

16. Ibid.

17. Baumrind, D. (1971). Current patterns of parental authority. *Developmental Psychology Monograph, 4* (no. 1, pt. 2); Kuczynski, L., and S. Lollis. (2002). Four foundations for a dynamic model of parenting. In J. R. M. Gerris (Ed.), *Dynamics of Parenting*. Hillsdale, NJ: Erlbaum; Russell, A., J. Mize, and K. Bissaker. (2002). Parent–child relationships. In P. K. Smith and C. Hart (Eds.), *Handbook of Childhood Social Development*. Oxford, UK: Blackwell.

18. Berk, L. E. (2005). *Infants, Children and Adolescents*. Boston: Pearson/Allyn and Bacon.

19. Erikson, E. H. (1950). *Childhood and Society*. New York: Norton.

20. Harlow, H. F., and R. Zimmerman. (1959). Affectional responses in the infant monkey. *Science, 130*, 421–432; Small, M. F. (1999). *Our Babies, Ourselves: How Biology and Culture Shape the Way We Parent*. New York: Anchor Books.

21. Bronfenbrenner, Strengthening family systems.

22. Bronfenbrenner, U. (1992). Child care in the Anglo-Saxon mode. In M. E. Lamb, J. J. Sternberg, C. P. Hwang, and A. G. Broberg (Eds.), *Child Care in Context* (pp. 281–291). Hillsdale, NJ: Lawrence Erlbaum.

23. Berk, Why parenting matters. (My emphasis.)

24. Ibid., 33.

25. Bronfenbrenner, U. (1985). The future of childhood. In V. Greaney (Ed.), *Children: Needs and Rights* (pp. 167–186). New York: Irvington Publishers.

CHAPTER 3

1. Russo, E. Researchers find no clear paths on road to unraveling schizophrenia. *The Scientist, 16* (2), 30–31. As cited in Coll, C. G., E. L. Bearer, and R. M. Lerner (Eds.). (2004). *Nature and Nurture: The Complex Interplay of Genetic and Environmental Influences on Human Behavior and Development*. Mahwah, NJ: L.E.A.; and Owen, M. J., and M. C. O'Donovan. (2004). Schizophrenia and genes. In R. Plomin et al. (Eds.), *Behavioral Genetics in the Postgenomic Era*. Washington, DC: American Psychological Association.

2. Kagan, J. (2004). A behavioral science perspective. In Plomin et al. (Eds.), *Behavioral Genetics in the Postgenomic Era*. Washington, DC: American Psychological Association (p. xix).

3. Schlaug, G. (2001). The brain of musicians: A model for functional and structural adaptation. *Annals of the New York Academy of Sciences, 930*, 281–299.

4. Herrenstein, R. J., and C. Murray. (1994). *The Bell Curve: Intelligence and Class Structure in American Life.* New York: Free Press.

5. Ridley, M. (2003). *Nature via Nurture: Genes, Experience, and What Makes Us Human.* New York: Harper Collins.

6. Ibid.

7. Scriver, C. R., and C. L. Clow. (1980). Phenylketonuria: Epitome of human biochemical genetics. *New England Journal of Medicine, 303,* 1336–1342.

8. Plomin et al. (Eds.), *Behavioral Genetics in the Postgenomic Era,* 14.

9. Ridley, *Nature via Nurture.*

10. Bearer, E. L. (2004). Behavior as influence and result of the genetic program. In Coll, Bearer, and Lerner (Eds.), *Nature and Nurture,* Mahwah, NJ: Lawrence Erlbaum Associates.

11. Robinson, G. E. (2004, December 13). The behavior of genes. *New York Times,* 29.

12. Galaburda, A. M. (2004, November 5). Norman Geshwind and dyslexia: A neurobiological legacy. Address presented at International Dyslexia Association Annual Meeting, Philadelphia.

13. Gottleib, G. (1998). Normally occurring environmental and behavioral influences on gene activity: From central dogma to probablistic epigenesist. In Coll, Bearer, and Lerner (Eds.), *Nature and Nurture,* 94.

14. Plomin et al. (Eds.), *Behavioral Genetics in the Postgenomic Era,* 366ff.

15. Ibid.

16. For one summary of current research, see the *New York Times,* December 7, 2004, D5.

17. Ridley, *Nature via Nurture.*

18. Shonkoff, J. P., and D. A. Phillips. (2000). *From Neurons to Neighborhoods: The Science of Early Childhood Education.* Washington, DC: National Academy Press.

19. As quoted in Rosenzweig, M. R. (2003). Effects of differential experience on the brain and behavior. *Developmental Neuropsychology, 24* (2–3), 534.

20. Galaburda, Geshwind and dyslexia.

21. G. M. Edelman. (1992). *Bright Air, Brilliant Fire: On the Matter of the Mind.* New York: Basic Books. As quoted in Coll, Bearer, and Lerner (Eds.), *Nature and Nurture,* 209.

22. Nemeroff, C. B., et al. (2003). Differential responses to psychotherapy versus pharmacotherapy in patients with chronic forms of major depression and childhood trauma. *Proceedings of the National Academy of Science, 100* (24), 14293–14296.

23. For a description of how television, computers, and contemporary lifestyles may be contributing to attention and learning problems in today's children, see: Healy, J. (1999). *Endangered Minds: Why Children Don't Think and What We Can Do about It.* New York: Simon and Schuster/Touchstone; and Healy, J. (1999). *Failure to Connect: How*

Computers Affect Our Children's Minds. New York: Simon and Schuster/ Touchstone.

24. Sunomi, S. J. (2004). How gene–environment interactions influence emotional development in rhesus monkeys. In Coll, Bearer, and Lerner (Eds.), *Nature and Nurture*, 9.

25. Ibid., 10.

26. Caspi, A., et al. (2003). Influence of life stress on depression: Moderation by a polymorphism in the 5-HTT gene. *Science, 301* (5631), 386–389.

27. Lesch, K. P. (2004). Neuroticism and serotonin: A developmental genetic perspective. In Plomin et al. (Eds.), *Behavioral Genetics in the Postgenomic Era.*

28. Weaver, I. C. G., et al. (2004, June 27). Epigenetic programming by maternal behavior. *Nature Neuroscience*, advance online publication, 1.

29. Robinson, Behavior of genes.

30. Ceci, S. J. (2003, November). Cast in six ponds and you'll reel in something: Looking back on 25 years of research. *American Psychologist, 58* (11), 855–866.

31. Molfese, D. L., V. J. Molfese, S. Key, and A. Modglin. (2002). Reading and cognitive abilities: Longitudinal studies of brain and behavior changes in young children. *Annals of Dyslexia, 52*, 99–11.

32. Greenough, W., K. Black, and C. Wallace. (1987). Experience and brain development. *Child Development, 58*, 539–559; and Wachs, T. D. (2000). *Necessary but Not Sufficient: The Respective Roles of Single and Multiple Influences on Individual Development*. Washington, DC: American Psychological Association.

33. Kuhl, P. S., et al. (1992). Linguistic experience alters phonetic perception in infants by six months of age. *Science, 255*, 606–608.

34. Molfese, D. L., V. J. Molfese, A. F. Key, and S. D. Kelly. (2003). Influence of environment on speech–sound discrimination: Findings from a longitudinal study. *Developmental Neuropsychology, 24* (2–3), 541–558.

35. Shaywitz, S. (2003). *Overcoming Dyslexia: A New and Complete Science-Based Program for Reading Problems at Any Level*. New York: Knopf; and Papanicolaou, A. C., et al. (2003). Brain mechanisms for reading in children with and without dyslexia: A review of studies of normal development and plasticity. *Developmental Neuropsychology, 24* (2–3), 593–561.

36. Posner, M. I. (2003). Educating the developing brain. Paper delivered at the annual convention of the American Psychological Association.

37. LeDoux, J. (2002). *Synaptic Self: How Our Brains Become Who We Are*. New York: Viking, p. 3.

CHAPTER 4

1. Mittelstaedt, M. (2004, July 31). Where the boys aren't. *Globe and Mail*, A3.

2. See Olfman, S. (Ed.). (2005). *Childhood Lost: How American Culture Is Failing Our Kids.* Westport, CT: Praeger. The whole collection speaks to many of the dimensions of these problems. For broad summaries of these trends, see especially Olfman, introduction to *Childhood Lost*, xi–xiv; Healey, J., and C. West. (2005). The war against parents. In Olfman (Ed.), *Childhood Lost*, 57–88.

3. Landrigan, P. J., and J. E. Carlson. (1995). Environmental policy and children's health. *Future of Children*, Summer/Fall, 34–52.

4. National Research Council. (1992). *Environmental Neurotoxicology.* Washington, DC: National Academy of Sciences Press. See also: McElgunn, B. (1999). Protecting the brain: Neurotoxicants and child development. *Interaction* (Canadian Child Care Federation), *13* (1), 22–24.

5. For connections between persistent organic pollutants and precocious puberty in girls and problems of normal sexual development in boys there are many sources. See: Colborn, T., D. Dumanoski, and J. P. Myers. (1996). *Our Stolen Future: Are We Threatening Our Fertility, Intelligence and Survival? A Scientific Detective Story.* New York: Dutton; Swan, S. H., E. P. Elkin, and L. Fenster. (2000). The question of declining sperm density revisited: An analysis of 101 studies published, 1934–1996. *Environmental Health Perspectives, 108* (10), 1996; Solomon, G. M. (2001). Early puberty in girls linked to DDT metabolites: A review of Kristevska-Konstantinova M., Charlier C., Craen M., Du Caju M., Heinrichs C., de Beaufort C., et al. "Sexual precocity after immigration from developing countries to Belgium: Evidence of previous exposure to organochlorine pesticides." *Human Reproduction,* 16 (5), 1020–1026. For emotional and psychological issues, see Levin, D. E. (2005). So sexy, so soon. In Olfman, S. (Ed.), *Childhood Lost*, 137–154.

6. In fact, the nutrient deficiencies in many diets, the pesticides and chemical food additives, and the chemical transformations in foods that result from forms of processing constitute serious mental health hazards for significant numbers of children. Because of the ubiquity of processed foods, even in the vast majority of U.S. schools these hazards can properly be called environmental dangers. It is very important that the now significant body of analysis that has been developed on these additives and processes, and the positive experiences with removing them, in schools as well as in homes, become part of what every educator, counselor, and therapist considers in assessing a given child or group of children. For brief introductions to and examples of the key issues in this field, see: Challem, J. (2003, January 18). Mean streets or mean minerals? *Nutrition Reporter*, www.thenutrionreporter.com. This article summarizes thirty years of research into the relationship among nutritional deficiencies, biochemical imbalances, brain function, and delinquent and criminal behavior. See also: Hersey, J. (2002). *Why Can't My Child Behave?* Alexandria, VA: Pear Tree Press; and Hersey, J. (2004, February 29). Hyperactivity, attention deficits, obesity and diabetes—On

the menu in American schools? www.school-lunch.org/obesity. html#jane. These articles summarize efforts in North America and the United Kingdom to reform school cafeterias and improve the contents of vending machines, and gives the supporting research. Also see: Hersey, J. (2004, November 4). Montana school cleans up the playground, then the food, www.feingold.org/article-pg.html, reporting on dramatic improvement of student behavior by dietary changes. And see: Hersey, J. (2003, April). At Wisconsin high school, students behave as they eat. *Education Reporter*, no. 207: "grades are up," "truancy is no longer a problem, arguments are rare, and teachers are able to spend their time teaching." And from the BBC: Junk food ban "calms pupils." (2002, November 5). *BBC News*; teachers at a London school reported that a ban on junk foods and fizzy drinks dramatically improved pupils' behavior. And from American television: Recipe for trouble: Food allergies. (2005, March 30). *Jane Pauley Show*, www.thejanepauleyshow.com/aboutshow/ 20050330.html, featuring Dr. Doris Rapp, whose books are also helpful on this issue, plus the stories of children and adults with serious food allergies.

7. Kohler, J. (2005, January 21). Colorado scientists find chemicals in waters. Associated Press. The USGS is in the process of conducting studies on water quality across the United States. For information on water quality in many jurisdictions, go to the USGS website, http://water.usgs.gov, and search accordingly.

8. Picard, A., and A. Favaro. (2005, February 14). Common foods laced with chemical: Levels of PBDEs rise, new research shows. *Globe and Mail*, A1; Picard, A. (2005, February 15). Flame retardants building up within us: Highest levels found in babies as PBDEs emanate from carpets, furniture to form dust balls. *Globe and Mail*, A19. Both articles were in response to a specially commissioned study by the *Globe and Mail* and CTV, in response to new alarms about flame retardants; they reported the possible problems associated with PBDEs as memory problems, thyroid problems, learning disabilities, stunted growth, and "the stunning rise in attention-deficit-hyperactivity disorder."

9. WWF (formerly known as the World Wildlife Fund). (2003, November 24). Highly toxic chemicals contaminate the nation, http://www.wwf.org.uk/News/n_0000001055.asp; WWF press release. (2004, October 19). WWF publishes results of blood tests on environment and health ministers, http://www.env-health.org/a/1462; Watson, J. (2003, November 24). Toxic cocktail lurking in our veins. *Scotsman*.

10. Tests reveal chemical cocktail in EU ministers' blood: WWF. (2004, October 19). Agence France Presse. The tests, part of the WWF's ongoing Chemical Checkup program, analyzed the blood samples for 101 chemicals of five types: bromated flame retardants, phthalates, perfluorinated chemicals, PCBs, and organo-chlorine pesticides. See: WWF. (2004, July 12). EU ministers give blood for chemical check up,

http://www.panda.org/news_facts/newsroom/news.cfm?uNewsId=14 132&uLangId=1. The results of the previous tests, in December 2003, were similar to those announced for the July tests: WWF. (2004). Factsheet: Chemical contamination, http://www.panda.org/downloads/ toxics/detoxfactsheetchemcheckup1.pdf.

11. "Home contaminants are important contributors to people's overall exposure and health effects because studies show that people in the United States spend 65% of their time in their residences," according to John Spengler of the Harvard School of Public Health. According to Spengler, this figure holds true for most other industrialized countries as well. For more information on John Spengler and the issue of body burden, and for information on toxic chemicals in everyday products, see: Betts, K. (2003, September 23). Cancer causing and hormone disrupting chemicals found in most U.S. homes. Organic Consumers' Association, http://www.organicconsumers.org/foodsafety/ endocrine100903.cfm. John Spengler's work is also described in a helpful summary of some of the work on body burden being done by leading U.S. researchers: Stevenson, M. (2005, March 5). I am polluted (Chemicals in our bodies). *Globe and Mail*.

12. Greater Boston Physicians for Social Responsibility. (2000). *In harm's way: Toxic threats to child development*. Cambridge, MA. Available at http://www.igc.org/psr.

13. Children's Environmental Health Network. (1998) Why children are not adults, Washington, DC: CEHN. http://www.cehn.org. CEHN is a national multidisciplinary organization whose mission is to protect the fetus and the child from environmental health hazards and promote a healthy environment.

14. Hill, B. L., and M. Keating. (2002). *Clean Air Task Force: Children at Risk*, Boston, MA: Spectrum, 5–16; Schmidt, C. W. (1999). Commentary: Poisoning young minds. *Environmental Health Perspectives, 109,* 187–192; Landrigan, P., et al. (1998). Children's health and the environment: A new agenda for prevention research. *Environmental Health Perspectives, 106,* 787–794; Bearer, C. F. (1995). Environmental health hazards: How children are different from adults. *Future of Children, 5* (2), 11–26.

15. The following references are excellent compendia, written in clear, everyday language, of children's special vulnerability to environmental dangers. They identify many of the key toxins on which research is substantial and the routes of exposure for children: Children's Environmental Health Network, Why children are not adults; Landrigan, P. J. (2004). Children as a vulnerable population. *International Journal of Occupational Medicine and Environmental Health, 17* (1): 175–177. For an older perspective, to view the evolution of research, see: Goldman, L. R. (1995). Environmental health issues. *Environmental Health Perspectives Supplements, 103* (S6). See also Heilprin, J. (2005, March 30). The EPA

says children may be more vulnerable than adults to carcinogens. Associated Press: "Under the previous EPA guidelines, last revised in 1986, cancer risks to children were assumed to be no greater than to similarly exposed adults.... In the first such update in nearly 20 years, the EPA said children 2 years old and younger might be 10 times more vulnerable than adults to certain chemicals. Children between the ages of 2 and 16 might be three times more vulnerable to certain chemicals."

16. Hu, H. (2002). Human health and heavy metals exposure. In Michael McCally (Ed.), *Life Support: The Environment and Human Health* (chap. 4). Cambridge, MA: MIT Press. For more details, see http://www.cdc.gov/nceh/lead/lead.htm.

17. On the ubiquity of lead poisoning and failures to address it, see: Needleman, H. L. (1998). Childhood lead poisoning: The promise and abandonment of primary prevention. *American Journal of Public Health, 88* (12), 1871–1877. See also: New York State Department of Health. *Physician's Handbook on Lead Poisoning Prevention*, http://www.health.state.ny.us/nysdoh/lead/handbook/phc1.htm. On the connections between lead and crime, see: Needleman, H. L., C. McFarland, R. B. Ness, S. E. Fienberg, and M. J. Tobin. (2003). Bone lead levels in adjudicated delinquents: A case control study. *Neurotoxicology and Teratology, 24,* 711–717. On lead and violence, see summary of the evidence, including Needleman's work in: Organic Consumer's Association. (2004, August 5). Strong links between lead poisoning and violent behavior. *Rachel's Environment and Health News*, no. 797, http://www.organicconsumers.org/school/lead081004.cfm.

18. Mann, J. (2000, May 26). Chemicals and crime: A truly toxic effect. *Washington Post*. See also http://www.fluoridealert.org/fluoride-lead.htm.

19. Challem, J. (2003, January 18). Mean streets or mean minerals? *Nutrition Reporter*: "Nutritional deficiencies and imbalances can impair brain function and set the stage for delinquent and criminal behavior. Experts have found that the right supplements can improve behavior."

20. Mann, J. (2000, May 26). Needleman explores the link between chemicals and crime. *The Washington Post*, Final Edition. See also, Masters, R., M. Coplan, B. Hone, and J. Dykes, (2000). Association of silicofluoride treated water with elevated blood lead. *Neurotoxicology, 21* (6), 101–110.

21. Hu, Human health and heavy metals exposure. 72.

22. Trasande, L., et al. (2005). Public health and economic consequences of methyl mercury toxicity to the developing brain. *Environmental Health Perspectives, 113* (5), 590–596. Mount Sinai pediatrician and lead researcher Leonardo Trasande estimated that between 316,588 and 637,233 children are born each year with umbilical cord blood mercury levels linked to IQ loss. The research found that the IQ losses linked to mercury range from one-fifth of an IQ point to as much as 24 points. As an example, Trasande said about 4 percent of babies, or about 180,000,

are born each year with blood mercury levels between 7.13 and 15 micrograms per liter. That level of mercury, the group concluded, causes a loss of 1.6 IQ points. See also: Barrett, D. (2005, March 1). Mercury damage to babies costs billions, study says. *Environmental News Network, Associated Press.*

23. Olmstead, D. (2005, March 15). The age of autism: Mercury in the air. UPI, http://www.upi.com/view.cfm?StoryID=20050314-052518-7615r. The Age of Autism is an ongoing UPI series tracking the roots and rise of autism. See also: Ackerman, T. (2005, March 18). Study links mercury from power plants to autism. *Houston Chronicle*, http://www.enn.com/today.html?id=7359. The study reported a strong correlation between higher mercury release levels and autism. The Olmstead article contains an interview with the lead author of the study, Raymond F. Palmer, an associate professor at the University of Texas Health Science Center in San Antonio. In answer to a question concerning data at the national level, Palmer said, "the data that I have at the states level, the 50 states, is consistent with the same idea. States that are reporting the highest levels of mercury emissions also have the highest rates of developmental disorders including autism."

24. Mercury study identifies problem spots. (2005, March 9). *Environmental News Network, Associated Press.* A four-year study in the northeastern United States and eastern Canada, funded by the U.S. Department of Agriculture's Northeastern States Research Cooperative, identified several mercury "hot spots" and suggests that contamination by the toxic metal is more pervasive than originally thought. The nine hot spots—four of them in Maine, one in New York, another in Massachusetts, and three in Canada—represent areas in which high mercury levels have been recorded in fish, loons, eagles, and other animals. The data caused researchers to question whether mercury from the sky is wreaking havoc on forest ecosystems as well.

25. Heilprin, J. (2005, March 23). EPA chided for disregarding study of benefits from mercury curbs. Environmental News Network, Associated Press. In regard to the EPA's decision, Rep. Edward Markey (D-Mass.) said he was outraged that the EPA would suppress the Harvard study while claiming stricter controls would cost industry far more than the projected health benefits of its regulatory proposal, and Sen. John Kerry (D-Mass.) asked, "Why is the EPA suppressing the evidence that mercury pollution can be controlled better and faster?"

26. Laslo-Baker, D., M. Barrera, D. Knittel-Keren, E. Kozer, J. Wolpin, S. Khattak, R. Hackman, J. Rovet, and G. Koren. (2004). Child neurodevelopmental outcome and maternal occupational exposure to solvents. *Archives of Pediatrics and Adolescent Medicine, 158* (10), 956–961.

27. Rapp, D. (1992). *Is This Your Child?* New York: Perennial Currents; and Rapp, D. (2003). *Our Toxic World: A Wake Up Call.* Buffalo, NY: Environmental Medical Research Foundation.

28. Ontario College of Family Physicians (OCFP). (2004, April). *Pesticides Literature Review*. Toronto. The PDF is available at http://www.ocfp.on.ca/English/OCFP/Communications/CurrentIssues/Pesticides/default.asp?s=1. See in particular chapter 10, "Pesticide health effects and children." For a summary of the report, see OCFP's news release: OCFP. (2004, April 23). Comprehensive review of pesticide research confirms dangers. Toronto. The PDF is available at http://www.ocfp.on.ca/local/files/Communications/Current%20Issues/Pesticides/News%20Release.pdf. See also: Mitchell, A. (2004, April 24). Pesticides too harmful to use in any form, doctors warn. *Globe and Mail*. Some quotes: "children are far more vulnerable to the effects of pesticides than adults"; "no evidence that some pesticides are less dangerous than others"; "the profoundly negative effects of some chemicals can be passed down through generations."

29. Schmidt, C. W. (1999). Poisoning young minds. *Environmental Health Perspectives, 107* (6), 302–307. (http://ehp.niehs.nih.gov/docs/1999/107-6/focus.html.) Schmidt is an award-winning science writer with a large body of work in public health, pharmacology, toxicology, and environmental risk assessment.

30. Rapp, D. *Is this your child?* 244–248.

31. Landrigan, P. J., and J. Slutsky. (1982). Are learning disabilities linked to environmental toxins? Learning Disabilities Worldwide (LDW), http://www.ldam.org/ldinformation/resources/O1-04_LDToxins.html. The article also cites the earlier work of Needleman, Leviton, and Bellinger: (1982). Lead-associated intellectual deficit. *New England Journal of Medicine, 306* (6), 367.

32. Pollution Watch [a collaboration of Environmental Defence and the Canadian Environmental Law Association] (2004, December). Shattering the myth of pollution progress in Canada: A national report; and Mitchell, A. (2004, December 8). Canada losing pollution fight, report shows: From 1995 to 2002, toxic emissions pumped into air, water and land rose by 50 percent. *Globe and Mail*. Paul Muldoon, executive director of the Canadian Environmental Law Association, said: "There's this rhetoric that this problem has been resolved, but the data don't support that."

33. League of Conservation Voters (2003, January). *2003 Presidential Report Card*. Washington, DC: League of Conservation Voters, p. 3.

34. As reported in the *New Scientist* of April 2–8, 2005, pp. 8–11 (and widely reported elsewhere). The *New Scientist* editorial "Save the Humans," in this same issue (p. 5), called the message of the Millennium Ecosystem Assessment (MA) "explosive" and concluded: "The most compelling reason for acting on the MA stems from one of its chief conclusions: there is a clear link between healthy ecosystems and healthy humans. Destroy those ecosystems and our economies—and our quality of life—will suffer."

35. In February, the EPA's own inspector general said that the Bush administration overlooked health effects and sided with the electric industry in developing rules for cutting toxic mercury pollution. See: Heilprin, J. (2005, February 4). EPA overlooked health impact. Environmental News Network, Associated Press. In May the attorneys general of thirteen states entered a joint lawsuit against the EPA, suing for more stringent rules and less reliance on "market forces" (i.e., the buying and selling of pollution units). At least three similar lawsuits were planned by coalitions of environmental groups. See: Groups seek tougher EPA rules on mercury from power plants. (2005, May 18). Environmental News Network, Associated Press.

36. Report of the Union of Concerned Scientists (2004, March). Scientific Integrity in Policy Making: Investigation of the Bush Administration's Abuse of Science. UCS: Cambridge, MA, p. 2. The Union of Concerned Scientists (UCS) noted that these actions have consequences for human health, public safety, and community well-being. And they reported at length on specific incidents they were able to document that involved "air pollutants, heat-trapping emissions, reproductive health, drug resistant bacteria, endangered species, forest health, and military intelligence." The UCS also stated that "there is strong documentation of a wide-ranging effort to manipulate the government's scientific advisory system to prevent the appearance of advice that might run counter to the administration's political agenda." This included "appointing underqualified individuals to important advisory roles including childhood lead poisoning prevention and reproductive health; applying political litmus tests that have no bearing on a nominee's expertise or advisory role; appointing a non-scientist to a senior position in the president's scientific advisory staff; and dismissing highly qualified scientific advisors." The UCS further adduced evidence that the administration "often imposes restrictions on what government scientists can say or write about 'sensitive' topics. In this context, "sensitive" applies to issues that might provoke opposition from the administration's political and ideological supporters.

37. Needleman, H. L. and P. J. Landrigan (1995). *Raising Children Toxic Free: How To Keep Your Child Safe From Lead, Asbestos, Pesticides and Other Environmental Hazards.* Farrar, Straus and Giroux: New York.

38. See: Burstyn, V., and G. Sampson. (2005). Technoenvironmental assaults on childhood in America. In S. Olfman (Ed.), *Childhood Lost.*

39. California Safe Schools. (2005, April 12). Children's advocates celebrate six years of protecting student health: Reformed pesticide policy sets national model, http://www.calisafe.org.

CHAPTER 5

1. Pecora, N., J. P. Murray, and E. Wartella. (2006, in press). *Children and Television: 50 Years of Research.* Mahwah, NJ: Erlbaum Publishers.

2. U.S. Congress. (1952, June 3–December 5). House Committee on Interstate and Foreign Commerce. *Investigation of Radio and Television Programs.* Hearings and Report, 82nd Congress, 2nd Session. Washington, DC: U.S. Government Printing Office; U.S. Congress. (1955, April 6–7). Senate Committee of the Judiciary, Subcommittee to Investigate Juvenile Delinquency. *Juvenile Delinquency (Television Programs).* Hearing, 84th Congress, 1st Session. Washington, DC: U.S. Government Printing Office; and U.S. Congress. (2003, April 10). Senate Commerce Committee, Subcommittee on Science, Technology, and Space. *Neurobiological Research and the Impact of Media.* Hearing. Washington, DC: U.S. Government Printing Office.

3. Himmelweit, H. T., A. N. Oppenheim, and P. Vince. (1958). *Television and the Child: An Empirical Study of the Effects of Television on the Young.* London: Oxford University Press.

4. Schramm, W., J. Lyle, and E. B. Parker. (1961). *Television in the Lives of Our Children.* Stanford: Stanford University Press.

5. Himmelweit, Oppenheim, and Vince. *Television and the Child,* 17–18.

6. Ibid., 20.

7. Australia: Murray, J. P., and S. Kippax. (1977). Television diffusion and social behavior in three communities: A field experiment. *Australian Journal of Psychology, 29* (1), 31–43; Murray, J. P., and S. Kippax. (1978). Children's social behavior in three towns with differing television experience. *Journal of Communication, 28* (1), 19–29; Murray, J. P., and S. Kippax. (1979). From the early window to the late night show: International trends in the study of television's impact on children and adults. In L. Berkowitz (Ed.), *Advances in Experimental Social Psychology.* New York: Academic Press. Canada: Williams, T. M. (1986). *The Impact of Television: A Natural Experiment in Three Communities.* New York: Academic Press; MacBeth, T. (1996). *Tuning in to Young Viewers: Social Science Perspectives on Television.* Thousand Oaks, CA: Sage Publishers.

8. Bandura, A., D. Ross, and S. H. Ross. (1961). Transmission of aggression through imitation of aggressive models. *Journal of Abnormal and Social Psychology, 63* (3), 575–582; and Bandura, A., D. Ross, and S. H. Ross (1963). Imitation of film-mediated aggressive models. *Journal of Abnormal and Social Psychology, 66* (1), 3–11.

9. Berkowitz, L., and E. Rawlings. (1963). Effects of film violence on inhibitions against subsequent aggression. *Journal of Abnormal and Social Psychology, 66* (3), 405–412; and Berkowitz, L., and R. G. Geen. (1966). Film violence and the cue properties of available targets. *Journal of Personality and Social Psychology, 3* (5), 525–530.

10. U.S. Congress, *Investigation of Radio and Television Programs*; idem, *Juvenile Delinquency.*

11. Maccoby, E. (1954). Why do children watch television? *Public Opinion Quarterly, 18* (3), 239–244; Lazarsfeld, P. E. (1955). Why is so little

known about the effects of television on children and what can be done? *Public Opinion Quarterly, 19* (2), 243–251; and Cressey, P. G., and F. M. Thrasher. (1933). *Boys, Movies, and City Streets.* New York: Macmillan.

12. Baker, R. K., and S. J. Ball. (1969). *Mass Media and Violence: A Staff Report to the National Commission on the Causes and Prevention of Violence.* Washington, DC: U.S. Government Printing Office; Surgeon General's Scientific Advisory Committee on Television and Social Behavior. (1972). *Television and Growing Up: The Impact of Televised Violence.* Washington, DC: U.S. Government Printing Office; Murray, J. P. (1973). Television and violence: Implications of the surgeon general's research program. *American Psychologist, 28* (6), 472–478; National Institute of Mental Health. (1982). *Television and Behavior: Ten Years of Scientific Progress and Implications for the Eighties,* vol. 1, *Summary Report.* Washington, DC: U.S. Government Printing Office; Group for the Advancement of Psychiatry. (1982). *The Child and Television Drama: The Psychosocial Impact of Cumulative Viewing.* New York: Mental Health Materials Center; and Huston, A. C., E. Donnerstein, H. Fairchild, N. D. Feshbach, P. A. Katz, J. P. Murray, E. A. Rubinstein, B. Wilcox, and D. Zuckerman. (1992). *Big World, Small Screen: The Role of Television in American Society.* Lincoln: University of Nebraska Press.

13. National Institute of Mental Health, *Television and Behavior*; Pearl, D., L. Bouthilet, and J. Lazar (Eds.). (1982). *Television and Behavior: Ten Years of Scientific Progress and Implications for the Eighties,* vol. 2, *Technical Reviews.* Washington, DC: U.S. Government Printing Office.

14. National Institute of Mental Health, *Television and Behavior,* 10.

15. Huston et al., *Big World, Small Screen,* 136.

16. Murray, J. P. (1980). *Television and Youth: 25 Years of Research and Controversy.* Boys Town, NE: Boys Town Center for the Study of Youth Development; Pecora, Murray, and Wartella, *Children and Television.*

17. Himmelweit, Oppenheim, and Vince, *Television and the Child*; Schramm, Lyle, and Parker, *Television in the Lives of Our Children.*

18. McLeod, J. M., D. Atkin, and S. H. Chaffee. (1972). Adolescents, parents, and television use: Adolescent self-report measures from Maryland and Wisconsin samples. In G. A. Comstock and E. A. Rubinstein (Eds.), *Television and Social Behavior,* vol. 3, *Television and Adolescent Aggressiveness.* Washington, DC: U.S. Government Printing Office; McLeod, J. M., C. K. Atkin, and S. H. Chaffee. (1972). Adolescents, parents, and television use: Self-report and other measures from the Wisconsin sample. In G. A. Comstock and E. A. Rubinstein (Eds.), *Television and Social Behavior,* vol. 3; Dominick, J. R., and B. S. Greenberg. (1972). Attitudes toward violence: The interaction of television exposure, family attitudes, and social class. In Comstock and Rubinstein (Eds.), *Television and Social Behavior,* vol. 3; Robinson, J. P., and J. G. Bachman. (1972). Television viewing habits and aggression. In Comstock and Rubinstein (Eds.), *Television and Social Behavior,* vol. 3.

19. Atkin, C. K., B. S. Greenberg, F. Korzenny, and S. McDermott. (1979). Selective exposure to televised violence. *Journal of Broadcasting, 23* (1), 5–13.

20. Walker, K. B., and D. D. Morley. (1991). Attitudes and parental factors as intervening variables in the television violence–aggression relation. *Communication Research, 8* (2), 41–47.

21. Gerbner, G. (1970). Cultural indicators: The case of violence in television drama. *Annals of the American Academy of Political and Social Sciences, 388,* 69–81; Gerbner, G., L. Gross, M. Morgan, and N. Signorielli. (1994). Growing up with television: The cultivation perspective. In J. Bryant and D. Zillman (Eds.), *Media Effects: Advances in Theory and Research.* Hillsdale, NJ: Erlbaum Publishers.

22. Gerbner et al., Growing up with television, 30.

23. CBS study: Belson, W. (1978). *Television Violence and the Adolescent Boy.* Farnsborough, UK: Saxon House–Teakfield Limited; NBC study: Milavsky, J. R., R. C. Kessler, H. H. Stipp, and W. S. Rubens. (1982). *Television and Aggression: A Panel Study.* New York: Academic Press; and surgeon general's study: Lefkowitz, M., L. Eron, L. Walder, and L. R. Huesmann. (1972). Television violence and child aggression: A follow-up study. In G. A. Comstock and E. A. Rubinstein (Eds.), *Television and Social Behavior,* vol. 3; Huesmann, L. R., L. D. Eron, M. M. Lefkowitz, and L. O. Walder. (1984). Stability of aggression over time and generations. *Developmental Psychology, 20,* 1120–1134; Huesmann, L. R., and L. D. Eron (Eds.). (1986) *Television and the Aggressive Child: A Cross-National Comparison.* Hillsdale, NJ: Erlbaum Publishers.

24. Eron, L. D., L. O. Walder, and M. M. Lefkowitz. (1971). *Learning of Aggression in Children.* Boston: Little, Brown.

25. Kenny, D. A. (1984). The NBC study and television violence. *Journal of Communication, 34* (1), 176–182; Cook, T. D., D. A. Kendzierski, and S. A. Thomas. (1983). The implicit assumptions of television research: An analysis of the 1982 NIMH report on "Television and Behavior." *Public Opinion Quarterly, 47* (2), 161–201.

26. Eron, L. D. (1963). Relationship of TV viewing habits and aggressive behavior in children. *Journal of Abnormal and Social Psychology, 67,* 193–196; Eron, L. D. (1982). Parent–child interaction, television violence and aggression of children. *American Psychologist, 27,* 197–211; Lefkowitz et al., Television violence and child aggression; Huesmann et al., Stability of aggression over time.

27. Lefkowitz et al., Television violence and child aggression.

28. Huesmann et al., Stability of aggression over time.

29. Bandura, Ross, and Ross, Transmission of aggression; idem, Imitation of film-mediated aggressive models; and, for example, Berkowitz and Rawlings, Effects of film violence.

30. Liebert, R. M., and B. A. Baron. (1972). Short term effects of television aggression on children's aggressive behavior. In J. P. Murray,

E. A. Rubinstein, and G. A. Comstock (Eds.), *Television and Social Behavior*, vol. 2, *Television and Social Learning*. Washington, DC: U.S. Government Printing Office.

31. Ekman, P., R. M. Liebert, W. Friesen, R. Harrison, C. Zlatchin, E. V. Malmstrom, and R. A. Baron. (1972). In G. A. Comstock, E. A. Rubinstein, and J. P. Murray (Eds.), *Television and Social Behavior*, vol. 5, *Television's Effects: Further Explorations*. Washington, DC: U.S. Government Printing Office.

32. Osborn, D. K., and R. C. Endsley. (1971). Emotional reactions of young children to TV violence. *Child Development, 42* (1), 321–331; Cline, V. B., R. G. Croft, and S. Courrier. (1973). Desensitization of children to television violence. *Journal of Personality and Social Psychology, 27,* 360–365.

33. Ellis, G. T., and F. Sekyra. (1972). The effect of aggressive cartoons on behavior of first grade children. *Journal of Psychology, 81,* 37–43; Hapkiewitz, W. G., and A. H. Roden. (1971). The effect of aggressive cartoons on children's interpersonal play. *Child Development, 42,* 1583–1585; Lovaas, O. I. (1961). Effect of exposure to symbolic aggression on aggressive behavior. *Child Development, 32,* 37–44; Mussen, P., and E. Rutherford. (1961). Effects of aggressive cartoons on children's aggressive play. *Journal of Abnormal and Social Psychology, 62* (2), 461–464; Ross, L. B. (1972). The effect of aggressive cartoons on the group play of children. Miami University, doctoral dissertation.

34. Drabman, R. S., and M. H. Thomas. (1974). Does media violence increase children's toleration of real-life aggression? *Developmental Psychology, 10,* 418–421; Thomas, M. H., R. W. Horton, E. C. Lippincott, and R. S. Drabman. (1977). Desensitization to portrayals of real life aggression as a function of television violence. *Journal of Personality and Social Psychology, 35* (6), 450–458.

35. Gadow, K. D., and J. Sprafkin. (1993). Television violence and children with emotional and behavioral disorders. *Journal of Emotional and Behavioral Disorders, 1* (1), 54–63; Grimes, T., E. Vernberg, and T. Cathers. (1997). Emotionally disturbed children's reactions to violent media segments. *Journal of Health Communication, 2* (3), 157–168.

36. Stein, A. H., and L. K. Friedrich. (1972). Television content and young children's behavior. In Murray, Rubinstein, and Comstock (Eds.), *Television and Social Behavior*, vol. 2; Friedrich, L. K., and A. H. Stein. (1975). Aggressive and prosocial television programs and the natural behavior of preschool children. *Monographs of the Society for Research in Child Development, 38* (4), no. 151.

37. Murray and Kippax, Television diffusion and social behavior; idem, Children's social behavior.

38. Williams, *Impact of Television*; Macbeth, *Tuning in to Young Viewers*.

39. Himmelweit, Oppenheim, and Vince, *Television and the Child*; and Schramm, Lyle, and Parker, *Television in the Lives of Our Children*.

40. Murray, *Television and Youth*; and Joy, L. A., M. Kimball, and M. L. Zabrack. (1986). Television exposure and children's aggressive behavior. In Williams (Ed.), *Impact of Television*.

41. Hearold, S. (1986). A synthesis of 1043 effects of television on social behavior. In G. Comstock (Ed.), *Public Communication and Behavior*, vol. 1 (pp. 65–133). New York: Academic Press; Murray, J. P. (1994). The impact of televised violence. *Hofstra Law Review, 22* (4), 809–825; Paik, H., and G. A. Comstock. (1994). The effects of television violence on antisocial behavior: A meta-analysis. *Communication Research, 21* (4), 516–546.

42. Bandura, A. (1962). Social learning through imitation. In M. R. Jones (Ed.), *Nebraska Symposium on Motivation*. Lincoln: University of Nebraska Press; Bandura, A. (1969). Social-learning theory of identificatory processes. In D. A. Goslin (Ed.), *Handbook of Socialization Theory and Research*. Chicago: Rand McNally; Berkowitz, L. (1962). *Aggression: A Social Psychological Analysis*. New York: McGraw-Hill; Berkowitz, L. (1965). Some aspects of observed aggression. *Journal of Personality and Social Psychology, 2,* 359–365.

43. Cline, Croft, and Courrier, Desensitization of children; Osborn and Endsley, Emotional reactions of young children; Zillmann, D. (1971). Excitation transfer in communication-mediated aggressive behavior. *Journal of Experimental Social Psychology, 7,* 419–434; Zillmann, D. (1982). Television viewing and arousal. In Pearl, Bouthilet, and Lazar (Eds.), *Television and Behavior*, vol. 2, *Technical Reviews*. Washington, DC: U.S. Government Printing Office.

44. Damasio, A. R. (1994). *Descartes' Error: Emotion, Reason, and the Human Brain*. New York: Putnam; Damasio, A. R. (1999). *The Feeling of What Happens: Body and Emotion in the Making of Consciousness*. New York: Harcourt Brace; Kosslyn, S. M., and O. Koenig. (1995). *Wet Mind: The New Cognitive Neuroscience*. New York: Free Press; LeDoux, J. (1996). *The Emotional Brain: The Mysterious Underpinnings of Emotional Life*. New York: Simon and Schuster; LeDoux, J. E. and W. Hirst (Eds.). (1986). *Mind and Brain: Dialogues in Cognitive Neuroscience*. New York: Cambridge University Press; Ornstein, R. (1997). *The Right Mind: Making Sense of the Hemispheres*. New York: Harcourt Brace; Panksepp, J. (1998). *Affective Neuroscience: The Foundations of Human and Animal Emotions*. New York: Oxford University Press; Steward, O. (2000). *Functional Neuroscience*. New York: Springer; Anderson, D. R., J. Bryant, J. P. Murray, M. Rich, M. J. Rivkin, and D. Zillmann. (2006, in press). Brain imaging—An introduction to a new approach to studying media processes and effects. *Media Psychology, 8* (1).

45. National Research Council. (1993). *Understanding and Preventing Violence*. Washington, DC: National Academy Press, pp. 115–116.

46. Osborn and Endsley, Emotional reactions of young children; Zillmann, Television viewing and arousal; Bryant and Zillmann, *Media Effects*.

47. Ekman, P., and R. J. Davidson. (1993). Voluntary smiling changes in regional brain activity. *Psychological Science, 4* (5), 342–345; Ekman, P., and R. J. Davidson. (1994). *The Nature of Emotion: Fundamental Questions.* New York: Oxford University Press; Ekman, P., R. J. Davidson, and W. J. Friesen. (1990). The Duchenne smile: Emotional expression and brain physiology II. *Journal of Personality and Social Psychology, 58,* 342–353; Davidson, R. J., P. Ekman, C. Saron, J. Senulis, and W. V. Friesen. (1990). Emotional expression and brain physiology I: Approach/withdrawal and cerebral asymmetry. *Journal of Personality and Social Psychology, 58,* 330–341.

48. Davidson, R. J., and A. J. Tomarken. (1989). Laterality and emotion: An electrophysiological approach. In F. Boller and J. Grafman (Eds.), *Handbook of Neuropsychology,* pp. 419–441. Amsterdam: Elsevier Publishers; Ornstein, R. (1997). *The Right Mind: Making Sense of the Hemispheres.* New York: Harcourt Brace.

49. Murray, J. P., M. Liotti, P. Ingmundson, H. S. Mayberg, Y. Pu, F. Zamarripa, Y. Liu, M. G. Woldorff, J. H. Gao, and P. T. Fox. (2006, in press). Children's brain activations while viewing televised violence revealed by fMRI. *Media Psychology, 8* (1); Murray, J. P., and M. Liotti. (2005). Risonanza magnetica funzionale dell'encefalo in bambini che assistono a scean de violenza televisiva. In G. Forti and M. Bertolino (Eds.), *La televisione del crimine,* pp. 465–469. Milan: Vita e Pensiero; Murray, J. P. (2001). TV violence and brainmapping in children. *Psychiatric Times, 17* (10), 70–71.

50. Talairach, J., and P. Tournoux. (1988). *Co-Planar Sterotaxic Atlas of the Human Brain.* New York: Thieme Medical Publishers.

CHAPTER 6

1. Sullivan, M. (2004, April). FDA wants new warnings on 10 antidepressants. *Clinical Psychiatry News, 1,* 8.

2. See chapter 9 in this volume, by L. Diller.

3. Angell, M. (2004). *The Truth about the Drug Companies: How They Deceive Us and What to Do about It.* New York: Random House; Healy, D. (2003). *Let Them Eat Prozac.* Toronto: James Lorimer and Co.

4. Rosen, G. (1968). *Madness in Society: Chapters in the Historical Sociology of Mental Illness.* New York: Harper and Row.

5. Ibid.

6. Fromm, E. (1970). *The Crisis of Psychoanalysis.* Greenwich, CT: Fawcett Premier Books.

7. Lurmann, T. M. (2000). *Of Two Minds: An Anthropologist Looks at American Psychiatry.* New York: Random House.

8. Talbott, J. (2004). Lessons learned about the chronic mentally ill since 1955. *Psychiatric Services, 55* (10), 1152–1159.

9. Valenstein, E. (1988). *Blaming the Brain*. New York: Free Press.

10. Healy, *Let Them Eat Prozac*.

11. American Psychiatric Association. (1994). *Diagnostic and Statistical Manual of Mental Disorders*, 4th ed. Washington, DC.

12. This act was originally created in 1975 and called the Education For All Handicapped Children Act. It was amended in 1997 and given its present name, Individuals with Disabilities Education Act (IDEA).

13. Healy, *Let Them Eat Prozac*.

14. Ibid.

15. Angell, *Truth about the Drug Companies*.

16. Ibid., 7–10.

17. Ibid.

18. Healy, *Let Them Eat Prozac*.

19. Horton, R. (2004, March 11). The dawn of McScience. *New York Review of Books, 51* (4), 7–9.

20. Healy, *Let Them Eat Prozac*.

21. Ibid., 192–194.

22. Ibid.

23. Gorman, C. (2005, February 28). Can the FDA heal itself? *Time*, 59.

24. Healy, *Let Them Eat Prozac*.

25. Sherer, R. (2002, May). Does DTC advertising benefit patients? *Psychiatric Times, 1*, 68.

26. Fuhrmans, V., and G. Naik. (2002, March 15). In Europe, prescription-drug ads are banned—and health costs lower. *Wall Street Journal*, B1, B4.

27. Todd, J., and Bohart, A. C. (1999). *Foundations of Clinical and Counseling Psychology*. Prospect Heights, IL: Waveland.

28. Ibid.

29. Coddington, D., E. Fischler, K. Moore, and R. Clarke. (2000). *Beyond Managed Care*. San Francisco: Jossey-Bass.

30. Abboud, L. (2004, March 24). Should family doctors treat serious mental illness? *Wall Street Journal*, D1, D4.

31. Tesoriero, H. (2004, October 7). New drug problem: Getting antidepressants. *Wall Street Journal*, D1, D7.

32. Landers, S. (2004, March 1). Experts urge caution in using SSRIs for depressed kids. *AMA News*, 27.

33. Fischer S. and R. Fischer, cited in Healy, *Let Them Eat Prozac*, p. 286.

34. Healy, *Let Them Eat Prozac*, p. 286.

35. Albert, T. (2004, June 28). Lawsuit claims Glaxo hid Paxil findings. *American Medical News*, 7–8.

36. Landro, L. (2004, June 17). How to find the latest results of clinical trials. *Wall Street Journal*, D1, D3.

CHAPTER 7

1. The argument presented in this chapter is the result of my close collaboration with Stanley Greenspan. See: Greenspan, S., and S. Shanker. (2004). *The First Idea: How Symbols, Language and Intelligence Evolved from Our Primate Ancestors to Modern Humans.* New York: Da Capo Press. In *The First Idea*, Greenspan and I develop this thesis in much greater detail. This research has been fully funded by the Harris Research Institute.

2. This report was Prepared with great care by the National Institute of Mental Health and the Substance Abuse and Mental Health Services Administration. See: *Mental Health: A Report of the Surgeon General.* (1999). Washington, DC: U.S. Government Printing Office, chap. 1.

3. Ibid., chap. 3.

4. Wittgenstein, L. (1953). *Philosophical Investigations.* Oxford: Basil Blackwell, p. 580.

5. Although, to be sure, there have been many relapses into viewing madness as the result of demons or sin. See: Midelfort, E. (1999). *A History of Madness in the Sixteenth Century.* Stanford: Stanford University Press; Porter, R. (2002). *Madness: A Brief History.* Oxford: Oxford University Press.

6. Simon, B. (1978). *Mind and Madness in Ancient Greece: The Classical Roots of Modern Psychiatry.* Ithaca, NY: Cornell University Press.

7. Ibid., 218.

8. Hippocrates. (1974). On the Sacred Disease. In S. Diamond (Ed.), *The Roots of Psychology: A Sourcebook in the History of Ideas.* New York: Basic Books, p. 160; Jouanna, J. (1999). *Hippocrates.* M. B. DeBevoise (trans). Baltimore: Johns Hopkins University Press.

9. Hippocrates, *On the Sacred Disease*, 160.

10. Ibid., 161.

11. Jouanna, *Hippocrates.*

12. Temkin, O. (1991). *Hippocrates in a World of Pagans and Christians.* Baltimore: Johns Hopkins University Press.

13. Rosen, G. (1968). *Madness in Society: Chapters in the Historical Sociology of Mental Illness.* New York: Harper and Row.

14. Greenspan and Shanker, *First Idea*, chaps. 1 and 2.

15. Greenspan, S., and S. Wieder, S. (1998). Developmental patterns and outcomes in infants and children with disorders in relating and communicating: A chart review of 200 cases of children with autistic spectrum diagnoses. *Journal of Developmental and Learning Disorders, 1*, 87–141; Greenspan, S., and S. Wieder. (2005). *Engaging Autism.* Cambridge, MA: Perseus Books.

16. Greenspan and Shanker, *First Idea*, chap. 2.

CHAPTER 8

1. I thank four people for their invaluable support in putting this chapter together. First, my heartfelt thanks to Ritt Goldstein, a courageous web and print journalist who has alerted millions of people to the dangers of "big pharma." Next, I thank my friends John Marx, professor of medical sociology at the University of Pittsburgh, and Henry Palmer III, CEO of the Centre for Community Change International and clinical professor at Southern New Hampshire University, for their illuminating feedback and references. Finally, warm thanks to my wife, Sharna Olfman, who wrestled through successive drafts with me until we finally got it right.

2. Erikson, E. (1956). The problem of ego identity. *Journal of the American Psychoanalytic Association, 4*, 56–121; Erikson, E. (1950). *Childhood and Society*. New York: Norton.

3. Burston, D. (2006). Psychological Issues. In M. Eagle (Ed.). *Ego, Ethics and Evolution: Erik Erikson and the Impossible Profession*, Westport, CT: International Universities Press.

4. Shapiro, E. and G. Fromm (1999). Erik Erikson's clinical theory. In B. J. K. Sadock (Ed.), *Comprehensive Textbook of Psychiatry*. New York: Williams and Wilkins.

5. Kirk, S. and H. Kutchins (1992). *The Selling of the DSM: The Rhetoric of Science in Psychiatry*. Hawthorne, NY: Aldine de Gruyter.; Marius, R. (1999). *Martin Luther: The Christian between God and Death*. Cambridge, MA: Harvard University Press; Kirk, S. K. (1992). *The Selling of the DSM: The Rhetoric of Science in Psychiatry*. Hawthorne, NY: Aldine de Gruyter.

6. Kirk, *Selling of the DSM*.

7. Spiegel, A. (2005, January 3). The dictionary of disorder: How one man revolutionized psychiatry. *New Yorker*, 56–66.

8. Mohr, W. K. (2001). Bipolar disorder in children. *Journal of Psychosocial Nursing and Mental Health Services, 39* (3), 12–23; Biederman, J. (2003). Pediatric bipolar disorder coming of age. *Biological Psychiatry, 53* (11), 931–934; Wozniak, J. (2003). Pediatric bipolar disorder: The new perspective on severe mood dysfunction in children. *Journal of Child and Adolescent Psychopharmacology, 13* (4), 441–451.

9. Kowatch, R. A., M. Fristad, B. Birmaher, K. D. Wagner, R. L. Findling, M. Hellander, and the Child Psychiatric Workgroup on Bipolar Disorder. (2005). Treatment guidelines for children and adolescents with bipolar disorder. *Journal of the American Academy of Child and Adolescent Psychiatry, 43* (3), 213–235.

10. Child and Adolescent Bipolar Foundation (CABF) website, http://www.bpkids.org.

11. Lewinsohn, P. M., J. R. Seeley, and D. M. Klein. (2003). Bipolar disorder in adolescents: Epidemiology and suicidal behavior. In B. Geller

and M. P. DelBello (Eds.), *Bipolar Disorder in Childhood and Early Adolescence.* New York: Guilford Press, p. 7–24

12. Kowatch et al., *Treatment Guidelines for Children.*

13. McLellan, J. (2005, March). Editorial. *Journal of the American Academy of Child and Adolescent Psychiatry, 44,* 236–239.

14. Kowatch et al., *Treatment Guidelines for Children.*

15. Knopf, A. (2005). Polypharmacy: New data evaluates prescribing patterns in children and adolescents. *Brown University Child and Adolescent Psychopharmacology Update, 7* (4), 1, 5–7; Vitiello, B. (2005). Pharmcoepidemiology and pediatric psychopharmacological research. *Journal of Child and Adolescent Psychopharmacology, 15* (1), 10–11; Zito, J. M. S. (2005). Recent child pharmacoepidemiological findings. *Journal of Child and Adolescent Psychopharmacology, 15* (1), 5–9.

16. Sinaikin, P. (2004, February). How I learned to stop worrying and love the *DSM. Psychiatric Times,* 103–105.

17. Goffman, I. (1961). *Asylums.* Chicago: University of Chicago Press; Scheff, T. (1966). *Being Mentally Ill: A Sociological Theory.* Chicago: Aldine.

18. Treacher, A. B. (1980). Towards a critical history of the psychiatric profession. In D. Ingleby (Ed.), *Critical Psychiatry: The Politics of Mental Health.* New York: Pantheon Books.

19. Karen, R. (1998). *Becoming Attached: First Relationships and How They Shape Our Capacity to Love.* New York: Oxford University Press; Greenspan, S. L. (1999). *Building Healthy Minds.* New York: Da Capo Press; Schore, A. (2003). *Affect Regulation and the Repair of the Self.* New York: Norton; Gerhardt, S. (2004). *Why Love Matters: How Affection Shapes a Baby's Brain.* New York: Brunner-Routledge.

20. Hewlett, S. A. W. (1998). *The War against Parents: What We Can Do for America's Beleaguered Moms and Dads.* New York: Houghton Mifflin.

21. Burstyn, V. (2005). Techno-environmental assaults on children's health. In S. Olfman (Ed.), *Childhood Lost: How American Culture Is Failing Our Kids.* Westport, CT: Praeger.

22. Olfman, S. (2003). All work and no play: How educational reforms and harming our preschoolers. In S. Olfman (Ed.), *Childhood in America.* Westport, CT: Praeger; De Gaetano, G. (2004). *Parenting Well in a Media Age: Keeping Our Kids Human.* Fawnskin, CA: Personhood Press.

23. Breggin, P. (1999). *Reclaiming Our Children: A Healing Plan for a Nation in Crisis.* Cambridge, MA: Perseus Books.

24. Burston, D. (2000). *The Crucible of Experience: R. D. Laing and the Crisis of Psychotherapy.* Cambridge, MA: Harvard University Press.

25. Cohen, D. (1997). Psychoiatrogenics: Introducing chloropromazine in psychiatry. *Review of Existential Psychology and Psychiatry, 23* (1–3), 206–233.

26. Whitaker, R. (2002). *Mad in America: Bad Science, Bad Medicine and the Mistreatment of the Mentally Ill*. New York: Basic Books.

27. Ibid., 226–232.

28. Lenzer, J. (2004, June 19). Bush plans to screen the whole population for mental illness. *British Medical Journal, 328*; Waters, R. (2005). Medicating Aliah. *Mother Jones*, 50–55, 86–87.

29. Whitaker, *Mad in America*; Waters, Medicating Aliah; Healy, D. (2003). *Let Them Eat Prozac*. Toronto: James Lorimer and Co.

30. Waters, Medicating Aliah; Healy, *Let Them Eat Prozac*; Hughes, C. W., G. J. Emslie, L. M. Crimson, K. D. Wagner, B. Birmaher, B. Geller, S. R. Pliszka, N. D. Ryan, M. Strober, M. Trivedi, M. Toprac, A. Sedillo, M. Llana, M. Lopez, and A. J. Rush. (1999). The Texas Children's Medication Algorithm Project: Report of the Texas Consensus Panel on Medication Treatment of Childhood Major Depressive Disorder. *Journal of the American Academy of Child and Adolescent Psychiatry, 38* (11).

31. Healy, *Let Them Eat Prozac*.

32. Waters, *Medicating Aliah*.

33. Hughes et al., Texas Children's Medication Algorithm Project.

34. Lenzer, *Bush Plans to Screen*; Waters, *Medicating Aliah*; Szasz, T. (2004, July/August). Pharmacracy in America. *Society*, 54–58.

35. Levine, M. (2002). *A Mind at a Time*. New York: Simon and Schuster.

36. Burstyn, V., Techno-environmental assaults.

37. Kirsner, D. (2000). *Unfree Associations: Inside Psychoanalytic Institutes*. London: Process Press.

CHAPTER 9

1. Methylphenidate/amphetamine yearly production quota (1980–2000). (2000). Washington, DC: Office of Public Affairs, Drug Enforcement Administration, Department of Justice.

2. Hallowell, E. M., et al. (1994). *Driven to Distraction: Recognizing and Coping with Attention Deficit Disorder from Childhood through Adulthood*. New York: Pantheon Books.

3. Hughes, A. L. (1994). Epidemiology of amphetamine use in the United States. In A. K. Cho and D. S. Segal (Eds.), *Amphetamine and Its Analogs: Pharmacology, Toxicology and Abuse*. San Diego: Academic Press, pp. 439–457.

4. Swanson, J. M., et al. (1993). Effect of stimulant medication on children with attention deficit disorder: A review of reviews. *Exceptional Children, 60*, 154–161.

5. Kaplan, R. D. (2003, April). A tale of two colonies. *Atlantic Monthly*.

6. Hughes, Epidemiology of amphetamine use.

7. UN International Narcotics Control Board. (2000). *Report of the UN International Narcotics Control Board*. New York: UN Publications.

8. Hughes, Epidemiology of amphetamine use.

9. Ibid.

10. Silvertone. T. (1993). The place of appetite-suppressant drugs in the treatment of obesity. In A. J. Stunkard and T. A. Wadden (Eds.), *Obesity: Theory and Therapy*, 2nd ed. New York: Raven Press.

11. Bradley, C. (1937). The behavior of children receiving Benzedrine. *American Journal of Psychiatry, 94*, 577–585.

12. Greenhill, L. L. (1991). Methylphenidate in the clinical office practice of child psychiatry. In L. L. Greenhill and B. B. Osman (Eds.), *Ritalin, Theory and Patient Management* New York: Mary Ann Liebert, Inc.

13. Methylphenidate/amphetamine yearly production quota (1980–2000).

14. IMS Health. (2000). Plymouth Meeting, PA (personal communication).

15. Methylphenidate/amphetamine yearly production quota (2004). (2005). Washington, DC: Office of Public Affairs, Drug Enforcement Administration, Department of Justice.

16. Safer, D. J., et al. (1996). Increased methylphenidate usage for attention deficit disorder in the 1990s. *Pediatrics, 98*, 1084–1088.

17. Per capita state methylphenidate prescriptions, 2001. (2001). Washington, DC: Office of Public Affairs, Drug Enforcement Administration, Department of Justice.

18. UN International Narcotics Control Board. (2000). *Report of the UN International Narcotics Control Board*. New York: UN Publications.

19. Pliszka, S. R., et al. (1996). Catecholamines in attention-deficit hyperactivity disorder: Current perspectives. *Journal of the American Academy of Child and Adolescent Psychiatry, 35*, 264–272.

20. Diller, L. H. (1998). *Running on Ritalin: A Physician Reflects on Children, Society and Performance in a Pill*. New York: Bantam Books, 106–107.

21. Swanson et al., Effect of stimulant medication.

22. Satterfield, J. H., et al. (1987). Therapeutic interventions to prevent delinquency in hyperactive boys. *Journal of the American Academy of Child and Adolescent Psychiatry, 26*, 56–64.

23. MTA Cooperative Group. (2004). NIMH multimodal study of ADHD follow-up: 24-month outcomes of treatment strategies for attention-deficit/hyperactivity disorder. *Pediatrics, 113*, 754–761.

24. Rapoport, J. L., et al. (1980). Dextroamphetamine: Its cognitive and behavioral effects in normal and hyperactive boys and normal men. *Archives of General Psychiatry, 37*, 933–943.

25. Bradley, Children receiving Benzedrine.

26. Rapoport et al., Dextroamphetamine.

27. Swanson et al., Effect of stimulant medication.

28. MTA Cooperative Group. (2004). NIMH treatment study of ADHD follow-up: Changes in effectiveness and growth after the end of treatment. *Pediatrics, 113,* 762–770.

29. Rush, C. R., et al. (2001). Reinforcing and subject-related effects of methylphenidate and d-amphetamine in non-drug abusing humans. *Journal of Clinical Psychopharmacology, 21,* 273–286.

30. Martin, W. R., et al. (1971). Physiologic, subjective, and behavioral effects of amphetamine, methamphetamine, ephedrine, phenmetrazine and methylphenidate in man. *Clinical Pharmacological Therapy, 12,* 245–258.

31. In 2003 and 2004, the newspapers of Harvard and the universities of Wisconsin, Virginia, and Colorado all reported increased use on campus of illegally obtained pharmaceutical methylphenidate and amphetamine, especially during exam time.

32. Volkow, N. D., et al. (1995). Is methylphenidate like cocaine? Studies on their pharmacokinetics and distribution in the human brain. *Archives of General Psychiatry, 52,* 456–463.

33. Strakowski, S. M., et al. (1998). Progressive behavioral response to repeated d-amphetamine challenge: Further evidence for sensitization in humans. *Biological Psychiatry, 44,* 1171–1177.

34. Lambert, N. M., et al. (1998). Prospective study of tobacco smoking and substance dependencies among samples of ADHD and non-ADHD participants. *Journal of Learning Disabilities, 31,* 533–544.

35. Wilens, T. E., et al. (2003). Does stimulant therapy of attention-deficit/hyperactivity disorder beget later substance abuse? A meta-analytic review of the literature. *Pediatrics, 111,* 179–185.

36. Barkley, R. A., et al. (2003). Does the treatment of attention-deficit/hyperactivity disorder with stimulants contribute to drug use/abuse? A 13-year prospective study. *Pediatrics, 111,* 97–109.

37. "For Preventing The Children of Poor People in Ireland From Being A Burden to Their Parents or Country, and For Making Them Beneficial to The Public," Jonathan Swift suggested ironically that "young healthy child" of "a year old" would have made "a most delicious, nourishing, and wholesome food, whether stewed, roasted, baked, or boiled."

38. New Federal Law Outlaws Schools from Forcing Parents to Drug Kids/IDEA 2004, www.Ablechild.org.

39. Hallowell, *Driven to Distraction.*

40. Michelson, D., A. J. Allen, J. Busner et al. (2002). Once-daily atomoxetine treatment for children and adolescents with attention deficit hyperactivity disorder: A randomized, placebo-controlled study. *American Journal of Psychiatry, 159* (11), 1896–1901.

CHAPTER 10

1. Rutter, M. (2005). Environmentally-mediated risks for psychopathology: Research strategies and findings. *Journal of the American Academy*

of Child and Adolescent Psychology, 44 (1), 3–18; Hammen, C., P. Brennan, and J. Shih. (2004). Family discord and stress predictors and other disorders in adolescent children of depressed and non-depressed mothers. *Journal of the American Academy of Child and Adolescent Psychiatry, 43* (8), 994–1002; Brennan, P., R. Le Brocque, and C. Hammen. (2003). Maternal depression, parent–child relationships, and resilient outcomes in adolescence. *Journal of the American Academy of Child and Adolescent Psychiatry, 42* (12), 1469–1477; Diamond, G., B. Reis, G. Diamond et al. (2002). Attachment-based family therapy for depressed adolescents: A treatment development study. *Journal of the American Academy of Child and Adolescent Psychiatry, 41* (10), 1190–1196; Sund, A., and L. Wichstrom. (2002). Insecure attachments as a risk factor for future depressive symptoms in early adolescence. *Journal of the American Academy of Child and Adolescent Psychiatry, 41* (12), 1478–1485; Kiser, L., E. Ostoja, and D. Pruitt. (1998). Dealing with stress and trauma in families. *Child and Adolescent Psychiatry Clinics of North America, 7* (1), 87–103; Field, T. (1994). The effects of mother's physical and emotional unavailability on emotion regulation. In N. Fox (Ed.), *Development of Emotion Regulation: Biological and Behavioral Considerations* (pp. 208–227). Monographs for the Society for Research in Child Development, no. 240.

2. Healy, D. (1999). The three faces of the antidepressants: A critical commentary on the clinical-economic context of diagnosis. *Journal of Nervous Mental Disorders, 187*, 174–180.

3. Rutter, Environmentally-mediated risks for psychopathology.

4. American Academy of Child and Adolescent Psychiatry. (1998, August). The depressed child. Handout no. 4.

5. American Psychiatric Association. (2000). Practice guidelines for the treatment of patients with major depressive disorder (rev.). *American. Journal of Psychiatry, 157* (4)S.

6. Vitiello, B., and S. Swedo. (2004). Antidepressant medications in children. *New England Journal of Medicine, 350* (15), 1489–1491.

7. Birmaher, B., N. Ryan, D. Williamson, D. Brent, J. Kaufman, R. Dahl et al. (1996). Childhood and adolescent depression: A review of the past 10 years. Part I. *Journal of the American Academy of Child and Adolescent Psychiatry, 35* (11), 1427–1439.

8. Ibid.

9. Zito, J., D. Safer, S. dos Reis, J. Gardner, M. Boles, and F. Lynch. (2000). Trends in the prescribing of psychotropic medications to preschoolers. *JAMA, 283* (8), 1025–1030.

10. Jensen, P., V. Bhatara, B. Vitiello, K. Hoagwood, M. Feil, and L. Burke. (1999). Psychoactive medication prescribing practices for U.S. children: Gaps between research and clinical practice. *Journal of the American Academy of Child and Adolescent Psychiatry, 38* (5), 557–565.

11. Albert, T. (2004, June 6). Lawsuit claims Glaxo hid Paxil findings, Amednews.com (on-line newspaper published by the AMA);

Splete, H. (2004). Anti-depressant use soars for preschool girls, boys. *Clinical Psychiatry News, 52* (5), 1.

12. Johnson, L. (2004, May 17). Behavioral drugs for kids on the rise. *San Francisco Chronicle.*

13. Angell, M. (2004). *The Truth about the Drug Companies.* New York: Random House, chaps. 1 and 2.

14. Bartlett, D., and Steele, J. (2004). *Critical Care.* New York: Doubleday, chap. 2.

15. Jellinek, M. (1999). Changes in the practice of child and adolescent psychiatry: Are our patients better served? *Journal of the American Academy of Child and Adolescent Psychiatry, 38* (2), 115–117.

16. Jensen et al., Psychoactive medication prescribing practices.

17. Greenhill, L. (2003). Introduction—Assessment of safety in pediatric psychopharmacology. *Journal of the American Academy of Child and Adolescent Psychiatry, 42* (6), 625–626; Greenhill, L., B. Vitiello, M. Riddle, P. Fisher, E. Shockey, J. March, J. Levine et al. (2003). Review of safety assessment methods used in pediatric psychopharmacology. *Journal of the American Academy of Child and Adolescent Psychiatry, 42* (6), 627–633.

18. Food and Drug Administration. (2004, October 15). FDA Public Health Advisory: Suicidality in children and adolescents being treated with antidepressants, www.fda.gov/cder/drug/antidepressants/SSRI-PHA200410.htm.

19. Dulcan, M., J. Bregman, E. Weller, and R. Weller. (2001). Treatment of child and adolescent disorders. In A. Schatzberg and C. Nemeroff (Eds.), *Essentials of Clinical Psychopharmacology* (chap. 22). Washington, DC: APA Press.

20. Bolling, M., and R. Kohlenberg. (2004). Reasons for quitting serotonin reuptake inhibitor therapy: Paradoxical psychological side effects and patient satisfaction. *Psychotherapy and Psychosomatics, 73,* 380–385.

21. This phenomenon, although it has not been widely written about, is in fact described in a study that discusses a biologically based loss of motivation in children on SSRIs: Garland, J., and E. Baerg. (2001). Amotivational syndrome associated with selective serotonin reuptake inhibitors in children and adolescents. *Journal of the American Academy of Child and Adolescent Psychiatry, 11* (2), 181–186.

22. Vitiello and Swedo, Antidepressant medications in children.

23. Ibid.; Whittington, C., T. Kendall, and S. Pilling. (2005). Are the SSRI's and atypical antidepressants safe and effective for children and adolescents? *Current Opinions in Psychiatry, 18* (1), 21–25; Whittington, C., T. Kendall, P. Fonagy, D. Cottrell, A. Cotgrove, and E. Boddington. (2004). Selective serotonin reuptake inhibitors in childhood depression: Systematic review of published vs. unpublished data. *Lancet, 363,* 1341–1345.

24. Zito, J., A. Derivan, and L. Greenhill. (2004). Making research data available: An ethical imperative demonstrated by the SSRI debacle. *Journal of the American Academy of Child and Adolescent Psychiatry, 43* (5),

512–514; Als-Nielsen, B., W. Chen, C. Gluud, and L. Kjaergard. (2003). Association of funding and conclusions in randomized drug trials: A reflection of treatment effect or adverse events? *JAMA, 290*, 921–928.

25. Office of the N.Y. State Attorney General Eliot Spitzer. (2004, June 18). Press release, available at www.oag.state.ny.us/press/2004/jun/jun18a.

26. Harris, G. (2004, September 10). Lawmaker says FDA held back drug data. *New York Times*; Rosack, J. (2004). Congress hammers FDA over handling of the SSRI's. *Psychiatric News* (newspaper of the American Psychiatric Association), *39* (20), 1, 8–10.

27. Whittington et al., Are the SSRI's safe and effective for children?

28. Helms, M. (2005, March 25). Shooting fuels debate over safety of Prozac for teens. Minnesota Public Radio; Dewan, S. (2004, February 15). Jurors in boy's murder trial consider if Zoloft is to blame. *New York Times*; Mahler, J. (2004, November 21). The antidepressant dilemma. *New York Times Magazine*; Meier, B. (2004, August 23). A drug on trial: Justice and science; boy's murder case entangled in fight over antidepressants. *New York Times.*

29. Greenhill, Introduction; Greenhill et al., Review of safety assessment methods; Jensen et al., Psychoactive medication prescribing practices.

30. APA press release. (2004, October 15). APA responds to FDA's new warning on antidepressants.

31. AACAP. (2005). Supplementary talking points for child and adolescents psychiatrists: Regarding the FDA black box warning on the use of antidepressants for pediatric patients.

32. This important point is demonstrated in all the articles listed in note 1. The books that follow cover the same ground. For the groundbreaking theoretical basis of this work, which integrates biology and theories of the mind, see: Bowlby, J. (1982). *Attachment*, 2nd ed. Vol. 1 of *Attachment and Loss*. New York: Basic Books; Bowlby, J. (1973). *Separation, Anxiety and Anger*. Vol. 2 of *Attachment and Loss*. New York: Basic Books; Bowlby, J. (1980). *Loss, Sadness and Depression*. Vol. 3 of *Attachment and Loss*. New York: Basic Books. A summary of the biological basis for this work can be found in: Fox, N. (Ed.). (1994). *The Development of Emotion Regulation*. Monographs of the Society for Research in Child Development 240, no. 59. A rendering of this work into practical parenting advice can be found in: Siegel, D., and M. Hartzell. (2003). *Parenting from the Inside Out*. New York: Penguin Books.

33. Kandel, E. (1998). A new intellectual framework for psychiatry. *American Journal of Psychiatry, 155* (4), 457–469; Kandel, E. (1999). Biology and the future of psychoanalysis: A new intellectual framework for psychiatry revisited. *American Journal of Psychiatry, 156* (4), 505–524.

34. Shonkoff, J., and D. Phillips (Eds.). (2000). *Neurons to Neighborhoods: The Science of Early Childhood Development*. Washington, DC: National

Academy Press; Siegel, D. (1999). *The Developing Mind.* New York: Guilford Press.

35. Rutter, Environmentally-mediated risks for psychopathology.

36. Ibid., 12.

37. Osofsky, J. (1998). For the sake of the infants and families: Violence prevention, intervention and treatment. *Zero-to-Three, 18,* 9–14.

38. Hoschild, A. R. (1997). *The Time Bind: When Work Becomes Home and Home Becomes Work.* New York: Henry Holt and Co. Without entering into a debate on the risks and benefits of day care for infants, I recommend the following review: Growing up in childcare. (2000). In Shonkoff and Phillips (Eds.), *Neurons to Neighborhoods.*

39. Olfman, S. (2003). *All Work and No Play: How Educational Reforms are Harming Our Pre-Schoolers.* Westport, CT: Praeger; Sacks, P. (1999). *Standardized Minds.* New York: Perseus Books.

40. Schwab-Stone, M., C. Chen, E. Greenberger, D. Silver, J. Lichtment, and C. Voyce. (1999). No safe haven II: The effects of violence exposure on urban youth. *American Journal of Child and Adolescent Psychiatry, 38* (4), 359–367; Villani, S., and N. Joshi. (2003). Television and movies, rock music and music videos, and computer and video games: Understanding and preventing learned violence in the information age. In M. Mattson (Ed.), *Neurobiology of Aggression: Understanding and Preventing Aggression* (chap. 13). Totowa, NJ: Humana Press; Grossman, D., and G. De Gaetano. (1999). *Stop Teaching Our Children to Kill.* New York: Crown Publishers.

41. Klesges, R. C., M. L. Shelton, and L. M. Klesges. (1993). Effects of television on metabolism: Potential implications for childhood obesity. *Pediatrics, 91* (2).

42. Lieberman, A. (1997). Toddlers' internalizations of maternal attributions as a factor in quality of attachment. In L. Atkinson and K. Zucker (Eds.) *Attachment and Psychopathology* (chap. 9). New York: Guilford Publications.

43. Vaillant, G. (2003). Mental health. *American Journal of Psychiatry, 160,* 1373–1384.

44. Knutson, B., O. Wolkowitz, S. Cole, T. Chan, E. Moore, R. Johnson et al. (1998). Selective alteration of personality and social behavior by serotonergic intervention. *American Journal of Psychiatry, 155,* 373–379.

45. Garland, E., and M. Weiss. (1997). Case study: Obsessive difficult temperament and its response to serotonergic intervention. *Journal of the American Academy of Child and Adolescent Psychiatry, 35,* 916–920.

46. Carey, W. (1997). Letters to the Editor: Obsessive difficult temperament. *Journal of the American Academy of Child and Adolescent Psychiatry, 36* (6), 722.

47. Sameroff, A., and R. Emde. (1989). *Relationship Disturbances in Early Childhood.* New York: Basic Books; Chess, S., and A. Thomas. (1986). *Temperament in Clinical Practice.* New York: Guilford Press.

48. Jellinek, *Changes in Practice.*

49. Borrego, J., A. Urquiza, R. Rasmussen, and N. Zebell. (1999). Parent–child interaction training with a family at high risk for physical abuse. *Child Maltreatment, 4* (4), 331–342.

50. Terr, L. (2003). "Wild child": How three principles of healing organized 12 years of psychotherapy. *Journal of the American Academy of Child and Adolescent Psychiatry, 42* (12), 1401–1409.

51. All small children have "trouble with transitions, though some more than others. This is such a frequent complaint that I often wonder whether we have all forgotten what it was like to be small and hauled from place to place, just as we were starting to feel comfortable. The average young child undergoes many more transitions in the course of a week than most of us over forty were ever required to do at that age, so it is no wonder that so many preschoolers have "trouble with transitions."

52. Main, M., and R. Goldwyn. (1984). Predicting rejection of her infant from mother's representations of her own experience: Implications for the abused-abusing intergenerational cycle. *Child Abuse and Neglect, 8,* 203–217.

53. Lieberman, A., and J. Pawl. (1993). Infant–parent psychotherapy. In J. Osofsky (Ed.), *Handbook of Infant Mental Health* (chap. 28). New York: Guilford Press. While infant–parent therapy was designed to be used with parents and children up to three, the principles—exploring how unconscious memories of an unhappy childhood color current parenting—can be applied to work with families with older children.

54. Kramer, P. (1993). *Listening to Prozac.* New York: Penguin Books, p. 292.

55. Brent, D., and B. Birmaher. (2004). Letters to the Editor: British warnings on SSRI's questioned. *American Journal of Child and Adolescent Psychiatry, 43* (4), 379.

56. U.S. Public Health Service. (2000). Report of the Surgeon General's Conference on Children's Mental Health: A national action agenda. Washington, DC: Department of Health and Human Services.

57. Harris, I. (1998). Pushing kids into the river. *Zero-to-Three, 18* (5), 1.

CHAPTER 11

1. Facts about eating disorders are presented in an appendix at the end of the chapter.

2. Gordon, R. A. (2001). Eating disorder East and West: A culture-bound syndrome unbound. In M. Nasser, M. A. Katzman, and R. A. Gordon (Eds.), *Eating Disorders and Cultures in Transition* (pp. 1–23) New York: Taylor and Francis.

3. Maine, M. (2004). *Father Hunger: Fathers, Daughters, and the Pursuit of Thinness.* Carlsbad, CA: Gurze Books.

4. Arnett, J. J. (2002). The psychology of globalization. *American Psychologist, 57* (10), 774–783.

5. Friedman, S. S (1997). *When Girls Feel Fat: Helping Girls through Adolescence.* Vancouver: Salal Books.

6. Gordon, Eating disorder East and West.

7. Brumberg, J. J. (1997). *The Body Project: An Intimate History of American Girls.* New York: Random House, p. 25.

8. Friedman, S. S. (2002). *Body Thieves: Help Girls Reclaim Their Natural Bodies and Become Physically Active.* Vancouver: Salal Books.

9. Gaesser, G. A. (2002). *Big Fat Lies: The Truth about Your Weight and Your Health.* Carlsbad, CA: Gurze Books.

10. www.Amazon.com (search 2004, October 8).

11. Northrup, C. (1995). *Women's Bodies, Women's Wisdom: Creating Physical and Emotional Health and Healing.* New York: Bantam.

12. Maine, M. (2000). *Body Wars: Making Peace with Women's Bodies.* Carlsbad, CA; Gurze Books.

13. American Psychiatric Association. (1994). *Diagnostic and Statistical Manual of Mental Disorders,* 4th ed. Washington, DC.

14. Underwood, N. (2000, August 14). Body envy: Thin is in and people are messing with their bodies as never before. *Maclean's,* 36.

15. Kilbourne, J. (1994). Still killing us softly: Advertising and the obsession with thinness. In P. Fallon, M. A. Katzman, and S. C. Wooley (Eds.), *Feminist Perspectives on Eating Disorders* (pp. 395–418). New York: Guilford Press.

16. Girls, Women & Media Project: What Are You Looking At? (2002, September 2). What's the problem? Facts about girls, women & media, www.mediaandwomen.org.

17. Segall, R. (2003, February 24). The new product placement. *Nation,* 30–33.

18. A. Balsamo (1996). *Technologies of the Gendered Body.* Durham, NC: Duke University Press.

19. Arnett, Psychology of globalization.

20. Jacobs, L. (1994). *Barbie in Fashion.* New York: Abbeville Press.

21. Ibid.

22. Hulburt, A. (2004, November 28). Tweens 'r us. *New York Times Magazine,* 31, 34.

23. Barboza, D. (2003, August 3). If you pitch it, they will eat. *New York Times,* sec. 3, p. 1.

24. Dittman, M. (2002, November). Selling to children. *American Psychological Association Monitor on Psychology,* 37.

25. Segall, New product placement.

26. Quart, A. (2003). *Branded: The Buying and Selling of Teenagers.* Cambridge, MA: Perseus Publishing.

27. National Center on Addiction and Substance Abuse at Columbia University [CASA]. (2003). *Food for Thought: Substance Abuse and Eating Disorders.* New York: CASA.

28. Plous, S., and D. Neptune. (1997). Racial and gender biases in magazine advertisements: A content analytic study. *Psychology of Women's Quarterly, 21,* 627–644.

29. CASA, *Food for Thought;* Then, D. (1992). Women's magazines: Messages they convey about looks, men, and careers. Paper presented at American Psychological Association, Washington, DC.

30. Linn, S. (2004). *Consuming Kids: The Hostile Takeover of Childhood.* New York: New Press.

31. Becker, A. E., and R. A. Burwell. (1999). Acculturation and disordered eating in Fiji. Paper presented at the 152nd Annual Meeting of the American Psychiatric Association.

32. Knapp, C. (2003). *Appetites: Why Women Want.* New York: Counterpoint, p. 100.

33. American Psychiatric Association. (2000). Practice guidelines for the treatment of patients with eating disorders (revision). *American Journal of Psychiatry, 157* (1), January suppl., 1–39.

34. Patrick, L. (2002). Eating disorders: A review of the literature with emphasis on medical complications and clinical nutrition. *Alternative Medicine Review, 7* (3), 184–202.

35. Sullivan, P. (2002). Course and outcome of anorexia nervosa and bulimia nervosa. In C. G. Fairburn and K. D. Brownell, K. D. (Eds.), *Eating Disorders and Obesity,* 2nd ed (pp. 226–232). New York: Guilford Press; American Psychiatric Association, Practice guidelines.

36. Sullivan. P. F. (1995) Mortality in anorexia nervosa. *American Journal of Psychiatry, 152,* 1073–1074.

37. Patrick, Eating disorders.

38. Croll, J., D. Neumark-Sztainer, M. Story, and M. Ireland. (2002). Prevalence and risk and protective factors related to disordered eating. *Journal of Adolescent Health, 31* (2), 166–175.

39. Centers for Disease Control and Prevention. (2002). Youth risk behavior surveillance—U.S., 2001. *Morbidity and Mortality Report (MMWR), 51* (SS-4).

40. Ibid.

41. Maine, *Body Wars.*

42. American Academy of Pediatrics. (2003). Identifying and treating eating disorders: Policy statement. *Pediatrics, 111* (1), 204–211.

43. Collins, M. (1991). Body figure perception and preferences among preadolescent children. *International Journal of Eating Disorders, 10,* 199–208.

44. Mellin, L. M., C. E. Irwin, and S. Scully. (1992). Prevalence of disordered eating in girls: A survey of middle-class children. *Journal of American Dietetics Association, 92* (7), 851–853.

45. Phelps, L., et al. (1993). Prevalence of self-induced vomiting and laxative/medication abuse among female adolescents: A longitudinal study. *International Journal of Eating Disorders, 14* (3), 375–378.

Index

About the Editor and the Contributors

Sharna Olfman is a clinical psychologist and an associate professor of developmental psychology at Point Park University, where she is also the founding director of the *Childhood and Society Symposium,* a multidisciplinary forum on wide-ranging issues affecting children in the wake of rapid technological change and globalization. Dr. Olfman is the founding editor of the *Childhood in America* book series for Praeger Press. She recently published *Childhood Lost: How American Culture Is Failing Our Kids* and *All Work and No Play: How Educational Reforms Are Harming Our Preschoolers.* Dr. Olfman is a member of the Council on Human Development, a partner in the Alliance for Childhood and an advisor to the Troubadour Centre. She has also written and presented widely on the subjects of gender development, women's mental health, infant care, and child psychopathology.

Michael Brody is a Board Certified, child and adult psychiatrist in private practice and professor of American Studies at the University of Maryland. He was, until the end of 2004, medical director and creator of Psychiatric Center, one the largest providers of outpatient care for the chronically mentally ill in the District of Columbia. He is Chairman of the Television and Media Committee of the American Academy of Child and Adolescent Psychiatry. He has published widely on child media issues. He has given testimony to Congress, the FTC, the FCC, the Department of Commerce, and the White House, on such topics as Columbine, educational TV, TV ratings, the V Chip, and children's privacy on the Internet. He helped write the AMA's publication *A Physician's Guide to Violence in the Media* and was a regular on NPR's *Media Matters*. He recently wrote and produced the film *Fifty Years of Children's Television, from Howdy Doody to Spongebob.*

Mary Burke is a child psychiatrist in private practice. She teaches at the California Pacific Medical Center and the Langley Porter Psychiatric Institution/University of California, San Francisco. She serves on the Executive Committee of the Northern California Regional Organization of Child and Adolescent Psychiatry, and on the Media Committee of the American Academy of Child and Adolescent Psychiatry.

Daniel Burston is an Associate Professor of Psychology at Duquesne University, Pittsburgh, and the author of three books from Harvard University Press: *The Legacy of Erich Fromm* (1996), *The Wing of Madness: The Life and Work of R.D. Laing* (1996), and *The Crucible of Experience: R.D. Laing and the Crisis of Psychotherapy* (2000). He is an Associate of the Center for Philosophy of Science at the University of Pittsburgh and serves on the editorial boards of the *Journal of the Society for Existential Analysis*, the *Journal of Humanistic Psychology*, and *Janus Head*.

Varda Burstyn is an award-winning author and public policy consultant who has written widely on the culture and politics of film, fine art, television, and sport. As a lifelong environmentalist and health activist, she has also written about and worked on documentary films concerned with new ideas in sickness and health, reproductive technologies, and genetic engineering. Her books include *The Rites of Men: Manhood, Politics and the Culture of Sport* and *Water Inc.*, an environmental thriller about the current water crisis. Her work has appeared in scholarly and popular journals, books, radio, television, and film.

Lawrence Diller is a behavioral-developmental pediatrician and family therapist. He has evaluated and treated more than 2,500 children and their families over the past twenty-seven years. He practices in Walnut Creek, a San Francisco Bay area suburb, and lives nearby in the town of Piedmont with his wife and two teenage sons. He is also an assistant clinical professor of pediatrics at the University of California, San Francisco. He has written many articles on children's behavior and psychiatric medication for the professional and lay literature that have garnered national and international notice. His book, *Running on Ritalin: A Physician Reflects on Children, Society and Performance in a Pill*, was featured in a *Time Magazine* cover story on Ritalin. He has since made numerous appearances on television and radio nationwide, including *Nightline*, PBS *Newshour*, *Good Morning America*, CBS *Early Morning*, the *Today Show*, *Frontline*, and NPR's *Fresh Air*. His two-part series, "Kids on Drugs," featured in the online magazine Salon.com won the Society of Professional Journalists "Excellence in Journalism" award in 2000. He provided expert testimony on Ritalin before a U.S. Congressional Committee in May 2000 and the President's Council on Bioethics in December 2002. His second book is called *Should I Medicate My Child? Sane Solutions for Troubled Kids with and without Psychiatric Drugs*.

David Fenton is a lifelong environmentalist. He was the Regional Environmentalist for the State of Oregon, a Legislative Lobbyist for the Oklahoma Audubon Council, and he has taught university courses on environmental studies, geography, and computer science. He has also directed communication and training departments for global technology companies, and has worked in high-tech fields around the world. He is a father and a grandfather and would like to help the world become a safer place for all children.

Jane M. Healy holds a PhD in educational psychology from Case Western Reserve University and has done postdoctoral work in developmental neuropsychology. Formerly on the faculties of Cleveland State University and John Carroll University, she is internationally recognized as a lecturer and consultant with many years of experience as a classroom teacher, reading/learning specialist, and elementary administrator. She is the author of numerous articles and the books *Your Child's Growing Mind: A Guide to Learning and Brain Development from Birth to Adolescence*, *Endangered Minds: Why Our Children Don't Think and What We Can Do About It*, *How to Have Intelligent and Creative Conversations with Your Kids*, and *Failure to Connect: How Computers Affect Our Children's Minds and What We Can Do About It*. She has lectured for schools and professional groups worldwide and has appeared on most of the major media in the United States, including the *Today Show*, *Nightline*,

Good Morning America, PBS specials, and NPR. She is frequently consulted about questions regarding the effects of new technologies on the developing brain. Nonetheless, Jane and her husband, Tom, claim they have learned most of what they know from their three sons, and six grandchildren.

Mel Levine is a Professor of Pediatrics at the University of North Carolina Medical School. He is the Director of the Center for Development and learning and also the Co-Chair of the Board of All Kinds of Minds, a nonprofit institute for the understanding of differences in learning, which he founded. Dr. Levine is the author of many books and articles on learning processes and differences in learning among school-age children. His books include *A Mind at a Time*, *The Myth of Laziness*, and *Ready or Not, Here Life Comes*. He advocates a non-labeling/phenomenological model for elucidating and managing learning difficulties. Dr. Levine places a strong emphasis on the diagnosis and cultivation of childhood cognitive strengths and affinities.

Margo D. Maine, cofounder of the Maine & Weinstein Specialty Group, is a clinical psychologist who has specialized in the treatment of eating disorders for over twenty-five years. She is a clinical consultant at the Institute of Living in Hartford, CT, and former director of their Eating Disorders Program. Her books include *The Body Myth: The Pressure on Adult Women to Be Perfect* (co-authored with Joe Kelly), *Body Wars: Making Peace with Women's Bodies*, and *Father Hunger: Fathers, Daughters and the Pursuit of Thinness*. Maine is a senior editor of *Eating Disorders: The Journal of Treatment and Prevention*, a founding Member and Fellow of the Academy for Eating Disorders, and past president of the National Eating Disorders Association. She is an Assistant Clinical Professor at the University of Connecticut, Department of Psychiatry, an adjunct faculty member at the University of Hartford, Graduate Institute of Professional Psychology, and a member of the psychiatry departments at the Institute of Living/Hartford Hospital's Mental Health Network and Connecticut Children's Medical Center.

John P. Murray is Professor of Developmental Psychology in the School of Family Studies and Human Services at Kansas State University. During 2004–2005, he served as a Senior Scientist and Visiting Scholar in the Center on Media and Child Health at Harvard Medical School. His current research is focused on using functional

Magnetic Resonance Imaging (fMRI) to map the brain activations of children while they view violent and nonviolent video programs. He has written fourteen books and about 100 articles on child development and media. His forthcoming book, *Children and Television: 50 Years of Research,* will be published in early 2006.

Stuart G. Shanker is a Distinguished Research Professor at York University, Toronto, where he is also the Director of the Milton and Ethel Harris Research Institute. One of the world's leading authorities on the philosophy of Ludwig Wittgenstein, he has been at the forefront of ape-language research and child-language studies. Shanker is the author of over twenty highly praised books, including *The First Idea: How Symbols, Language, and Intelligence Evolved from Our Primate Ancestors to Modern Humans* (co-authored with Stanley Greenspan), and he is the co-general editor of the ten-volume *Routledge History of Philosophy.* Shanker co-chairs the Council of Human Development.